NATIONS OF THE MODERN WORLD

CEYLON — S. A. Pakeman
Formerly Professor of Modern History, Ceylon University College; Appointed Member, House of Representatives, Ceylon, 1947–52

MODERN EGYPT — Tom Little
Managing Director and General Manager of Regional News Services (Middle East), Ltd., London

ENGLAND
A Portrait — John Bowle
Professor of Political Theory, College d'Europe, Bruges

MODERN INDIA — Sir Percival Griffiths
President of the India, Pakistan and Burma Association

MODERN IRAN — Peter Avery
Lecturer in Persian and Fellow of King's College, Cambridge

JAPAN — Sir Esler Dening
H.M. Ambassador to Japan, 1952–57

MALAYA — J. M. Gullick
Formerly of the Malayan Civil Service

MOROCCO — Mark I. Cohen
and
Lorna Hahn

NIGERIA — Sir Rex Niven
Colonial Service, Nigeria, 1921–59; Member of Northern House of Assembly, 1947–59

PAKISTAN — Ian Stephens
Formerly Editor of The Statesman *Calcutta and Delhi, 1942–51; Fellow of King's College, Cambridge, 1952–58*

SOUTH AFRICA — John Cope
Formerly Editor-in-Chief of The Forum; *South African Correspondent of* The Guardian

SUDAN
REPUBLIC — K. D. D. Henderson
Formerly of the Sudan Political Services; Governor of Darfur Province, 1943–53

TURKEY — Geoffrey Lewis
Senior Lecturer in Islamic Studies, Oxford

THE UNITED
STATES OF
AMERICA — H. C. Allen
Commonwealth Fund Professor of American History, University College, London

YUGOSLAVIA — Muriel Heppell
and
F. B. Singleton

PAKISTAN

By
IAN STEPHENS

THIRD EDITION

FREDERICK A. PRAEGER, *Publishers*
New York · Washington

BOOKS THAT MATTER

Published in the United States of America in 1967
by Frederick A. Praeger, Inc., Publishers
111 Fourth Avenue, New York, N.Y. 10003

The original edition of this book was published in 1963, and a second edition in 1966, by Frederick A. Praeger, Inc., Publishers. This third edition has been extensively revised and brought up to date.

Library of Congress Catalog Card Number: 67–29713

PRINTED IN GREAT BRITAIN

Preface

THIS is not offered as a learned book, needing source-notes. But learned readers may want to know the basis for facts and quotations which seem to them new. Carefully recorded basis exists, and particulars could nearly always be given if asked for. The previously unpublished material drawn on derives from the author's editorship of *The Statesman* newspaper between 1942 and 1951, and from his having been Historian to the Pakistan Army between 1957 and 1960.

The book's structure also needs explaining. Pakistan is an exceptional country, politically and geographically. Part I describes some problems raised by this, dealing with them subject by subject, not chronologically. Part II, by contrast, is straight historical narrative. So is most of Part III. In Part II, events during the three years or so before the Partition of the Indian subcontinent was decided on in 1947 are examined fully, this being necessary for understanding why Pakistan came to exist, what her character is, and why she maintains certain attitudes in foreign affairs. The way a country won its independence can affect its whole ethos, as (for example) the U.S.A. shows. On the other hand in Part III, about eleven years of Pakistan's domestic politics are telescoped into one chapter, those affairs having been made largely meaningless by the military revolution of October 1958, and, moreover, having been gone into in other books, e.g. by Callard, Khalid Bin Sayeed, Binder. There has also been telescoping over Kashmir. What in a concrete sense happened, during the opening phase (1947–9) of that extremely important Indo-Pakistan dispute, is described in detail. But the subsequent debates at the U.N. and elsewhere, protracted and verbose, are almost ignored, because so far they have led to nothing. Particulars can be got in Korbel, Bazaz, Birdwood, Sarwar Hasan, Ferguson (see the Bibliography).

Prefixes before men's names have been kept brief. And those in use at the time are preferred to honorifics got later. If the person has died, but was alive as lately as 1935, the prefix stays. Thus we have 'Mr. Jinnah', 'Mr. Gandhi', which is how those leaders were referred to during most of their lifetimes. But prefixes are shorn from historical personages; 'Curzon', for instance, or 'Syed Ahmad Khan'.

Military men of modern times raise difficulty, owing to their pro-
motions and knighthoods; though consistency has been sought,
some anomalies remain. And exception is made of participants in
the drama who have themselves written books. From them – as
from all authors – prefixes go, rude though this may seem to persons
so distinguished as 'Ismay', 'Tuker', 'Caroe'. Spelling of Pakistanis'
names is normally as the man concerned liked it – 'Liaquat', for
instance. Some Western scholars, Arabist pedants we might say,
tamper with such usages. Being no Arabist, the present writer
abstains; 'Liaquat' accordingly retains its 'u', 'Ayub' has only one
'y', and so forth. The exception is 'Mohammad', which can be
spelt in so many ways that it has been systematised into one. More
questionable, is the omission of dots to show where quotations have
occasionally been shortened. Honest qualms are still felt about this,
and perhaps the decision was wrong. If so, the author apologises. But
dots can vex the eye, they waste space, and may seem priggish. The
utmost care has been taken that no such shortening distorts a
quotation's sense.

  A Bibliography is offered, near the end before the Index. Like
most such things, it claims no completeness, and the books it mentions
vary in importance. A few of them are referred to quite often in the
text, these mainly being books by the aforementioned men who
participated personally in the drama, especially when what they
wrote reproduces, or was based on, diaries or notes actually taken at
the time. Foremost among such books – giving them in the order
they came out in – are those by Tuker, Campbell-Johnson, Menon,
Ismay, Moon. Others of more than ordinary importance – in alpha-
betical order, now – are by Azad, Binder, Birdwood, Bolitho, Brecher,
Callard, Caroe, Connell, Ferguson, Korbel, Lumby, Mosley, Sarwar
Hasan, Siddiqi, Spear, Stephens, Symonds, and Woodruff. Two
more need mentioning here, because they might well have been referred to in the text, had they not come out while the writing of this
present one was in its final stages : Rushbrook Williams' *The State
of Pakistan*, and Hugh Tinker's *India and Pakistan*.

  It is hoped that the Index will prove serviceable. On factual detail, it is fairly dull. But it does not try to do much about philo-
sophical and other abstract terms, of the sort mentioned in Chapters
1, 3, 5, and 10. Indexing such things takes space and time, and may
not be much good.

  The author records his enthusiastic thanks to his secretary, Miss
M. B. Stiff, for her hard work and intelligently critical aid throughout; and also to Miss E. A. Furlong, for her prompt and capable help
over research-items.

Acknowledgements are also gratefully made to the following authors and publishers for permitting quotations from the books named in brackets : Messrs. George Allen and Unwin (*Pakistan, A Political Study*, by Keith Callard; *The Transfer of Power in India*, by E. W. R. Lumby); Messrs. Jonathan Cape (*Verdict on India*, by Beverley Nichols; *The Men Who Ruled India*, by Philip Woodruff); Messrs. Cassell and Co. (*While Memory Serves*, by Sir Francis Tuker; *Auchinleck*, by John Connell); Messrs. Chatto and Windus (*Horned Moon*, by Ian Stephens; *Divide and Quit*, by Penderel Moon); The Clarendon Press (*The Oxford History of India*, edited by Percival Spear); Messrs. Faber and Faber (*The Making of Pakistan*, by Richard Symonds); Messrs. Robert Hale (*Mission with Mountbatten*, by Alan Campbell-Johnson; *A Continent Decides*, by Lord Birdwood); Messrs. William Heinemann (*The Memoirs or Lord Ismay*); Messrs. Macmillan and Co. (*The Pathans*, by Sir Olaf Caroe); Mr. Philip Mason (Foreword to *The Springing Tiger*, by Hugh Toye); Messrs. Orient Longmans (*India Wins Freedom*, by Abul Kalam Azad; *The Transfer of Power in India*, by V. P. Menon); Princeton University Press (*Ceylon: Dilemmas of a New Nation*, by W. Howard Wriggins); Messrs. Weidenfeld and Nicolson (*Into a Dangerous World*, by Woodrow Wyatt).

October 31st 1962

PREFACE TO THE SECOND EDITION

The main changes made for this edition have been in Chapters 16 and 19, parts of both of which have been enlarged and recast. Items in the preceding 1962 Preface have also been altered; some additions have been made to the Bibliography; and minor corrections and improvements have been undertaken throughout the text.

CAMBRIDGE *October 15th 1963*

PREFACE TO THE THIRD EDITION

A revised paperback edition of this book was published by Penguin Books Ltd. in 1964 (Preface dated May 15th). For this present third hardback edition further extensive revisions have been made, especially in Chapters 1, 2, 3, and 16. Changes in Chapters 15 and 17 are also considerable. Chapter 19 has been shortened, but augmented by Chapter 20, much of which is new.

The changes in Chapters 1, 2, and 3 are mainly in the minor

factual allusions, several of which had got out of date. These have
been set right and some fresh generalities added. Most of the
population statistics however have had to stay unaltered, being
based on what are still the latest Pakistani and Indian Censuses
(1961). An exception is the '104 million' for Pakistan's total population (pp. 13 and 50); this is a 1966 estimate. The complete reconstruction of the second part of the 'Defence and Foreign Affairs'
Chapter (16) is due to the general transformation of the international
scene in recent years and particularly, in Pakistan's case, to China's
attack on India in November 1962 and the effects of this on
American and British policy. Elsewhere throughout the book smaller
corrections have been done, these naturally being fewest in the
middle, that is, in the chronological narrative describing what happened in 1946–48, immediately before and after the Partition of the
Indo-Pakistani subcontinent when British rule ended. The Bibliography too has been much changed, several important recently-
published books going in, but others being expunged so as to limit its
length.

This brings us to two final points which need explaining. No
attempt has been made to weave into the text specific mentions of
books published since the writing was finished of the second hardback edition in October '63. To do this would have needed what
seemed excessive minor verbal reconstructions, as well as fresh re-
quests to authors and publishers for permission to quote. So in this
one respect the present edition does not claim to be topical. But
details about these newly-published books can readily be got by looking through the new Bibliography for publication-dates later than
1963. The other point is what some may consider a chronological
flaw. Chapter 16, as reconstructed, pushes right forward to 1967,
whereas Chapter 18, on 'Politics and Constitution 1947–58', still
stops nine years earlier. However, to complete the 'Defence and
Foreign Affairs' story in one run – supplemented by a few topical
touches in Chapter 20 – seemed in a way logical, and perhaps no
apology is needed other than this explanation implies.

CAMBRIDGE   *April 30th 1967*

Contents

Illustrations

Photographs 1–3, 5–15, 18, 20 and 27 are reproduced by courtesy of the Pakistan High Commission, London. The others were taken by the author. All are inserted between pages 144 and 145.

MAPS

PART I

Chapter 1

The Idea

PAKISTAN is an independent sovereign country in south Asia of over 104 million people, which was brought into being in 1947, to fulfil a religious or cultural aspiration. The idea was to provide a homeland for the Indian subcontinent's Muslims, or most of them; a place where, after the British imperial power had gone, they could freely develop their way of life in an Islamic environment apart from the Hindus, who outnumbered them by about three to one.

So Pakistan, in a sense, is a very extraordinary country – a fact which gets less attention, here in the West, than it deserves. Few others in the modern world can be said to have been created to embody a belief or doctrine or theory; to owe their existence to what some would call – depending on how the word is defined – an ideology. Most people indeed, glancing over an atlas, would find it hard to recognise more than two.

Obviously one of these – a much bigger, better-known instance – is Soviet Russia. Marxist belief, though atheist, has some of the attributes of religion; and it too, like the Pakistan-concept, pervaded the intellectual air for quite a while, before it found a physical body to put its spirit into. Until the huge collapsed form of Czarist imperialism in 1917 offered it the chance of life, gave it a territory and a still workable governmental structure to function by, it remained an abstraction, Stateless, an affair of breath and ink and agitation, of talk in back rooms by men burning with zeal for a cause – and of tomes standing seldom opened in public libraries. The Soviet Union holds place as the supreme example of the ideological State; and the fact of its being totalitarian, as well, makes it the more outstanding: more so than Red China – a secondary affair, for its doctrines come from Russia – and obviously than the antique Buddhist theocracy in Tibet, which Red China overthrew; or – to take other ancient examples – than the Papal States in their medieval heyday, or the seventeenth-century Jesuit theocracy in Paraguay; or again – to return to this century – than Franco's Spain. And more so, as we shall see, than Pakistan is or wants to be.

The other striking twentieth-century example, puny in geographical terms beside Russia but not so in zeal, is Israel. Like the Pakistan-concept, and only ten months later, Zionism got the chance to become the directing-force of an independent sovereign State through the weakening of an old-established empire: of the British Empire after World War II. And there are further similarities. Like Pakistan, Israel regards herself as under threat; she lives in fear of being swamped by a larger, unfriendly neighbour or neighbours – a condition of mind which (temporarily at least) gives her enhanced cohesion. She is a country, too, where the prestige of the Army stands very high, and where proportionately very large sums are spent on it; and one which, during her first years of life, was so busy with survival as not to have managed to formulate a written Constitution. She is a country whose population includes many refugees, persons displaced and upset, physically and mentally, by actual or foreseen tyrannies or injustices elsewhere; and, moreover, one where, from the start, a tense inner struggle for mastery has been going on – fascinating for the uncommitted onlooker to watch – between traditionalists and progressives, between the rabbis (or mullahs) on the one hand, and modernisers on the other.

But over one big matter there is divergence. For something distinct from religious and cultural spirit infuses Zionism; it is inspired, too, by a sense of race, by beliefs about a chosen people; and in this, with grim irony, it bears some resemblance to its appalling former foe in Europe, German Nazism. Islam, on the other hand – the creed from which the Pakistan-concept takes origin – agrees wholeheartedly with Communism in being without qualification and emphatically raceless, a brotherhood open for all mankind; which means that, unlike Judaism, it remains, potentially at least, a proselytising force, bent upon enlarging itself – as it so formidably did in past centuries. Here we have a fresh fact of major importance, and one which does much to explain the peculiar obstacles and prejudices which the idea of Pakistan, from the time of its first becoming active in the 1930's, has met not only from Hindus, but also, though less consciously – so this writer at any rate reckons – from Christian people in the West.

Hindus, of course, fully understand why they fear Islam, despite their huge numerical preponderance on the subcontinent. Its believers, arriving by sea and then by land, began to inflict a catastrophic series of defeats on their gifted forbears as long ago as A.D. 712, when a general of the Caliph invaded Sind; and for about 550 years, from the thirteenth to eighteenth centuries, Muslim conquerors exercised from Delhi almost uninterrupted, impious sway over large parts of Bharat Mata, of holy Mother India, of the revered land, the very earth itself which forms an essential part of the Hindu religion,

and through which flow the three sacred river-systems.[1] The shame
of it has caused deep wounds in the Hindu mind. Hinduism's resulting unrelieved antagonism to Islam, its patient, age-long determination to subjugate or absorb or expel it, and Islam's corresponding
resistance, are plainly both the main reason for the obstacles which
the Pakistan-concept met, and why the concept ever developed; the
cause, in fact, of the appalling bloodsoaked partition of the subcontinent in 1947 ─(in which about 500,000 persons died, and
14,000,000 had to migrate. These things will be discussed in later
chapters.)

But the attitude towards Islam of Westerners, American and European – a less obvious but important matters – needs some discussing
here and now. Their lack of interest in a country so exceptional as
Pakistan, so populous, so strategically important, a country, too,
which in 1954 allied itself with them militarily; their frequent symptoms of a vague emotional repugnance; their inclination to turn
elsewhere, towards other less significant parts of the map, combine,
on reflection, into something strange, which asks for inquiry. And
there seems reason to suspect that an antagonism of religious origin –
though it does not wholly explain it – may be involved here too.

British statesmen and administrators, of course, before Pakistan
came into being, disliked the prospect of the administrative unity of
the Indian subcontinent, which their predecessors had done so much
to create, being wrenched apart. The thought of the Indian Army
having to be divided was particularly distressing, to civilians as to
soldiers. It had just come through World War II with glory; its
prestige stood higher than ever; and internationally it had great
stabilising potentialities. There was nothing religious in this; but it
meant that the Pakistan-concept stirred distaste in British governing
circles. And much doubt was felt, and indeed disbelief, not only by
leading British people but by foreigners, on whether, in the event, so
clumsy-looking a new political creation as Pakistan – consisting, as
evidently it would, of two very dissimilar bits of country about
1,000 miles apart – could survive. And if it did not, that would make
a nasty mess on the map of South Asia, which war-weary Westerners
would presumably have to try to tidy up.

And then, as well, after Pakistan had come into being, influential
men experienced in the subcontinent's affairs, as a result of Government service or careers in business, tended to become silent. Most
senior Government personnel just retired, whether military or
civilian, were exhausted and disillusioned; they had gone through

---

[1] Those of the Ganges, the Cauvery, and the Indus. Some Hindus add two more,
the systems of the Narbadda and the Godaviri.

very rough times, and the Partition and the riots had destroyed
assumptions that their whole lifework was based on. Moreover, rules
still to some extent bound them; their positions might depend on
reticence about their knowledge or about papers that they held.
'Well, that's that; no use crying over spilt milk; let's turn to something else'. Phrases such as these well express what many of them
felt. There was also a widespread notion in high places, which affected the Press, that as Britain had ceased to rule, she should not risk
jogging the successor-Governments' elbows by fussy comments from
afar. These were respectable reasons for silence; and yet another
supplemented it, one of calculated expediency, which from its nature
happened to be adverse to Pakistan. For plainly the new India, much
the larger successor-State, would occupy a position on which great
international issues hinged: issues of Communist ideology and the
'cold war'; of competition between foreign countries hitherto uninterested in the subcontinent for strategic, cultural and trading
opportunities; and in Britain's case, the critical issue of how much
of her large stake in the Indian investment-field she could preserve.
To avoid irritating the Government of such a country would be
prudent.

All these were practical considerations unconnected with religion,
but in themselves failing fully to explain – so this writer believes –
most Westerners' dislike of the Pakistan-concept. And, as well, the
mere average Westerner – not the prominent politician or civil servant or businessman, but the person of no particular position – tends
to forget about Asia, or at any rate its remoter regions: a by-product,
this, of the Occidental bias in his schooling, and in the newspapers
and wireless that mould his adult ideas. Europe, and its affluent North
American offshoot, is usually assumed to be the only part of the
globe that matters; the large non-Christian parts are ignored. In
childhood, he has been taught of Greece and Rome – with just
enough of the Levant thrown in to illustrate Christianity's background, but not to let him grasp that Jesus was an Asiatic; then,
hustled past the discreditable 'dark ages', he reaches Europe's
medieval epoch, with its distinctive culture evolved under the
Church's leadership – but gets hardly a glimpse of what was simultaneously going on elsewhere. Much is recounted about the Renaissance and Reformation; and more about the wonderful European
technological discoveries and overseas expansion of the last four
centuries – all leading straight to the West's pre-eminence of today,
or yesterday, and regardless of the fact that, for one millennium out
of the two thus dealt with, the now developed lands of north-western
Europe were but an unimportant appendage of the Eurasian land-

mass, steeped (comparatively speaking) in ignorant squalor, when set against the accomplished civilisations farther east, in Asia.

Hindu and Buddhist empires, Confucian ones – here, at last, we come to the religious factor already foreshadowed – were indeed far away; far enough for the Westerner's ignorance to be excused. But some of the former Muslim empires were nearer. Direct contacts did exist. And it may well be that uneasy half-remembrance of this, and of the sometimes alarming quality, militarily and religiously, of the proselytising Faith which inspired them, underlies the Westerner's tendency to turn aside, alienated or uncomfortable, when the ideology of the Pakistani State is touched on. At any rate, there is a point here, and in this writer's opinion an important one, worth looking at in the opening chapter of this book.

Suppose an average Westerner, a novice in eastward travel, arrives at Istanbul, the best-known city in the Muslim country nearest to Europe. As he is driven off to his hotel, he sees, startling against the clear evening air – perhaps with a symbolic crescent moon riding above it – that wonderful notched skyline of domes and minars. And the spectacle jolts both his eye and mind, violently. Those structures, or some of them, he recalls, stand on the masonry of what once were Christian churches. And as he looks about, further thoughts stir; dim memories of tales half-heard about conversion by the sword of Levantine Christian communities during Islam's first outrush from Arabia 1,300 years ago; later tales – more meaningful, here in Istanbul – of fierce non-Christian hordes, Turkish ones now, not Arab, sweeping across the plains of Hungary to the gates of Vienna; or – glancing further west, nearer home – tales of rape, and lootings, by slave-raiding Barbary pirates along Europe's southern shores – shores rich in Greek and Roman history; or tales of the conquest by the Moors of Spain.

And he will forget now, if he knew, about that Moorish civilisation's superiority to its contemporary Christian rivals further north; its splendid arts, the grace and richness of its architecture, its pioneering technology – in baths and sanitation for instance, or street lighting; the prestige of its University of Cordova; or the crucial role played by Islamic scholarship along the Mediterranean, as guardian of the heritage of Greece, in fostering the European Renaissance. It is the rough military fact of seizure of European soil by, for him, an alien, infidel régime, that grips his thoughts.

And he will recall again, drawing his mind back to Istanbul and gazing anew at those shapes on the skyline – so unfamiliar, compared with his accustomed buildings of Gothic or Classical design – the (for

B

him) tragic collapse, 500 years ago, before Islamic onslaught, of the
Byzantine Empire. Or, delving deeper into European group-memory,
where the hurt of it still festers a little, he may think of the high
hopes, the chivalry, the faith and then the disillusioned, ignominious
end of the Crusades.

It can scarcely be questioned that, though detailed attempts to
analyse them would be absurd, thoughts like these do distort the
Westerner's attitude towards Islam, and therefore towards the interesting country dealt with in this book.

But Pakistanis, oddly enough – here we reach the unexpected
obverse of the medal – see matters quite otherwise, geographically
and historically; see them in a friendly, not a hostile light – which
is a big discovery that our hypothetical Western novice makes, travelling east, if his first major landfall happens not to be (say) Istanbul
or Cairo, but Karachi or Lahore, Delhi or Dacca. He will then have
entered the Oriental world not through some stiff-hinged opening in
Islam's historic boundary-wall with Christendom in the Mediterranean, but (so to speak) by a side-door, via the muddle of the open
fields and unfenced orchards behind, in South Asia.

Here, no particular local remembrance exists of any doctrinal
clash or conflict between Islam and Christianity – though politically
some resentment may linger, among the elderly, against the arro-
gant aspects of recent British imperialism. Religiously, however, it
is an area where the Muslim is well aware – even the simple illiterate
Muslim, and his posture when praying reminds him of it – that his
affinities lie westwards; an area where Islam competes confusedly
with creeds and cultures to the east, so very alien, both to itself and
to the Western spirit generally, that by contrast the hard-edged
difference between things Muslim and Christian may at moments
seem to waver, even to dissolve; an area where, in particular, Islam
confronts with continual blank incomprehension, from its egalitarian
and raceless standpoint, from its austere iconoclastic monotheism,
the intricacies of the Hindus' caste system, their prohibitions on
inter-marriage and inter-dining, their multiplicity of gods, their (to
the Muslim) nauseating idol-worship.

And although our Western novice in his initial bewilderment finds
the brownish people around him, whether Hindu or Muslim, all much
alike, he soon realises that some Muslims approach him, if not as a
brother doctrinally, then as a fairly close cousin. By comparison with
Hindus, or with Buddhists or Sikhs, Jains or indeed Parsis, it is clear
that he, a Christian, stands forth for them in a special relationship.
He is not, in their view, quite a pagan. While in his inexperience

he may not yet know it, he shares with them a good deal of scripture, which is not annulled by what, to them, is the final holy book, the Koran. The Founder of Christianity – he may be surprised to learn – ranks for them as one of the major prophets of Islam. Jerusalem for them, too, is a place of holiness. What other religion, educated Indo-Pakistani Muslims might ask, has this sort of nearness to Christianity? Do the Jews revere Jesus? Old Testament personages – Adam and Eve, King Solomon, the Queen of Sheba, Noah, Ishmael – are common to both Faiths. So-called Christian names are Muslim names too : Ibrahim and Musa, Daud and Yakub and Ishaq translate into their English equivalents very easily. To some Muslims, in fact, the Christian may appear scarcely more outside the Islamic pale than do people claiming to be Muslims, such as those controversial nineteenth-century sectarians the Qadianis, or more properly Ahmadis, of the Punjab.

Nor should the novice suppose that the Muslims around him in South Asia, or what is called the Middle East, are less important than those closer to Europe, in the Near East. Here lies a frequent misconception, deriving, in part, from the noisy arrogance of Arab nationalism in recent years, but perhaps more from the lopsided way in which Oriental affairs are treated in Western publications, by people who assume that, if a place lies nearer Washington or London or Paris, its interest increases. Indo-Pakistan Muslims, Persian or Afghan Muslims, Indonesian Muslims do not look at the map that way. Their minds, naturally, turn it round. South, or Central, or South-east Asia is their starting-off point. And in this they have such weighty facts as population-strength to back them. The combined number of Muslims in their area – Iran, Afghanistan, the two wings of Pakistan, the Indian Union, the U.S.S.R., China, Burma and Thailand, Ceylon, Indonesia, Borneo and so forth – amounts to no less than 280 millions. Against this, the Westerner may discover with surprise, the better-known Mediterranean or Turco-Arab sector of the Islamic world – that is, Yugoslavia and Albania, Turkey, Lebanon, Syria, Jordan, Iraq, the Persian Gulf States, Saudi Arabia, the Yemen, Egypt, and the four 'Maghreb' countries (Libya, Tunisia, Algeria and Morocco) strung along the North African shore – can offer only 107 millions.[2] And, as Indo-Pakistani Muslims construe history – a subject which may mean more to them than to the British, who have never been under foreign rule – the achievements of their régime at Delhi, of the successive sultanates of Kutb-ud-Din and the

[2] The figures are co-ordinated estimates for 1959. Central African countries not contiguous with the Mediterranean, e.g. the Sudan and Nigeria, have been excluded.

'slave kings', of the Khiljis, Tughlaks, Sayyids, Lodis, Surs, culminating during the sixteenth and seventeenth centuries in that of the
Moghuls, probably the greatest of all, were (to put it mildly) at least
equal, in liberality as well as splendour, to those of the Ottomans,
nearer to Europe.

And this, of course, leads to another resemblance, as the Pakistani
sees it, between you, as a Westerner, and himself, especially if you
are British. Although as indicated he may dislike some manifestations
of the British Raj that he experienced or has heard about, nevertheless he recognises in you an affinity in military and administrative
aptitudes. He looks on you, in fact – looks on you nowadays with a
lively sympathetic interest – as a fellow ex-imperialist.

True, your régime was short, 200 years or so, about a third of his.
And its imprint on the Indian scene, artistic and architectural, religious and racial, was less. In a sense, you Westerners were with-
drawers always, your governmental and commercial folk leading a
camp-like existence, setting up no permanent home, the men doing
their jobs up and down the subcontinent till middle life, then retiring on the proceeds, always retiring, to your far-off little island;
the women, thanks to the Suez Canal and latterly to aircraft, putting
in ever more ephemeral and disconnected appearances – disconnected, it seemed, mentally as well as physically, for few British women
ever developed any sense of 'belonging'; none of you, with the
rarest exceptions, settling down for good on its soil, or mingling
intimately with the people, personally, intellectually or matri-
monially, as the Muslim invaders did.

Nevertheless, your forbears, like his, and like the Portuguese and
the French, arrived in India as Western conquerors; and they too, like
his, ruled successfully for a while over intelligent, cultivated and
sturdy Hindus much more numerous than themselves. The bond of
fellow-feeling between him and you is thus felt to be strong.

The Muslim in South Asia, then, is very conscious that his sources
– religious and cultural certainly, and he may believe racial too –
are Occidental. Unlike the Hindu – entwined by ancient rituals and
tradition with the venerated land and waters of Mother India – he
feels keen interest in outside countries to the west of him, where his
own religion started; or, at the least, he does not feel neutral, or alien
from them. Because pressed by geography into touch with Oriental
cultures so distinct from his own, and particularly with Hinduism –
which contrasts with Islam on practical details of life in an extreme
way, as later pages will illustrate – he has much in mind his links
with the non-Indian world; not merely with Arabia or Turkey, but

with Europe. The average Westerner on the other hand, parochially European and aloof, has no conception of the profound cleavage between Hinduism and Islam, or of the reasons for it, or of the resultant leaning of Indo-Pakistani Muslims towards friendliness for the West – until he himself visits the subcontinent, and is embarrassed to discover how little he knows.

And perhaps some Muslim there, observing his predicament, might politely press upon him the question why Westerners should be so ignorant of simple Asian realities? Can it be that unwittingly they live under remote control by their early Church? Are they swayed subconsciously by the dread which, centuries ago, bishops and abbots felt of Islam's capacity to expand? Does there, even now, lurk in the shadows of the European mind a remembrance of such unrelished facts as that, in A.D. 732, the Muslim conquerors of Spain, thrusting northwards under their leader Abdur Rahman, got half way across France, to a point beyond Poitiers, only 200 miles from the English Channel? And our Western novice might find such questions difficult to answer.

But deep and probably unique though the cleavage is between Islam and Hinduism, nevertheless something describable as a joint Hindu-Muslim or Indian culture did exist, both under the British régime, and more genuinely perhaps in the sixteenth and seventeenth centuries under Moghul emperors such as Akbar and Shahjehan. The point needs emphasising, to keep a correct balance. Over long periods, the two religious systems have functioned alongside one another without overt antagonism, and sometimes with mutual sympathy. Akbar, indeed, conscious doubtless that hostility between his subjects would mean political instability, went so far as to try to unify them under a new religion of his own devising, the Din Illahi. The attempt proved abortive; but important interchanges between the two systems took place. The Moghul rulers sought Hindu princesses as wives; several of them interested themselves in Hindu philosophy, and patronised Hindu poetry and painting; their architecture not merely borrowed Hindu forms, but blent these superbly with traditional Islamic ones. The Hindu Faith itself evolved an iconoclastic, monotheistic, casteless offshoot, in Sikhism; while Islam, on Indian soil, answered by shedding some of its Arabian austerity, drew God nearer and more lovingly towards man through the mystical devotions of the Sufis, and allowed itself un-Islamic practices such as worship at the tombs of saints.

To some extent, these processes were an outcome of geography. Communications on the vast subcontinent before the mid-nineteenth century were arduous and slow; and the Muslims there lived far removed from their own religion's fountainhead on the very different Arabian subcontinent to the west. India is almost a self-contained physical unit, held apart from the rest of Asia by the often stormy ocean waters and the gigantic Himalayan wall. Indeed, perhaps the surprising thing – granted the geographical facts and the unifying orderly minds of administrators – is that, over the six relevant centuries, no final decisive mingling occurred. But the simile of oil and water applies. For long spells of time, Islam and Hinduism could lie tolerantly or at least unexplosively side by side, or one above the other; but they would not mix, their disposition was always separate. So true is this that a distinguished Muslim of judicial mind could remark, in the 1920's, eight centuries after the two systems were first brought into juxtaposition, that whereas 'any of us Muslims' from India, when travelling in Afghanistan, or Persia, or Central Asia, or among the Arabs, or Turks, 'would at once be made at home, and would not find anything to which we are not accustomed', yet here in their own region in South Asia 'we find ourselves, in all social matters, total aliens when we cross the street, and enter that part of the town where our Hindu fellow-townsmen live'.[3] There are some who would carry the matter ruthlessly further; who would say that the cleavage between the two systems is so complete that nothing short of a smashing-up will do; that stability on the subcontinent will remain unattainable until they are replaced by a third one, equally capable of holding men's allegiance. A century ago, vaunting Western imperialists such as Meredith Townsend would have seen in muscular Christianity the proper substitute; today, imperialists of another kind will point to Communism.

It must however, as well, be conceded that the Western intellectual – not our unsophisticated traveller, but someone trained in political theory – does have reasons, not yet touched on, especially if he is religiously agnostic and politically of the Left, for looking on Islam – and thus on the Pakistan-concept – with disapproval. To him, or at any rate to some such people, it is of necessity narrow, regressive, chained to a hoary past. This assumption is partly due to the distinctive nature of Muslim law; to the far-reaching way in which, as a religion, Islam projects itself into what, for the Westerner, are fields merely secular.

The problems involved here are complex, and beyond the scope of a book such as this unless condensed. In Western Europe and America, law comes from Roman rather than Christian sources; most

[3] Sir Abdur Rahim; subsequently President of the Indian Legislative Assembly.

of it is not, as a Westerner sees it, religious in source or purpose. Two distinct spheres exist, ordinarily identifiable without much difficulty: those of the State, and of the Church. But in Islamic countries – before most of them became semi-Westernised under colonialist pressure, and public or State law broke off from personal law – law like everything else was part of religion. Human beings were believed to be living under the rule of Allah, as divinely revealed through his Prophet Mohammad in the Koran and the associated Sunna or customs, and as interpreted by theologians in the religious laws known as the Sharia. The Faith therefore stretched forth very far, into all sorts of practical day-to-day details.

Islam is not unique in this; and writers such as Cantwell Smith perhaps make needlessly heavy weather of it. But the Western Leftist intelligentsia tends to single Islam out, because of social items accounted objectionable, to be mentioned in a moment. Judaism also projects itself authoritatively into affairs of daily life, including politics, in ways disconcerting to the Westerner, as a visit to Israel will show. And Byzantine Christianity does it to some extent too, as the British public discovered during the Cyprus troubles of 1954–59. And if Communism may be classed as a religion, then it certainly does so as well. The phenomenon seems characteristic of the East. We find it in a religion so devoid of dogma, so loosely organised as Buddhism. Wriggins, discussing nationalism and religion in Ceylon, emphasises that Buddhists there have 'no indigenous tradition of the separation of Church and State, which has done so much in western Europe to promote the notion of Caesar's province, as distinct from the realm of religion; in Asia, the two have not been different worlds, but they interpenetrated and merged'.

The problem may be approached another way, by reference to historical events in Europe since the fifteenth century. The Islamic world has had no Reformation and Counter-Reformation, no Renaissance; has made no conscious, comprehensive effort to adapt itself to the facts of science, such as Christendom began to do at about that time. Nor, except at second hand, has it had any convulsive political experience such as the French Revolution, from which our concept of the secular national State in the West emerged. Groups of Muslim modernists have often attempted reform, in Turkey, Egypt, India and elsewhere, but Islam as a whole has remained resistant, still in much the same shape, formally, as at the outset of the Abbasid Caliphate, a mere 118 years after the Prophet's death in A.D. 632.

And then there are the objectionable social items, already foreshadowed, which antagonise Westerners, such as polygamy, and purdah or feminine segregation (these things are not really Koranic, and will be discussed further in Chapter 3); or the often-adduced but in fact virtually discarded Koranic injunction about cutting off a habitual thief's hand or limb, a thing only rarely heard of nowadays, in countries like Afghanistan, Saudi Arabia and the Yemen. Even the word Islam itself is suspect to some Westerners, for it means submission, or resignation – to God's will – and is therefore thought to pave the way towards fatalistic acceptance by the masses of autocracy. And on top of all this, in Pakistan's case, has come her association, over a period of years, with 'Islamic', a word which carries a formidable meaning for scholars. 'Muslim' merely signifies someone ready to make the Faith's workmanlike short declaration that 'There is no god but God, and Mohammad is his Prophet'. But 'Islamic' implies full acceptance not only of the Koran and the Sunna, but of the Sharia, the vast mass of religious law evolved by Islamic schoolmen a thousand years or more ago, and expounded by the ulema, the professional theologians.

Pakistan's present Constitution, as enacted by the military régime in 1962, did not declare Pakistan 'Islamic'. The omission seems to have been deliberate. Some months later the term was re-introduced by an amendment. It had been conspicuous at the opening of the politicians' Constitution of 1956; and undeniably, the eight years' dreary controversy between the mullahs and the modernisers before that earlier Constitution was agreed to, and then that formal 'Islamic' assertion did her much international damage. It meant that many Westerners still vaguely suppose her a country dominated by reactionary clergy busy formulating fatwas (holy edicts), awaiting chances to start jihad (holy war), and bent on thrusting outmoded dogmas down an unbeliever's throat.

The amount of dogma in Islam is in fact relatively small; less than in Christianity. There are few bewildering items such as the Trinity for a doubter to swallow. And the picture formed by Western intellectuals of Pakistan as 'theocratic', medieval and retrograde owes much to utterances by leading Indian politicians, notably Mr. Nehru, an Edwardian-style agnostic and Socialist from Harrow and Cambridge, but in origin nevertheless Hindu and Brahmin. Since Tilak's time more than fifty years ago, contacts between Westernised Hindus and British Leftists have been many and close, the latters' ideas about the problems of a vast, complex subcontinent often having filtered almost wholly through the minds of the former. However, it remains true, and to Pakistan's detriment for propagandist purposes, that no other major Muslim State has associated itself with the word 'Islamic' in quite this way :[4] not Indonesia – her only rival in population-strength – nor any of the (to a Western eye) better-known ones bordering the Mediterranean. Turkey indeed – her ally – deliberately took quite the opposite path. Under Ataturk's reforms of the 1920's she put harsh domestic curbs on the practice of Islam; abolished the Caliphate; banned theologians from participation in politics, proscribed many things traditional to the Muslim way of life such as the Arabic script, purdah for women, and public use by men of brimless headgear like the fez (a necessity when at prayer); and unequivocally proclaimed herself a secular State of Western type. What are we to make of so striking a contrast?

Much less, in this writer's view, than people who have not lived in Pakistan might think. Those who have, would probably concur that she quite lacks the 'feel' of an intolerant, reactionary society, or indeed of one capable in the normal course of becoming so; and that this was as true under the Constitution of 1956 as it is now. The outward structure of life is Western and liberal. Foreign visitors hear little about the theologians and are cordially received. Christian missionaries experience fewer difficulties than in the professedly secular Indian Union. At no time in Pakistan's twenty years of life – except perhaps briefly in Khwaja Nazimuddin's Prime Ministership, during the anti-Ahmadi riots of 1953 in Lahore – has there been any practical possibility of her falling under the sway of the mullahs, influential and active though some of them such as Maulana Maudoodi are.[5]

The power of such people, actually, has proved perceptibly less than in that other ideological State of the 1940's, which most Western progressives regard so much more amiably, Israel. There, rabbinical authority enforces a Sabbatarianism perhaps drearier than in Victorian Scotland; from dusk on Friday until Saturday night, most public transport ceases, and cargoes remain unhandled at the ports; cars driving through orthodox districts may be stoned. If as Crossman asserts, 90 per cent of Israelis are agnostics, it is strange that they should endure such things. Pakistan, by contrast, has not even bothered, since British rule ended, to shift her weekly rest formally to the Muslim prayer-day, Friday, as in most Muslim countries. Some

[4] Unless we include Iraq, which did so in her provisional Constitution of 1958. Islam, of course, is the State religion in many predominantly Muslim countries; but that does not carry the theological implications of dubbing the country 'Islamic'. The distinction may seem fine; but it is real.

[5] Authorities such as Binder subdivide the mullahs into two groups: the ulema proper, or traditionalists; and the Maudoodi group, or Jama'at-i-Islami, whom he terms fundamentalists.

of the banks close that day, but otherwise she continues happily to shut up shop on the Westerners' Sunday, and transport plies uninhibited every day of the week. In Israel again – though not in Pakistan – pig-breeding has been made illegal; and medical teaching is recurrently threatened with difficulties because of religious objection to dissection of corpses. And marriage of a Jew with a non-Jew on Israeli soil cannot occur, because the official rabbinate has prevented provision for civil marriages. And enforcement of rules about kosher food makes many Israeli meals meatless, not from poverty, as may widely apply in Pakistan, but because imports of preserved meat not certified as slaughtered in the ritual Jewish way are banned. And no Pakistani equivalent exists, either, for the Israelis' choice of a national language. They rejected Yiddish and Ladino; as also possible modern substitutes such as Polish, German, English, or Arabic. Instead, they decided to enclose their living thought within the antique structure of Hebrew, a language which indeed they have enlarged with characteristic skill since the 1920's, but which, except for liturgical purposes, has been dead for more than two thousand years.

Another striking point, which should allay the Western intelligentsia's misgivings, is that the Pakistan-concept, throughout its evolution, has in fact been modernist not only in general spirit, but in leadership. The foremost men in the Muslim revival during the seventy years or so before the new State was born – Syed Ahmad Khan, Syed Ameer Ali, Sir Mohammad Iqbal – were all reformers, persons unorthodox in outlook, disapproved of by the theologians. Iqbal, who died as recently as 1938, was a particularly adventurous thinker. All of them wanted change; worked actively for the overthrow of things outmoded within the Muslim Faith and social structure; were enthusiasts for integrating the community's thought with the latest scientific knowledge. On the other hand the theologians, whom Westerners usually assume encouraged the concept, actually opposed it almost to a man: not merely because those who advocated it were reformers, but on the broader ground of principle that it was nationalist, and nationalism, by implying fragmentation of the Muslim world into separate States, runs counter to Islamic theory. Indeed we may find in Pakistan, when experienced enough to know where to look for it, a strange, and for the connoisseur fascinating barrier between her professional theologians and her Westernised upper-middle classes, such as probably no other 'under-developed' Afro-Asian country can offer. It consists not so much of lack of mutual sympathy between these groups, as of an often total incapacity for a meeting of differently-educated minds. This anomaly, a by-product of scholastic events in the later nineteenth century, explains much of the otherwise unpredictable quality of Pakistani national life, which so baffles many Western observers. It will be discussed further in Chapter 18.

Most of the movement's leading personages, during those first seventy years or so, though suspect in the theologians' eyes, were nevertheless practising Muslims. That can scarcely be said of the great man who personally brought Pakistan into being, Mr. Jinnah, whom as a nation-builder future historians may have to reckon the Asian counterpart of Bismarck or Cavour. During much of his life he paid scant heed to conventional religious observances, and indeed was said, at one time, to hold opinions not very unlike Ataturk's. Circumstances in the Turkey of the 1920's and in the India of the 1940's were, however, very dissimilar. What concerned him – utterly absorbed him in his latter years, calling forth all the strength of an extraordinary will – was to preserve the culture of the subcontinent's Muslim community against (as he saw it) the rising threat of suffocation by militant revivalist Hinduism, a culture and a religion combined, wholly inimical to everything Muslim, which was using the ballot-box as its instrument, and hypocritically concealing itself behind the Congress party's secular cloak. 'In my judgement,' he said in 1939, 'democracy can only mean Hindu raj all over India; to this, Muslims will never submit.' Till his death, it was a standpoint from which he never deviated. He based his policies on the 'two-nation' theory. This was not of his devising, its origins can be found in Syed Ahmad Khan's works of sixty years before, but he developed it to its fullest. It postulated that the subcontinent's Muslims now constituted a genuine nation distinct from the Hindus, as entitled to self-government, on the evidently now imminent break-up of the British Empire in India after World War II, as were, say – though he may not have put it in these terms – Czechoslovaks or Yugoslavs on the Austro-Hungarian Empire's break-up after World War I. It was a proposition woven mainly from politics, culture, economics and history, with not much religion necessarily in it. And that of course explains the confusion about the nature of the Pakistani State, which has since perplexed not only foreigners, but many Pakistanis themselves.

Pakistan's first Prime Minister, Mr. Liaquat Ali Khan, though more disposed than Mr. Jinnah towards religious observance, was unmistakably modernist. So were most of the country's leading politicians from 1947 to 1958. As Callard puts it, 'the background of the men who organised the campaign (for Pakistan) was not theology and Islamic law, but politics and the common law; not Deoband,[6]

---

[6] A Muslim theological college near Saharanpur in Northern India.

but Cambridge and the Inns of Court.' F.-M. Ayub Khan, President
since the military revolution of 1958, is a practising Muslim, and (like
some other Sandhurst men) can talk very attractively to his compatriots about religion in simple soldierly terms. But like soldiers
everywhere, he has little use for abstractions, and keeps his feet
firmly planted on this solid earth. Nor has he hesitated, for purposes
of social betterment, to push through drastic changes in customs
which had become linked with religion, by means mainly of the
remarkable Muslim Family Laws Ordinance of March 1961, which
put restrictions on polygamy and divorce. It would be laughable to
suppose that his régime, composed until the lifting of martial law in
1962 entirely of realists recruited from Government service, the
professions, and business, would let itself be swayed, in decisions of
State, by reactionary counsels from the mullahs. So far as generalisations on such intangibles are valid, it may be said that the attitude
of Pakistan's senior military officers and civil servants – the con-
scientious men who have in fact throughout enabled the country to
surmount the hazards of her early years – differs on the average
little from that of Westerners in similar positions : religion, they
would tell you, is an excellent thing in its place, but it needs to be
kept there.

    This matter of the Pakistani State's involvement with Islam, in
any case, needs shifting round, so as to appear as it would in South
Asia. One may imagine a patriotic Pakistani, riled by the foreign
intelligentsia's suspicions, launching zestful counter-attacks. Are
there not Western nations, he might ask, where religion and Government are also rather entwined: England, for instance? Would he be
wrong in supposing that the Head of State there, on taking office, has
to avow his (or her) intention to preserve a particular Christian sect,
the Anglican : a sect which, incidentally – or is this mere ribaldry? –
owes its origins partly to the accident that a monarch of early times,
Henry VIII, had exceptionally many wives? And have not this
sect's leading dignitaries since been appointed, not even really by the
Head of State, but by the leading politician in office plus some civil
servants, who nowadays might not be members of that Christian sect
at all, nor indeed of any, but be Jews, or agnostics? And are not
twenty-six of these particular dignitaries, to the exclusion of those of
the other Christian sects, automatically made participants in politics, by membership of the Upper House? And is there not also a
funny custom – or perhaps this exaggerates? – whereby the selfsame
Head of State, when he (or she) travels north, after crossing a river
called the Tweed, forthwith changes sect, and becomes a practising

member of the Presbyterian Church of Scotland? In their country, in Pakistan, they might cheerfully point out, matters are not pushed so far. Though the President must under the Constitution be a Muslim, which seems reasonable, he need not, when he moves about, alter the details of faith and worship. Shias or Ismailis or Ahmadis would not mind his remaining, throughout his domestic travels, if he was so at the start, a Sunni. And have not the organs of public opinion in Britain, the newspapers and wireless, a habit of giving the views on national affairs of Britain's various kinds of mullah – the archbishops and bishops and moderators, the deans, canons and reverends – much prominence, implying that, because of these gentlemen's ecclesiastical status, what they say on politics has special weight? Might not a visitor to Britain from Mars, listening to the radio bulletins, be led to believe, not that Christians are a minority on this planet, which they are, but that it is peopled almost wholly by them and indeed, usually, by Anglicans?

Such pleasantries may help a Westerner to put things right. The real explanation of the undeniable anomaly that Pakistan, though an ideological State created for Muslims, is not dominated by reactionary mullahs – and is indeed as bent as any other in Asia on participation in the evolving, modern world – lies in her relations with India. Here we come back to the heart of the matter; to the cardinal fact of Pakistan's national life : her fear, as she sees it, and as emphasised earlier, of being swamped beneath a massive, hostile, nearby Hindu culture. A man could be an enthusiastic Pakistani, and of Muslim upbringing, yet irreligious, a convinced disbeliever in Islam. There is the well-known case of the rich Muslim of Delhi, in adult life an atheist, who in 1949 – well after the horrors of the Partition-time riots were over – announced his intention of emigrating to Pakistan, at heavy financial loss. When asked why, he said he could not abide the new Sanskritised Hindi, he wanted Urdu; and he enjoyed beef. Mr. Jinnah, in one of his most publicised interviews, vividly illustrated the cultural differences' extent. 'Islam is not merely a religious doctrine,' he explained, 'but a realistic and practical code of conduct – in terms of everything important in life : of our history, our heroes, our art, our architecture, our music, our laws, our jurisprudence. In all these things, our outlook is not only fundamentally different, but often radically antagonistic to the Hindus'. Our names, our clothes, our foods – they are all different; our economic life, our educational ideas, our treatment of women, our attitude to animals – we challenge each other at every point. Take one example. We eat the cow. the Hindus worship it. Englishmen imagine this is merely a picturesque convention; it is nothing of the sort. Only a few days ago, in this city, the cow-question became a matter for the police.'

Pakistan, then, may be looked on not as a militant country, poised towards proselytisation or renewed conquests – in spite of Islam's real latent tendencies towards such things – but essentially as a defensive one, on guard; brought into being to maintain a culture that most of her inhabitants highly value; and to be a refuge to which like-minded Muslims everywhere on the subcontinent could go. Are not the facts of population-size, Pakistanis would ask, alone proof enough of this defensiveness? Though Hindus may well consider Islam formidable, when they look back on the past, surely Muslims, looking out on the present, have even better cause for finding Hinduism so? The subcontinent contains about 380 million Hindus, but only 125 million Muslims. Or, to put it differently, in terms of the 1947 frontiers : the Indian Union's Hindus amount to about 370 millions, Pakistan's Muslims to only 83 millions.[7] How, on such figures, Pakistanis would ask, could any Indian honestly fear Pakistani attack? Are not the Muslims the people to be afraid? Nor, of course, is numerical superiority the Hindus' only advantage. Pakistanis would hasten to adduce other important things, such as comparative industrial and financial power, and educational advancement – things we must leave over for later chapters.

At the start of this book, we described Pakistan as something very unusual in the twentieth-century world(an ideological State) one founded in large part on sentiments of a religious or doctrinal sort; and comparisons were made with Communist Russia, and with Israel. It remains true that she is such a State; but – as will by now have been guessed – it is probably less so than was originally supposed. For the more valid the secular aspect of the 'two-nation' theory has proved to be, the greater becomes her similarity with the other countries on the earth's surface, all the ordinary non-ideological ones. This antithesis keeps many Pakistanis, and outside commentators on Pakistan, in confusion. Partly, the trouble is that mere words, abstractions, are being struggled with; translated words, too. 'Nation' is no easy thing to define, even in English; nor 'religion'. And when those terms are shifted from a Western environment into unfamiliar Eastern ones, for use by people having very different kinds of historical background, the difficulty worsens. What mainly matters, is how the people concerned feel.

Judged by that test, it seems undeniable that Pakistan, however ideological she may be, is also in the secular sense a nation – simply

[7] 1961 statistics.

because she has survived as such. For twenty years, despite extra-ordinary pressures and adversities, she has continued in full being within her allotted frontiers, sustained by the strong feelings of her leaders and people for preserving her independence. Opinion among them still oscillates as to which of the two cements for their State has the firmer permanent binding-power : Islam, or nationalist spirit. And during the critical years 1940–7 which preceded her birth, when British rule was expiring, many of the subcontinent's Muslims – Western-educated ones, as well as the masses – were mentally in a complete muddle about their future. They belonged – this they knew – to one of the four main civilisations into which humanity is tradi-tionally grouped: Islam; Christendom; Hinduism plus its Buddhist and Sikh offshoots; the distinctive Sino-Japanese civilisation of the Far East. And they increasingly realised that, though on the sub-continent Hindus and Muslims had at times lived tolerantly beside one another under British imperial sway (as under Moghul sway before), the chances, after it had gone, of their amicably combining into a single self-governing democracy were infinitesimal. But many were unready, yet, to swallow in full the idea of the Western-style nation-State. It seemed neither small enough, nor big enough, to grip their loyalties. It lacked the customary pull of affection for family, tribe, province, or linguistic unit; nor did it offer the com-fortable sense of inclusion in a broad frontierless Islamic brother-hood. It remains, for large numbers of them, an idea that needs getting used to.

And who would blame them? The idea is alien to Asia and Africa; an import from Europe of recent date. Outside the Indo-Pakistani subcontinent as within, its emotional hold is unsure. And everywhere during the last three or four decades the impact of change has been unprecedented. Even in the West, there has been no time for orderly adjustment. In regions such as South Asia, the stresses have of course been greater. Whether illiterate or sophisticated, its inhabitants have experienced innovations unequalled in history, chronology telescop-ing upon itself in brutal fashion, the twentieth century thrusting right through into (say) the seventeenth.

Present signs however suggest that, in Pakistan as in the other two ideological States mentioned, nationalism is proving stronger than doctrine. Mr. Stalin's eliminations of the theorists of the Bolshevik revolution, and the empiricism of Mr. Khrushchev and his successors, have altered the Soviet experiment. Marxist-Leninist dogma is not applied as it was. Revolution everywhere is less blatantly worked for; peaceful co-existence is spoken of; old-style patriotic sentiment has been allowed to revive. To the Chinese, Russia has become 'revisionist'; but their own Communism is derivatory, its teachings came from Russia, and its present course early in 1967 under Mr. Mao's new urgings is unpredictable. And in Russia, the contrasts in daily life with that prevailing in non-Communist countries has in recent years much narrowed. Similarly with Israel. From the time of the Sinai campaign in 1956, if not earlier, the indications have been that the rabbis, the traditionalists and the romantics are losing in their struggle with the practical men and modernists, with those bent on accommodation with the contemporary world as it is. Some of the 'sabra', the young pioneers on the so-called communal farms, the most interesting people in the State, tend now to proclaim an Israeli patriotism only. They ignore or even repudiate the Jewish Faith, and favour cutting their links with such Jews as, despite the creation of Israel, choose to remain 'of the Dispersion'.

If what is exceptional about Pakistan were to disappear, some would feel sorry. The world would be a duller place were every country to become of a type. But as with Israel, so with Pakistan, much that seemed to threaten their existence two decades ago is now taken for granted. The longer each State survives, the greater become habits of cohesion. Less need is found for a sustaining faith; the younger folk look forward and out, rather than back. But for the persisting nearby antagonism of a numerically bigger Arab culture in the one case, and of a Hindu culture in the other, most of what is ideological and peculiar in these two otherwise so different and estranged creations of twentieth-century statecraft might shrivel away.

Chapter 2

The Land

THE last chapter stressed what an exceptional country Pakistan is, because of the ideological basis on which she was set up. But she is exceptional too – probably indeed unique – in another way; one which, so far, we have touched on but not examined: in her geography; in the fact that she consists of two distinct blocks of territory, her so-called East and West 'wings', unconnected with one another, and, moreover, about 1,000 miles apart.[1] It was this very peculiar disjunction, more than anything else, that gave rise to the many doubts, widely voiced at the time of her birth, on whether she could survive.

And it still causes misgiving, for there is something more. The two wings themselves, besides being startlingly far apart physically, differ much in character : on such important matters as their size, and their respective population-densities; their climate, their kind of landscape, the things their agriculture produces; a good deal of their history; their more pressing strategic hazards; and their inhabitants' language, dress, diet, and (to some extent) physique and temperament too.

The West wing is a large sprawling object on the map, very conspicuous, about as large as France and Britain together. It covers 310,000 square miles.[2]. The East wing on the other hand might almost be overlooked; it is only about a sixth as big, covering a mere 55,000 square miles. Yet it is this latter wing, the East one, which paradoxically contains most of Pakistan's inhabitants: no fewer than 50,840,000, as against the West's 42,880,000. The respective population-densities of the two wings, the smaller and the larger, thus work out at 922 and 138 per square mile – a really astonishing contrast, which, however, the contrasts of terrain and rainfall in large measure explain.

It has been rightly said that, whereas in West Pakistan the villager gets about by camel, in East Pakistan he does so by boat. For the one region is dry; the other wet. East Pakistan is a delta, perhaps the

---

[1] A convenient generalisation. At their nearest point, about 725 miles. Distance between Karachi and Dacca, 1,175 miles.

[2] Excluding a further large area which, for practical purposes, is part of Pakistan, namely Pakistani-held Kashmir, 31,000 square miles; but including the former federal area of Karachi, 8,000 square miles.

biggest in the world; a land almost totally flat, through which two immense river-systems, the Ganges and the Brahmaputra, join up to find, uncertainly, their eventual meandering exits to the sea; a land, therefore, cut through by countless watercourses, big and little, straight or twisty, and dotted over with lakes and swamps.

During much of the rainy season, between May and October, vast tracts of it, especially round the Meghna estuary, get almost submerged : nothing breaks the surface of an apparently limitless inundation, except here and there a slow-moving country boat, and branches of half-drowned trees, and marooned homesteads and hamlets standing up fifteen feet or so from the hidden fields on artificial earthy rises. But by autumn, the ponderous, sagging belts of monsoon-cloud have gone, an open heaven shines above, and the waste of dun-coloured waters is transformed to a land of infinite sunny greenness – mainly the vivid green of rice-plants, growing in their mud-rimmed shallows of breeze-ruffled water. Two and sometimes three rice-crops are raised yearly, on soils regularly enriched, with little or no ado on the farmer's part, by the silt laid down in the annual flooding. And if the green is not of rice, it is probably of rough-looking jute. Around the homesteads of thatch and palm-frond, pleasant sorts of trees cluster : dark-leaved mango; banyans, pipals, tamarinds; clumps of feathery bamboo; tall-boled toddy-palms and date-palms. In pools on the adjacent low ground, black water-buffaloes wallow. Above the level horizons, the empty dome of blue sky may sometimes be crossed by an indolent white cloud, or, nearer, by flights of spindly-legged waterfowl.

Undeniably the scene, in these bright winter or spring months, has much charm, marred however perhaps by its repetitiveness, by what seems an unending uniformity. Only in the far south-east corner near the Burmese frontier does one find hills : real, sudden hills; the lovely but cruel, steep-folded, jungle-draped, leech-infested hills of the Chittagong Tracts and the Arakan, in which, during 1943–5, the Allied Forces waged bitter campaigns against the Japanese. From amongst the tea-gardens of Sylhet, hills are indeed also visible; but they stand mostly just beyond the Indian frontier, in Assam or Tripura. Elsewhere, the observant may notice slight deviations from the monotonous flatness in two places : the Madhupur area, between the Meghna tributary and the main Brahmaputra channel; and the Barind, up against the Indian frontier between Brahmaputra and Ganges. Here, the land surface is a trifle higher, and the soil rather less fertile, for the underlying alluvium is older; one sees rough, uncultivated scrub land, and some stretches of virgin forest. And along the sea face in the south, over an area about 150 miles broad

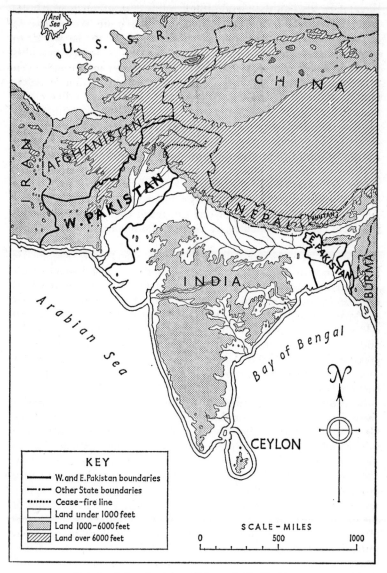

South Asia showing W. and E. Pakistan

[Please see also maps facing p. 284]

by 60 deep, though the terrain is if possible flatter than ever, its surface alters startlingly and completely. The fields cease. We leave what is perhaps the most populous agricultural region in the world, to enter primitive, practically uninhabited jungle – a fact which makes the East wing's over-all density of 922 persons per square mile even more remarkable. This is the Sundarbans, the vast double delta-mouth of Brahmaputra and Ganges; a maze of turbid saline creeks and channels, into whose watery edges crowd down great stilt-rooted trees such as the mangrove, festooned with creepers; or the nipa-palm and the towering sundri, which gives its name to the region. Voyaging along the intersecting channels, one glides within what seem tubes or corridors of solid foliage. It is story-book tropical jungle in extreme form; the kind of thing which rich tourists from New York or Southampton might spend weeks on luxury liners travelling to the Amazon to see, but which anyone can reach cheaply in less than a day from Dacca, or Calcutta, by local paddle-steamer.

Calcutta, the former 'second city' of the British Empire, is however not in Pakistan. It is capital of the part of Bengal which went to the Indian Union in 1947, and Dacca of the part which became Pakistani, to which was added most of the Sylhet district of Assam. The resulting East wing of Pakistan, though as stated oddly small compared with the West wing, is larger than the Indian Union's State of West Bengal : 55,000 square miles, as compared with 34,000. And besides being the larger, it has a more productive agriculture, and is healthier than West Bengal because less malarious.

Both these advantages are due to huge, extraordinary shiftings of river-courses within historic times. Until the seventeenth century, the Ganges' main exit to the sea was down what has since become a minor and brackish though internationally famous channel, risky to navigate because liable to get choked by silt: the Hooghly. Then, for obscure reasons that geographers quarrel about, the river began gradually pushing south-east across the delta from near Nawabganj, until now, via its Padma channel and the southernmost reaches of the Brahmaputra, it emerges as a mighty stream into the Bay of Bengal about 175 miles away, just short of Chandpur. Similarly the Brahmaputra itself, farther up course, has shifted too; a major though less extensive move, and in the opposite direction – westwards. Until the 1780's, its main stream ran through Mymensingh to enter the Meghna tributary near Bhairab Bazar, instead of down the then unimportant channel known as the Jamuna, about 70 miles to the west, to join the Ganges directly, as now. And two other tributaries, at about the same period, changed course as well, and in sudden, calamitous fashion – the Damodar and the Tista; notorious streams, amply entitled, from their many devastations over the centuries, to borrow a name from China and call themselves Rivers of Sorrow. In 1770 the Damodar, which drains stormwater from the Hazaribagh-Ranchi hills of Bihar into the lower Hooghly, suddenly swung its outlet 80 miles farther south, incidentally thereby much increasing the silting upstream in the Hooghly's middle reaches. And seventeen years later the Tista, which emerges abruptly through narrow gorges on to the Bengal plains from a titanic Himalayan catchment-area around Everest, abandoned its established course to the Ganges altogether, and forced open a fresh bed for itself, about 150 miles long, into the Brahmaputra beyond Rangpur.

All this together has worked out badly for what is now West Bengal. Compared with East Pakistan, it is a land of dead or dying rivers; of navigation-channels filled with debris dropped by slow-moving water, which need frequent costly dredging; of fields not exposed to regular summer floods, and so unrefreshed by annual layers of fertilising new silt; of countless mosquito-breeding swamps and stagnant backwaters – and thus of malaria. And if a big new Indian barrage is soon to be built across the Ganges at Farakka, to increase the water-flow down the Hooghly by 35,000 cusecs,[3] that, it seems, would inevitably cause great harm in East Pakistan. Farakka is only ten miles upstream from the Pakistani frontier, and according to some reports work there had already started in 1966. This evoked sharp Pakistani protests. Pakistan has also complained about the effects on East Pakistan of new Indian embankments along the Brahmaputra in Assam.

Although in the ways described East Pakistan is a pleasanter place than West Bengal, it has the more violent climate. Whereas the latter's average rainfall at about 55 inches annually may be reckoned merely adequate or plentiful, East Pakistan's except in Rajshahi district is undeniably excessive. Some places along the Chittagong coast and up in its hilly hinterland, and beside the Meghna estuary, and around Sylhet town, and near Rangpur in the far north, may get as much as 150–200 inches. And above Sylhet district, just across the Indian frontier in the Khasi hills of Assam, rises the most rain-drenched bit of country in the world, around the famous village of Cherrapunji, which averages about 425 inches, and on occasions (e.g. in 1861) has been known to exceed 900 (equalling about 75 feet of water). Moreover, some of East Pakistan's rain does not come

[3] Cusec = cubic foot of water per second.

quietly, in steady downpours; it arrives in storms of extraordinary force, during the weeks either before, or after, the rainy season proper. (West Bengal gets these storms too; but because precipitation there is less, they are fewer.) The storms of April and May, known as 'nor'-westers', are curious local cyclonic disturbances characteristic of the Bengal basin, which fascinate meteorologists. But although the huge electrical discharges from them, the walls of suddenly descending water (with hailstones perhaps), and the blasts of wind may appal, they only become calamitous in a large way if coincident with high tides at the main river-mouths – as one did in May 1941 around Barisal and Noakhali, drowning about 7,500 people. However the storms of autumn, developing in the Bay of Bengal during the withdrawal of the rains proper, are much more wide-ranging systems; true tropical typhoons or hurricanes, analogous to those of the China Seas and the Caribbean. Perhaps the worst year on record for them was 1960, when two big ones in succession – which is very unusual – struck the East Pakistan coast within four weeks. The total deathroll then was estimated at 14,000; and so fierce was the wind, as to blow a 10,000-ton cargo vessel eight miles inland, riding on the invading waters, where it stood thereafter for months, marooned among the rice-fields, testifying to the storm's quality. Vast material damage was done over a large area, temporarily crippling East Pakistan's economy. Other years of catastrophic casualties and damage from typhoons during the last century or so have been 1864, 1876, 1919, 1942, 1961, 1963 and 1965.

Obviously East Pakistan's over-lavish rainfall, her propensity for being flooded, and for occasional devastating storms, and the fact that her rivers are not moribund like West Bengal's, but active, in continuous process both of creating new land, and of changing course, means that getting about there can be quite a job; and in fact the only really efficient travel-media are not by ground, but by air or water. In a region made essentially of mud, dried or drying, indigenous 'road-metal' and railway ballast are non-existent; the nearest stone is found about 400 miles north of the sea, and it costs much to transport. And when built, the roads and railways, so as to circumvent great unbridgeable water-channels and the more particularly flood-prone tracts, may take routes very devious and slow. Even in the old days, before Partition in 1947, the most frequently done journey in Bengal – the journey between Calcutta and Dacca – was an exasperating one. There was no through motor-road. By the shorter of the two rail-plus-river routes, it covered 225 miles and took about thirteen hours, the change from train to steamer being a nuisance. Yet by air, the two cities are only about 145 miles or fifty minutes apart. And political severance in 1947 of course made things much worse, if only because of delays due to frontier-formalities; and from the engineering aspect, the undivided British province's communications system was now broken up in ways often wholly irrational.

Because of all this, much of East Pakistan is in actuality remote, inaccessible, out of touch with the world, to an extent hard to realise when the region's mere size, and relatively compact outline, are looked at on an atlas. And here we reach another paradox. For although so densely populated, East Pakistan is essentially rural; much more so than West. Towns are few, and small, and mostly of negligible importance except for marketing; what matters is the fertile fields, and their assiduous cultivation from immensely many scattered hamlets and homesteads. Chittagong indeed is of growing significance as a port; and the Chalna anchorage, near Khulna, is also being developed. But there is only one sizable town, Dacca, which if its new industrial offshoots at Narayanganj 10 miles or so away are included, may be claimed to have 720,000 inhabitants; that is to say, about a third of those of Karachi, and about a fifth of those of Calcutta, which lies – it is startling to reflect on – a mere 40 miles beyond the Indian frontier.

Now for the West wing. Whereas East Pakistan is in the main tropical, and has a moist, warm, languorous climate of 'oceanic' type in which temperature-changes are slight, none of West Pakistan lies in the tropics at all. And it is dry country, harshly arid indeed in parts; with a 'continental' climate which means big, abrupt changes of temperature between different times of day and different seasons, as well of course as between heights – and the heights, in contrast to the East wing's, differ greatly. Its non-tropical position on the map, when pointed out, surprises most Europeans and Americans. The principality of Chitral, its uppermost bit, stands about as far north as Athens or San Francisco; and the terrain there being mountainous, the climate, the flora and fauna, and the people's complexions and clothing-requirements are rather like those of upland regions within the temperate zone, such as (say) the Sierra Nevada of Spain, or America's Colorado. Indeed, parts of Chitral may well be described as less than temperate, because near its frontier with Afghanistan it includes one of Asia's really big mountains: Tirich Mir, over 25,000 feet high, in the Hindu Kush system.

But generalisations about the West wing, such as were offered about the East, are unfitting. It is too vast and varied for them; it wants scrutinising sector by sector. Physiographically, it contains

several other towering snowy mountain ranges besides the Hindu
Kush – the Karakoram, parts of the Himalaya proper, and the not
negligible Safed Koh; deserts burningly fierce, as in Africa or Arabia;
immense green irrigated fertile plains; and much jumbled stony
plateau country. Climatically, at the right times of year, it can be
delightful, as healthy and exhilarating as anywhere in the world:
crisp, frosty dawns; afternoons of cloudless sunshine; a pleasant
breeze; skies sparkling with stars at night. But at other times and
places it can be perishingly cold; or almost insufferably hot, dried
up, and dusty; or, in the north during the few weeks in late summer
when cloud-laden monsoon airs push dubiously across the plains, as
moistly, enervatingly warm as Bengal at its worst.

Due east of Chitral – the tract referred to just now – and even
more mountainous, is the Gilgit agency; still nominally part of the
disputed principality of Kashmir, but in fact administered by Pakistan for the last twenty years; a great attraction internationally for
glaciologists, rock-climbers, and the more intrepid sort of tourist, for
it contains, in the Karakoram range, the biggest concentration of
lofty peaks that exists : thirty-three summits over 24,000 feet high,
crammed into an area about the size of the Swiss Alps; so many,
that most of them have not even got names. The spectacle is terrific.
Probably the best known are K2, at 28,250 feet the second highest
mountain in the world; Rakaposhi; the four main Gasherbrum
summits; Distaghil; Masherbrum; and Kanjut Sar. The region also
includes the two charming, romantically secluded little mountain
principalities of Hunza and Nagar – not far from the frontier with
China – which have captivated many writers' fancy. To get to the
Gilgit agency is still an adventure. Soon it may not be; an all-weather
road is being built up the difficult right bank of the Indus via Swat
Kohistan. But hitherto, since 1948 – the former track via Gurais
being straddled by the U.N.-supervised 'cease-fire' line, and so un-
available – there have been only two ways of reaching it. Either, in
summer, to go by jeep over the Babusar pass, which however is
snow-blocked for most of the year; or else to fly, by what is
probably the most spectacular air-route in the world, with grim
spiky ice-tipped crags shouldering in on either side, and, to starboard,
the huge white bulk of Nanga Parbat above them, almost 27,000 feet
high.

That terrible mountain, which has killed nearly as many brave
climbers as all the other great peaks of Asia combined,[4] is not
in the Karakoram; it is the westernmost summit of the Himalaya.
The two ranges are geologically distinct. And no other summit

[4] 37, up to 1960.

approaching Nanga Parbat in height is to be found eastwards in the Himalaya for 450 miles, until we reach Nanda Devi in Uttar Pradesh. It stands thus majestically alone, towering above its neighbours, a fact which intensifies its beauty – but also its murderous power for inducing unpredictable sudden storms.

To its south and south-east, and to its south-west – we are still nominally on Kashmir soil here – the land falls away in a tangle of what locally are reckoned foothills, though a less slighting term would be used for them in Europe, for many are taller than Mt. Blanc: Baramula, Uri and Poonch, Kotli and Mirpur, Rajaori and Bhim-bar, towards Chambh and Akhnur and Jammu – country battled over during the Indo-Pakistani fighting about Kashmir in 1947–8 and 1965; and away towards the Hazara district of the former Frontier Province and the Pathan tribal principalities of Swat and Dir in the south-west. Scenically, all this land is rather similar. As in Bengal among the flatness, so here among Himalayan foothills, the same theme, seemingly without end, repeats itself: narrow-floored valleys, in cross-section V-shaped, whose sides rise steeply through conifer-clad slopes to crests which, in places, are always snow-topped, reaching maxima at 17,000 feet or so. Roads, as a rule, wind deviously along the valleys' sides, the floors below being too torrential and boulder-strewn to take them; and many of them are new: built for strategic purposes created by the Kashmir dispute. Some would consider it characterless, tedious country – except perhaps at two points, where it excitingly widens to permit abrupt egress of mighty rivers to the plains : the Indus; and further west, its almost equally big tributary the Jhelum.

Enclosed, after their emergence, between Indus and Jhelum as between a pair of arms, lies the curious block of country known as the Potwar plateau; rimmed to east and south by the relatively puny, though impressive escarpments of the geologically complex Salt Range, which average about 3,000 feet and near Sakesar reach 5,000. Large-scale irrigation, naturally, is impracticable in such broken terrain; and the plateau's pebbly surface and thin soil, lying usually at a height of about 1,700 feet and based on a rough porous pudding-stone, includes big tracts incapable of cultivation. But rain-fed crops of surprising quality are often raised in the hollows, or on artificial terraces. The plateau also breeds a fine hardy race of men, too numerous however for its agriculture to sustain, so that many find employment in the Army. During spring especially, when patches of the tawny undulating landscape become vivid green under growing wheat, or yellow with mustard, this perhaps on first acquaintance unalluring region displays a strange charm of its own, receding unevenly into its remote powder-blue distances under wide windy azure skies. And away to the east, when visibility is good, shines in provoking beauty the snow-topped Himalayan fore-range called the Pir Panjal, unattainable for Pakistanis, a symbol of South Asia's 'cold war'. For between them and it wriggles the cease-fire line; the splendour of mountain is inside the part of Kashmir held by India's forces. Administratively, the Potwar plateau centres on Rawalpindi, an important town through which runs the grand trunk route for road and railway between Lahore and Peshawar; another road takes off north for Murree and Muzafferabad. And nearby, since 1960, Pakistan's new federal capital has been a-building as substitute for Karachi : Islamabad, impressive even now, a thriving modern creation and with about 60,000 inhabitants.

Continuing south-east from the Potwar, through the escarpment and across the Jhelum river towards Gujrat, we emerge on the West Pakistan plains; from a geographer's point of view, merely one sector of the immense Indo-Gangetic flatness, the great curving belt of alluvial lowland drained by Indus and Ganges which spans the whole north of the subcontinent; and on which it is possible – or was, before events in 1947 interfered with communications – to go uninterruptedly by train from Karachi via Delhi to Calcutta, about 1,700 miles, without ever catching sight of a hill. Nevertheless, variety exists, interesting when knowledgeably looked for: in West Pakistan's case, as you go (say) from Gujrat to Karachi, not so much from any discernible slight alteration in levels, or in crops, or in people's physique or dress – though these may be noticed – as from the striking paradox that, travelling from far inland towards the sea, you move through a landscape getting progressively drier. Though you should be exchanging comparatively arid country for moist, the opposite is happening.

The upper Punjabi part of Pakistan's West wing however gets fairly good rainfall, averaging along the foot of the Himalayas about 35 inches a year. It comes at two seasons : the smaller amount is brought, soon after midwinter usually, by western 'depressions' which push through from the Mediterranean via Afghanistan and Persia; the larger, in July-August as already indicated, by the warm monsoon air-current from the Indian Ocean, as it bumps for a few weeks, in its expiring northernmost effort, against the wall of the lower Himalaya between Kathua and Nathiagali. And besides this, and more dependably, West Punjab gets huge volumes of water – as indeed Sind does too, though at second hand – pouring down the large rivercourses from the summer snow-melt in the high Himalaya and

Karakoram. As a result of this double-sourced water-supply, from the skies and along the ground, and of the bold irrigation-works to exploit the latter, initiated by the British and extended by the Pakistanis, the scene presented to the railway traveller's eye, as he sits by his window, from when he leaves the Salt Range till reaching Rahim Yar Khan or thereabouts in Bahawalpur State, is in general of a splendid fertility.

Afterwards, what he sees becomes more and more either mere sandy wilderness dotted with sparse acacia-scrub, for mile after weary mile, or a strip of contrived fertility, with wilderness just out of sight nearby; for the railway serves strings of settlements to which water is brought from the great irrigation-works on the lower Indus at Sukkur and Kotri. Beyond these, on either flank, desert stretches away far; on the eastern flank to merge with the notorious great Thar of Rajasthan beyond the Indian frontier. You can find in Bahawalpur and Khairpur States, and in parts of Sind, country which in its sterile desolation would be indistinguishable from the Nubian or Libyan wastes of North Africa. And as Egypt and the Sudan depend for livelihood almost solely on the Nile, so does this region on the Indus. All the way from Multan to the sea, about 450 miles, the average annual rainfall probably does not exceed 7 inches. And even this is completely undependable in arrival; it comes at any time of the year in abrupt heavy deluges, mostly to rush profitlessly away along eroded gulleys, or to evaporate under the fierce sunshine that soon returns. The impossibility of effective agriculture in such a climate, except by river-fed canals or tube-walls, is shown by Karachi's rainfall records: during a typical series of four years, the city got respectively 0·7, 9·4, 20·8 and 7·0 inches, delivered mainly in sudden seasonless storms.

Set between sandy waste on the one side, and the saline creeks fringed with stunted mangrove which indent its coast on the other, Karachi is a remarkable place, ranking among the dozen or so really big conurbations of Asia, internationally renowned both as seaport and airport, and with a population of over two millions. But it is no longer capital of anything, Pakistan's federal Government having shifted as mentioned to Rawalpindi and nearby Islamabad in 1960, and the province of Sind having been abolished in 1955. And historically it must be accounted an upstart. Whereas Lahore, the capital of the West wing, and Dacca of the East, are cities rich in tradition and ancient buildings – Lahore outsandingly so, on the entire subcontinent only Delhi surpasses it – Karachi can make no such claims. As lately as the end of the eighteenth century, it was no better than a fishing hamlet. From then onwards however its growth was almost continuous. First came British mercantile initiative after Napier's conquest of Sind in the 1840's; then, sudden lucrative demand for the cotton of its hinterland during the American civil war; then in 1878, completion of the North-Western Railway, and consequent opening up of the Punjab to modern trading ventures; in the decade after 1886, the new canal-colonies in the Punjab, followed by the Sukkur barrage of Upper Sind in 1932; and, as final and biggest factor of all, the huge influx of mostly destitute Muslim refugees from India after Partition in 1947. However, until President Ayub's military régime took drastic action in 1959, Karachi during the preceding years of Pakistan's existence, when serving as her federal capital, was certainly no credit to her, and misled foreigners about the kind of country they were arriving in; for the conditions in which the refugees lived, huddled without sanitation in shacks along the sidewalks remained appalling. The problem seemed beyond the politicians' capacity to cope with; and it was in truth formidable, for statistics indicated that, over the thirteen years since 1946, the city's population had more than quadrupled.

Baluchistan, by contrast, is very thinly inhabited indeed. A large tract of high and arid country to the north and west of Karachi, about equal in area to Italy, its population is only about 1,384,000, that is to say, less than two-thirds of Karachi's, the density per square mile being only about ten. Except for the narrow Makran coastal strip, and the small and in summer atrociously hot Sibi plain – which in logic ought to be reckoned part not of Baluchistan at all, but of Sind – it consists of poorly watered, stony plateau at an average elevation of about 5,000 feet, traversed by complex mountain systems which, here and there, rise to peaks of 11,000 feet or so. It is, in fact, the easternmost finale of the high tablelands of Persia. Impressive barriers separate most of it from the great Indus valley below: towards the north, curving like a scimitar round its shoulder, is the Sulaiman range; farther down, against its flank, rests the arrow-straight precipitous limestone Kirthar range. Between them however the Sibi-Bolan gap lies open, up which road and railway wind deviously to Quetta, its only sizable town; a place famous for its Army staff college, and for earthquakes. (In 1935, about 30,000 people died in one.)

The distance from the head of the gap at Bolan, on over high country to Chaman close to the Afghan frontier, is only seventy miles. Thus the plateau narrows markedly at this one point; and the constriction, in effect, almost cuts Baluchistan into two : in the south, a large rectangle; in the north-east, a smaller triangle or wedge. These segments differ considerably from one another, both in scenery, and in inhabitants. Though both consist of lofty flattish country, crumpled by a confusion of large, bare, often strongly coloured hills – olive-green, slate-black, russet-red, ochreous – the confusion becomes increasingly wilder and more devoid of semblance of meaning in the south, until, as you near the rectangle's base, what you see verges on the impossible, and might be a creation of dream. 'Gigantic cap-crowned pillars and pedestals,' writes Holdich, 'are balanced in fantastic array about the mountain slopes, with successive strata so well defined that they possess all the appearance of massive masonry construction; standing stiff, jagged, naked and uncompromising'; and beyond them, 'that brazen coast washed by a molten sea'.

The highest ground of the rectangle is however near Kalat, farther north, the pivot perhaps of such coherent mountain structure as exists. And between the great crests and spurs, from there to the coast, you may find hidden in deep defiles occasional pleasant fertile strips, green with date-groves, and cereal crops laid out in little terraced fields. Of the main river-beds – which often go dry – only one, the Mula, drains into the Indus. This thrusts through the Kirthar range by a spectacular gorge: in ancient times it was an important route for trade, and for marching armies. The others run either direct into the Arabian Sea, or wander vaguely off north-west to sink into the futile sun-scorched pools and marshes, perpetually evaporating, of the Mushkel depression against the Persian frontier. In that far-off tract may also be seen the strange, extinct volcanoes of the Chagai hills, and the wind-rippled sands of the Kharan desert.

Almost throughout, despite Southern Baluchistan's nearness to the sea, its climate remains 'continental', alternating fiercely between cold and extreme heat. And winds can be very strong, for – unlike the Indo-Gangetic plain – Baluchistan as a whole is shielded by no Himalayan rampart from air-drift circulating from the immense open steppes or snows of Asiatic Russia, and Tibet, and inner China. In its wedge-shaped north-eastern segment particularly, the cold in winter – despite bright sunshine – has a piercing, bone-searching quality difficult to believe by those unacquainted with it; and temperatures before dawn may fall far below zero.

Although there are some higher mountains in that segment than in the southern one – among them the conspicuous Takht-i-Sulaiman, and Zarghun, which reaches nearly 12,000 feet – its geophysical layout is less improbably extravagant. A typical landscape of the Zhob – its best-known tract because traversed by a strategic road, and (as far as Fort Sandeman) also by railway – would be a wide stony level, dotted with small sparse bushes and dried grass, and slightly up-tilted from the horizontal towards the nearest mountain wall; a wall which, above its short talus screen, stands up immense and brown and almost bald, its abrupt lower surface perhaps weirdly sculptured by wind-erosion, but with upper slopes and clefts enriched by scattered clumps of dark green juniper, wild olive, and the chil-goza or 'edible' pine. Beyond and behind, you would glimpse re-moter ranges, huge hogsbacks, most of them snow-topped in winter and spring – the whole conveying an impression of vast vacant windy space.

But as you motor on north from Fort Sandeman via Sambaza – probably under escort, for the Afghan frontier lies near, and there might be ambushes – that impression dissolves. Soon after you cross the stream of the Gomal, which flows in from the left, the landscape begins to contract. It becomes an intense confined affair of crag and scree and precipice; Baluchistan's broadly horizontal theme has been abandoned for a vertical one. Of course, from the higher points, grand distant views can be got; but they lack curved sur-faces, nearly everything seems jagged. You are in Waziristan here, the most notorious tract of tribal territory; in the heartland of the Pathan or Pakhtoon people, the speakers of Pashto or Pakhtu; and it has none of that withdrawn, not quite credible, dreamlike quality of Southern Baluchistan. It is hard, practical, cruel as a knife.

This same vertical type of terrain stretches north ahead of you. In detail, it can be very varied; and sometimes, in an unexpected way and despite the harshness, of a breath-taking beauty – as when all of a sudden it discloses, cupped between arid tawny steeps, delicious little green hollows, blessed with tinkling streams, tiny well-tended fields, good orchards, perhaps a few shade-giving cedars; or reveals, far-off, glimpses of snowy Sikaram in the Safed Koh, nearly 16,000 feet high. But even at moments of enchantment such as these, it retains that first, special feeling of sharp-edged immediacy. All the way ahead of you, about 250 miles by air it stretches, to the Pathan tribal principalities of Dir and Swat, first mentioned near the start of this descriptive tour of Pakistan's West wing; stretches through tracts of gory historical renown such as the Tochi, Kurram, Tirah, Khyber, Bajaur, and Malakand; spills over on the left, beyond the international frontier or Durand Line, into Afghanistan; drops down on the right to include the wide, richly fertile, populous vales of Bannu, Kohat, and Peshawar, each gripped within its half-circle of fine bold hills; and actually, though you may not have noticed it, lies for miles behind you as well, because the north-east triangle of

Baluchistan, almost as far back as Quetta, if inhabited at all, is in-habited mainly by Pathans; that being the second factor – ethnic instead of scenic – which distinguishes it from the larger southern rectangle, whose people are altogether non-Pathan in speech and race.

Chapter 3

Some Social Problems

'PATHANS, or Pakhtoons; the speakers of Pashto' . . . who are one of Pakistan's leading peoples. The quoted words, from page 46, recall us to consider – though in the end we may doubt if we have a full answer – something puzzled over in Chapter 1 : nationhood. What is a nation? And what, in this particular context, is nationhood's connection with language?

Like most Asian countries, Pakistan has many languages. As a moment's thought will show, a nation is not necessarily just a linguistic group; it need not consist only of a collection of people using the same language. Other things are involved. Nevertheless, language does seem a big factor. So we must ask if inclusion in the body-politic of many languages – not merely two or three, but (say) a dozen – is an obstacle, perhaps in the long run a fatal one, to healthy nationhood? Obviously, it must slow things down; must make for inefficiency. Almost certainly too, in times of stress, it could weaken or break up cohesive nationalist feeling, the living sentiment which makes members of a nation believe they are one. And there may be a physical aspect as well, a question simply of distances. Can the idea of nationhood, when transplanted from its original fairly small European seedbeds to new Asian or African fields, really function over very large geographical tracts, in the parts of the world so lavishly multilingual as South Asia is? Modern communications can help to surmount the physical difficulty : the radio, aircraft, even the village bus. But may there not be a point where the idea of nationhood on the European model gets so overstretched as to be a mere theorists' bubble, sure to collapse at the first practical puff of adversity : a puff, for instance, from a language-riot?

Perhaps the question should be approached from the other end. Would we be right, would it be realistic to regard the Pathans, the Pashto-speakers, as in a sense themselves a nation? The claim is sometimes made, and with vigour, from the Afghan capital rather than from Peshawar; and arguments of weight could be adduced in its support. For besides sharing a language, they share a literature or folklore; they share a good deal of well-remembered local history, tradition, and tribal custom; and, so far as their notorious feuds and factions and a dividing international frontier allow, they possess some sense of cohesion. Further, over a period of fifty years or so, starting in 1747, they were in fact united under a dynasty founded by one of themselves, by a great Pathan soldier-of-fortune, Ahmad Shah Durrani; and remembrance of the Durrani Empire in its hey-day, passed down among them from father to son, is still alive. Such things, by normal Western standards, would form a large part of what is generally accounted the essential stuff of nationhood. In the Europe of two generations or so ago, advocates of self-determina-tion for, say, the Yugoslavs might have been hard put to it to adduce more.

If, however, it is accepted that the Pathans are a nation, what happens to the twenty-year-old State which this book is about? What becomes of the Pakistan-concept, of Mr. Jinnah's theory; of the supposition of 1947 that a major new feat of constructive statecraft had been achieved in South Asia, spanning (though in disconnected form) the vast area from near Zahidan in Persia, almost to Buthi-daung in the Arakan, and based on religious and cultural affinity, on a sense of membership of a distinctive ethos, of participating in a special Muslim 'way of life'? Obviously, we step here into deeply controversial waters. And it is right to do so, at the start of a fresh chapter, because the Pathans and their affairs bring into sharp focus a formidable long-range conundrum which must be faced, when we try to estimate Pakistan's future, peering ahead to guess which of several imaginable shapes the political map, in her part of Asia, might have a century or so hence.

In Europe are to be found several rather similar nationalisms or sub-nationalisms, regionalisms, provincialisms or separatisms – which-ever term we prefer – based, as with the Pathans, primarily on a shared language: Welsh regionalism; Walloon and Breton, Basque and Catalan regionalism; or – to come back to Asia, to Pakistan's big neighbour India – Telegu or Mahratti, Tamil or Gujerati, Assamese or Naga regionalism. But, in Pakistan's case, the Pathan version deserves particular study, and perhaps signifies danger, for two reasons. The Pathans live far enough from Hindustan, from India, to feel little or none of other Pakistanis' fear of being culturally and religiously swamped by a numerically stronger con-tiguous Hinduism, a feeling which hitherto has probably formed the chief cement of Pakistani nationhood; and they are on the other hand conscious that, in Afghanistan, just across an adjacent inter-national frontier, live large numbers of fellow Pashto-speakers – perhaps 7 millions of them, a substantial part of the whole Pathan people.[1] Admittedly, Punjabis in Pakistani Punjab, and Bengalis in

[1] Afghan Census statistics are unreliable.

D

East Pakistan, are likewise conscious that fellow-Punjabis, or fellow-Bengalis, live just beyond another nearby international frontier, that of India. But with them, though language and folklore and tradition are still to some extent a bond, religion (except with the East Pakistani Hindus) very emphatically is not. So, plainly, the Pathans imply the possibility of some headaches for Pakistan.

Another patient however might be a worse sufferer from these. For if – which may turn out not to be so – the present map of Asia is wrongly drawn, and linguistic nationalism is in fact the ultimate political reality, then not merely Pakistan – and India too – but Afghanistan is due for some drastic internal unpicking. Ramshackle in structure, poor, backward, with only about 15 million inhabitants as against Pakistan's 104 millions,[2] she survived the hazards of the nineteenth century merely because Britain and Russia happened to want a Central Asian buffer to prevent their rival imperial interests clashing. No Afghan State as such ever existed before Ahmad Shah Durrani's day in 1747. She has been likened to an Asian Switzerland – a comparison interesting but not wholly valid. Big mountains jut up in the middle; and (as with the Swiss) the population which fans out round this central hump subdivides into three or four different linguistic groups, Pashto being spoken in the south-east, Persian in the west, and the tongues of Turkistan in the north. But whereas the sophisticated Swiss are bound willingly together by democratic principle, the people of Afghanistan find themselves under one régime through dynastic chance. Thus, any major unpicking on linguistic lines of South Asia's existing frontiers, were it to happen, might cause the Afghan kingdom to fall apart. The northern tract, logically, would then join with the U.S.S.R.'s Central Asian republics; the western with Persia; and the rest with Pakistan's present tribal tract – where the Pakistani Pathans, having the higher standards of living and education, would doubtless take the lead. On the other hand, were the Pakistani State to be thus enlarged, its delicate internal ethnic and linguistic balance would be upset; Peshawar would become nearly as important as Lahore; and the 'one-unit' reform in the West wing – to be described in a moment – might be imperilled.

Such speculations however need no further pursuing here; Pakistani-Afghan relations will be touched on again in Chapters 12 and 16. The point, now, simply is that the Pashto language, and those who speak it, pose peculiar problems for Pakistan; problems both international and domestic. These, as yet, have caused no serious trouble; but it can readily be surmised that they might.

[2] Both 1966 estimates.

'Linguism', however – to use a term current throughout the sub-continent – has been less of a worry for Pakistan so far than for India, owing partly to the latter's greater ethnic diversity and size. And it is interesting that the two countries should have chosen to deal with it in opposite ways : India negatively, by conciliating it, by breaking up her internal map to accord with it; Pakistan positively, by overriding it, in the bold but perhaps brittle 'one-unit' reform achieved in 1955, whereby what in effect were linguistic Punjabi, and Pathan, and Sindhi provincial governments and legislatures in the West wing vanished, that wing being made a single entity – which the East wing always had been. Other considerations besides the linguistic indeed inspired this reform: federal considerations arising from the two wings' geographical disjunction for instance, and fears that the mullahs might exploit local disagreements for retrograde purposes. But resistance to linguism was a factor. Which of the two methods will prove the wiser, the Pakistani or the Indian, will be for future historians to decide. Hitherto, the Pakistani has seemed much the more successful.

How dangerously near the surface may lie passionate emotions about language is shown by recalling some of India's afflictions from this cause since Independence : the 'fast unto death' by Potti Sriramulu in Andhra on the east coast in December 1952, resulting in bloodshed and disorder, before Mr. Nehru consented to creation of a separate Telegu-speaking province or 'state'; worse riots on the other side of the peninsula in 1956–7 by both Mahrattas and Gujeratis, for similar reasons and with similar results; the protracted tribal revolts near the eastern frontier of the Nagas and then of the Mizos (partly linguist); the upheaval of July 1960 against Bengali-speakers in Assam, when administration collapsed and thousands of Bengali families fled, conditions for a short while almost resembling those during the Partition-time migrations of 1947; retaliatory civil disobedience in that area in May-June 1961, to enforce official acceptance of Bengali as one of the 'state' languages; agitation in November 1963 throughout South India – Madras, Andhra, Mysore, Kerala – against adoption of Hindi as India's national language; fierce rioting in Madras in February 1965 and widespread disturbances elsewhere from the same cause; disorder in Mysore and Maharashtra in 1966 owing to Mahratti-speaking areas being within the boundaries of the former 'state'. Little Ceylon, too, has witnessed dreadful scenes, as a result of clash of interests between the Sinhalese-speakers and the Tamils. The barbarities during the riots of 1958 seemed at first incredible, to people used to the island's normally easy-going friendly ways.

Pakistan has experienced nothing like this. Her only major disorders describable as linguistic were in Dacca in February 1952, resulting from the attempt by Prime Minister Nazimuddin to rank the Bengali language officially below Urdu. Influenced no doubt partly by that, she has since (unlike India and Ceylon) avoided making any single language her 'national' one. Instead, she has adopted two – or it might be said, three. Under the 1956 Constitution, Urdu and Bengali got equal rank; and English, as well, was given a free run for twenty years. It remains her high-level lingua franca, still the working instrument for most Governmental affairs and for intercommunication between the two wings, for the superior courts of law, federal politics, big business, major industrial projects and so on. And the Constitution of 1962 confirmed these arrangements.

Bengali is a true regional language – analogous to Pashto, or the languages in India and Ceylon that the rioting has been about. But Urdu must be classed separately. It has no compact local roots; instead, it enjoys a loose wide web of intelligibility, strongest in Pakistan perhaps around Karachi and Lahore and Rawalpindi, but stretching across the entire northern plain of the subcontinent from Baluchistan to Chittagong – including India's Uttar Pradesh, and Bihar, and West Bengal, and with an outlier in the far south at Hyderabad in the Deccan. It too, like English, though at a less sophisticated modern level, is a lingua franca. So the assumption from 1947 to 1952 that it would eventually be made Pakistan's national language was reasonable – though hurtful to Bengali regionalist pride. Historically, it is a fascinating, composite thing : a product of the successive Muslim invasions from the Central Asian uplands which overran the subcontinent from the twelfth century. In underlying structure it derives from the dialect of Hindi spoken in those days round Delhi; but this has been surmounted by a vocabulary largely Persian, Turkish and Arabic, and it uses Persian-Arabic script. During Moghul times, it developed a rich poetic literature. At the outset, however, in its first simple form, it came into being merely as a means of converse between the conquering Muslim soldiery and the indigenous Hindu populace; and Urdu zaban, translated, means 'camp language'.

Pakistan's other main regional languages, besides Bengali and Pashto, are Punjabi and Sindhi. Sindhi has a considerable literature. But both were weakened by the exodus to India in 1947 at Partition-time of the millions of Hindus and (in Punjabi's case) of Sikhs who also spoke them. For the Sikhs indeed – nearly all of whom migrated to India – Punjabi is not only the language of common speech but of religion, in a way comparable to Hebrew for the Jews; and it possesses a distinctive religious script, Gurmukhi. There are also, in Pakistan, dialects spoken by such large populations as almost to rank as languages : for example Multani, a kind of Punjabi current in the south-western tip of the Punjab and in Bahawalpur State, which however in Rawalpindi or Ambala would be scarcely intelligible. And smaller languages exist galore, often tucked away in the plateaux and mountain ranges of the west and north, and perhaps used by quite tiny numbers of people. For philologists, some of these are sheer joy, because so mysterious in origin and in reasons for survival. Brahui, for instance, in Baluchistan, which though surrounded by languages of normal Aryan type – Baluchi, Jatki, and the southern dialects of Pashto – is inexplicably akin to the Dravidian tongues of southern peninsular India, 1,000 miles or more away, with nothing in the least resembling it to be found over all that intervening distance; or Urmuri, a minute isolated blob of non-Pathan speech, still persisting alive and unabsorbed in the wild fierce heart of the Mahsud country, at Kaniguram in Waziristan; or away in the far north, Khowar, the main language of Chitral, whose sources are disputed; or the astonishing variety of obscure small languages in the upper part of the Gilgit agency, such as Brusheski, the best-known of the several languages to be found in the thinly populated Hunza valley alone.

Description of Pakistan's language-problems, so far, has proceeded rather glumly. If, in fact, the most vital element in modern nationhood is a common speech, then is not the whole political map of South Asia nowadays – consisting as it does of States extravagantly multi-lingual – built on a falsity, and sure, sooner or later, to rearrange itself? And even if that is not so, may not India and Pakistan be physically too bulky, as yet, for their own strength; be trying to embody within themselves more discrepant language-units than they can digest? Those are the kind of thoughts so far offered. It might be added that Europe, minus Russia, is after all of about the same size and population as the Indo-Pakistani subcontinent; and that when, in its eastern part, during the nineteenth century, the multilingual Ottoman Empire began breaking up, what emerged from the confusion was a group of geographically quite small States based mainly on language : Serbia, Greece, Rumania, Bulgaria; States less populous than (say) the Pashto-speaking, Sindhi-speaking Gurkhali-speaking, Assamese-speaking or Sinhalese-speaking areas in South Asia today. And the break-up of the Austro-Hungarian Empire in 1918: did not that merely push the process one step further so that – linked with the nationalist Western Europe already extant – there came into being the familiar chequer-board of the independent linguistic States which Europe consists of now? Why, therefore, should it be assumed that multilingual South Asia, when the British Empire in that area broke up during the 1940's in a comparable way, should behave differently, indeed should evolve on contrary lines?

But if you take a closer look at Europe, with mind alert to present-day technical facts rather than to historical happenings of fifty or sixty years ago, you may find that thoughts of quite another sort come up. Board a jet aircraft; glance from aloft at that chequer-board; reflect on all the twisty little frontiers down below there, and the annoyances and dangers they represent; recall that in this plane you can cross some of Europe's famous independent, separate, sovereign States from end to end in a matter of minutes. Is not the chequer-board nowadays, when considered in terms of modern communications, an absurdity, completely out of date? And have not its internecine rivalries, twice this century, plunged humanity into the worst wars ever known, temporarily reducing Europeans themselves, by the end of the second one, to dependency on America or Russia? And have not Europeans, since, been laboriously struggling to abate their excessive nationalism, by setting up collective bodies such as the Common Market, hoping thereby to regain the primacy in the world that they have lost, but to which their energies and skills perhaps entitle them?

So possibly the future lies with the big geographical units after all. The people of South Asia may have struck lucky, stumbling by accident on a truly up-to-date political device, the large multilingual State; something enabling them to short-circuit what hitherto have been the standard processes of history, and to put themselves – if Europe does not mend her ways – in the van of human progress.

However that may be on the long view, it is nevertheless obvious, on the short, that multilingualism is awkward for Pakistan – even though, so far, it has caused her less trouble than it has India and Ceylon. And two other features of Pakistan's population-structure are awkward too: the size of the minorities – or minority; and the number of the refugees. Time is slowly softening both these angularities; but they are important, and need examining.

Except for the Hindus in the East wing, Pakistan's minorities are small. The huge tragic two-way migrations of bewildered fugitives in the Punjab during the Partition-time savageries of 1947 had at least one incidental advantage : that the halves of that sundered province, the Pakistani and the Indian, each became religiously homogeneous,. Nearly all the Muslims fled from East Punjab; nearly all the Hindus and Sikhs from West Punjab, and from other parts in Pakistan's West wing. It would thus be fair to say that the West wing has no substantial minority or communal problem – though it has indeed a perceptible sectarian or inter-Muslim one, as we shall see shortly. Its total Hindu population is only 622,000; some of these Hindus still live in 'up-country' cities such as Lahore, Rawalpindi and Peshawar; rather more in maritime Karachi; and the rest mostly in rural Sind. As mentioned, virtually no Sikhs remain – though small groups of them sometimes briefly reappear on pilgrimage from India, revisiting their shrines. West Pakistan also has a scattered Christian community, amounting in 1961 to about 543,000, on friendly terms generally with their Muslim neighbours; also a few Parsis, notably in Karachi.

The core of Pakistan's minority problem, as indicated, consists of the Hindu community in the East wing : 9,380,000 strong, plainly an indigestible lump, almost a fifth of that wing's total population. Like the Indian Union's proportionately even larger Muslim community (43,000,000), these people – whatever may be the high-minded intentions towards them of the respective Governments – are in general unhappy, maladjusted still to the new conditions, their loyalty often suspect, and sufferers doubtless, at the lower bureaucratic and social levels, from much petty victimisation and injustice.

Owing however to the caste system, these East Pakistani Hindus are themselves in a sense split, which makes the problem they pose rather less massive than it seems. More than half of them, about 6 millions, belong to what census officials euphemistically call the 'scheduled castes'; that is to say, they are untouchables, people so low in the stratified Hindu social structure as, in an orthodox Brahmin's view, to be virtually beyond it, excluded, outcaste. During the acute crises in Indo-Pakistani affairs in 1950 and 1965 these unfortunates showed no particular enthusiasm for their high-caste brethrens' cause; and though they were frightened, not a great many of them fled. A further factor here is that most of the East wing's Muslims may perhaps themselves be of remotely similar origins and half-aware of it; descendants of low-caste Hindus who, centuries ago, escaped the net of Brahminical tyranny to embrace Buddhism, turning to Islam later; or else, after about 1200 A.D., became Muslims directly.

But though socially divided in this way, the bulk of Pakistan's Hindu minority, in geographical terms – unlike the widely scattered Muslim minority in India – forms a compact block; and there can be no denying that it involves a major unsolved problem for Pakistani statesmanship. Many of the high-caste Hindus in the East wing are people of great personal gifts, who before 1947 played a prominent part in the exciting political and intellectual and artistic life of undivided Bengal, holding big posts in Calcutta university, in the law and other professions, and in some of the mercantile firms. In East Pakistan, there is much less scope for them; and the hard realities of Indo-Pakistani affairs make it difficult to foresee a time when, in spirit, they could regard themselves – or be regarded – as fully integrated Pakistani nationals. And there are 4 millions of them; that is to say, about half as many as the population of Australia, or Peru, or Morocco; about three times more than the population of independent Jamaica, or Lebanon. Even now, twenty years after Partition, the dissatisfied, unassimilated Hindu community of the East wing remains one of the major flaws, the obvious weaknesses, of the Pakistani State. On the other hand it may be remarked that, except during 1950 and 1964, when grave anti-Hindu disorders in East Pakistan synchronised with equally grave anti-Muslim disorders in West Bengal, Bihar and Orissa, the Hindu minority in Pakistan has not been the victim of major attack, whereas in India, rioting against the Muslim minority has been frequent over the years, notable other recent examples, besides those mentioned, being the outbreaks at Jubbulpore in Madhya Pradesh in February 1961, at Agra and elsewhere in Uttar Pradesh later in the same year, and in parts of West Bengal and Assam in 1962.

Pakistan's East wing also contains communities of Christians, about 128,000 in 1961, and of Buddhists, about 383,000, the latter mainly in the Chittagong hill tracts near the Burmese frontier. Buddhism, like Christianity, and like Islam, does not believe in caste, so these two small communities present no real problem and fit in easily. But alas, even now, it would be untrue to say this, in a comprehensive way, about Pakistan's refugees; about the vast number, estimated at 8 millions, of immigrant Muslim fugitives from the Indian Union. Historically, these hapless folk fall into four groups: those who arrived en masse and in fear of their lives during the climax of the Partition-time killings in 1947, mainly from East Punjab and the Delhi area; the similar but smaller number who came in soon after, from the southern tracts of Kashmir State, when organised butcheries of Muslims broke out there, followed by localised Indo-Pakistani war; third, the steady influx, which went on for years and has not even now quite dried up – and which proved the most baffling problem of all – of Muslims from all over the Indian Union who felt impelled to leave from a mixture of motives: discriminatory unemployment or fear of it, for themselves or their children; or its converse, a plain, down-to-earth wish to better themselves; or starry-eyed Islamic idealism; or a vague sense of spiritual suffocation under Hindu majority rule, mixed with dread of horrors to come – more anti-Muslim riots, for instance. These three streams of humanity went mainly to the West wing. The fourth one, which went East, was for the most part a trickle; but it swelled to quite a torrent in 1950 and again in 1964–5, because of the anti-Muslim riots in and around West Bengal already mentioned, which ended in war. Some of the people then uprooted moved across later to the West wing by air or sea. That wing thus has the great bulk of this still partly unsolved problem on its hands, perhaps 80 per cent of the refugees being there, the burden serving as a sort of counterpoise to that which weighs heavily on the East wing, of the large unconciliated Hindu minority.

Refugees' bodily ills and discomforts; refugees' morale : these things are really much the same all the world over, a matter of basic human wants. The twentieth century, pre-eminent for mass-creation of the 'displaced person', has forced such evils much on our attention. But except in scale, the perplexities wrestled with by the authorities in India and Pakistan after 1947 were not dissimilar to those faced by Governments and welfare organisations elsewhere. Subdivided along economic lines, the subcontinent's displaced persons, the human debris of the 1947 catastrophe, classify themselves as those always poor, and those who once were rich (and may be rich again): on the one hand, the largely illiterate masses, urban and rural, the peasants and landless labourers, artisans and petty merchants; on the other, the educated upper and middle classes, aristocrats, landlords, professional and business men. And most fairminded Pakistanis would probably concur that, until 1958, when the Army took over, their politicians did less well than India's in improving the plight of at any rate the poorer fugitives. The atrocious squalor that persisted unremedied for years in Karachi, the (then) federal capital, has already been mentioned; and conditions remained very bad for some while around Lahore, and elsewhere.

Reasons for this contrast were not however, solely, the instability and incompetence of Pakistan's Administrations from 1952 to 1958. The populations exchanged during the Punjab upheaval differed both in size and quality. Pakistan, the smaller country, received fugitives in more overwhelming mass – about 8 millions as mentioned, against 6 millions – and proportionately many of them were urban types, small shopkeepers and street-vendors, craftsmen, factory hands from towns such as Amritsar and Ferozepur and Bhatinda, Jullundur and Ludhiana, Amabala and Panipat and Delhi, who proved less adaptable, less good at fending for themselves and more apt to get demoralized than the villagers. Impartial witnesses of the tragic Punjab scenes of 1947 seem agreed that the sturdiest, most self-disciplined of the fugitives were the Sikh cultivators on trek eastwards by bullock-wagon from the canal-colonies of the Multan and Lyallpur districts and from Montgomery (now re-named Sahiwal). Despite abandonment of their good lands, a grievous blow, they showed astonishing fortitude and resilience.

Among the educated upper classes, most of whom possessed skills or influence sufficient to lift themselves fairly soon above mere physical want, distresses have been subtler. The humiliation of having, even for a while, to depend on public charity; the tiny daily dents to self-esteem involved in sharing perhaps cramped quarters with distant relatives or 'in-laws' after loss of a home; the continuous mental harking back to the past, in the old folk almost unrestrainable; among the younger, the flowering of memories of happy times and surroundings now lost. Almost certainly, too, some disillusion about Pakistan itself : for during the bad years of shady political deals and ramifying general corruption between 1952 and 1958, many bright hopes and idealistic assumptions brought over by the fugitives fell broken. The persistent feeling of never quite belonging. And diverse cultural dislocations and shocks, as well: the dismay, for instance, of aristocratic parents from (say) Agra or Bareilly, settled now in Lahore, and themselves nurtured in the chastest Urdu, on hearing their offspring bawl to one another across the breakfast-table in, to their ears, coarse Punjabi voices.

Like all the world's great religions, Islam has its internal schisms. But being simpler doctrinally than Christianity, it is less riddled with them; they have never involved it in slaughter and destruction on the scale of Europe's seventeenth-century religious wars. So schism among Pakistan's Muslims, while occasionally a nuisance, constitutes no profound problem. The main split, between Sunnis and Shias, happened very long ago, about A.D. 657, and over a question more of politics than religion – namely, the community's leadership; about what should be the method of succession to the Caliphate. Shias chose the hereditary principle, operative through the Prophet's family; Sunnis the elective. And from then on, differences between them in ceremonial and custom gradually developed.

These sometimes cause strife or unpleasantness. In pre-Partition days, recurrent Shia-Sunni disorders were almost traditional in Lucknow. And trouble is liable to flare up near the head of the Kurram valley on the North-West Frontier, where certain tribes or sectors of tribes are Shias, who live surrounded by Sunnis. But in general, Shia-Sunni relations in Pakistan are easy enough; and of course, with the abolition of the Caliphate by Kemalist Turkey in 1924, the original cause of the dispute faded. Numerically, the split was always an unequal one, unlike that in Europe between Protestants and Catholics. Shias are in the majority only in a few parts of the Muslim world, such as Persia; in most of it Sunnis preponderate, and indeed, throughout Islam generally, they massively outnumber all the other sects combined.

Ismailis are an offshoot from the Shias, under the hereditary leadership of the Aga Khan. Widely distributed over the globe though not in large numbers, they are economically close-knit, and tend to be secretive about their affairs; a fact which may arouse dislike, and if those upon whom it focuses are wealthy or influential, suspicions of nepotism too. That is also true of the Ahmadis; and here another consideration comes in: recent sharp doctrinal disagreements. Some Sunnis in Pakistan go so far as to assert that Ahmadis are not Muslims at all, and to demand their classification as a separate community, like the Christians or Parsis. This book is no place for theological debate; but briefly, it may be said that claims made by or on behalf of the nineteenth-century founder of the Ahmadi sect, Mirza Ghulam Ahmad, who lived at Qadian in East Punjab, are considered by some to impugn the supreme decisive prophethood of Mohammad himself.

Serious anti-Ahmadi rioting raged for days in Lahore in March 1953, necessitating imposition of martial law. In part, this complex episode had little really to do with disapproval of the Ahmadis' doctrines, and was a political side-wind from the controversy then blowing in Karachi over the federal shape, and Islamic flavour, of Pakistan's proposed new Constitution. The Ahmadi leadership had shown no enthusiasm before August 1947 for the Pakistan-concept, and that aroused ire. But neither had the orthodox ulema, nor Maulana Maudoodi's fundamentalists; and the latter, in 1953, put themselves in the very forefront of the anti-Ahmadi agitation. Undeniably the Ahmadi sect's tenets shock many ordinary Muslims, and disapproval of them is understandable. Ahmadis however are a vigorous lot, active in proselytising; and much of the contemporay Muslim religious propaganda which Christian missionaries, not very successfully, find themselves struggling against outside Asia – in Africa, for instance – is of Ahmadi derivation.

Like other religions, Islam also has its monastic orders : groups of people voluntarily bound under a common rule to lead a life of piety, either through mystical contemplation, or through mundane good works. They are usually termed Sufis; and the Sufi orders seem to have been the main instrument by which, from about the twelfth century, most of the spontaneous conversions to the Muslim Faith of Hindus and Buddhists in South Asia were brought about. Islam in its original Arabian form, as a stark transcendental monotheism, could make no very obvious appeal religiously to the polytheistic or pantheistic Indian mind – though socially, of course, it opened up for the lowlier folk an escape-route from the prison of caste. The God of Islam as explained by orthodox schoolmen must to many Hindus have appeared very impersonal, unattainable, bleak, and far away. But the wondering Sufi friars and preachers offered an alluring way round this difficulty : they believed He could be brought lovingly nearer; that He might be personally approached along the path of mystical devotion. In consequence, Islam in South Asia is massively infused with the Sufi spirit, exhibiting a warmth and immediacy, and a tolerance of simple superstitions, alien to the arid Westerly subcontinent of its birth. Historic shrines, and the tombs of saints or pirs, may be venerated in Pakistan and India with a fervour which a Catholic from South Europe might find unremarkable, but which Wahabi puritans from Arabia would be outraged by.

On one important point, however, Sufi monastic institutions differ startlingly from those of Europe or America : there is no celibacy, nor any feeling that such a state has religious merit. Guardianship of the shrines is often hereditary, passed down from father to son; in effect from a married abbot to his progeny. Doubtless the main reason for this lies in a simple fact of history. The Founder of the Muslim Faith – like Guru Nanak and Guru Gobind Singh, the chief Founders of Sikhism – was a married man; moreover, he latterly had several spouses at a time. Thus to a Muslim, as to a Sikh, on the strength of incontrovertibly high example, celibacy seems not only unrequired for religious fulfilment, but silly, and even rather wrong. On the other hand, for Christians, it is axiomatic that the Founder of their Faith was celibate; to suppose anything else is inconceivable. And Gotama, the Founder of another great religion, Buddhism, felt it important to renounce matrimony, dramatically, as his first step towards spiritual achievement. And reverence for ascetic abstinences of all kinds is strongly exemplified, as well, in Hinduism – a fact which, during the present century, helped Mr. Gandhi in his politics. So the great religions diverge markedly in their standpoint on this one large human matter. And that, logically, leads us straight to consider a quite different set of Pakistani social problems : those connected with sex; with polygamy and the status of women; and – most formidable of all – with population-growth.

Much mutual misunderstanding over these things exists between

East and West. Westerners find Muslims in some ways strangely prudish about them; in others disconcertingly blunt. Wide gulfs of difference also separate Muslims and Hindus, which complicates the subject further. Basically, sex for the Muslim is a practical thing. For the Hindu, with his pantheist view of the world, it is all mixed up with holiness; is a manifestation of the divine. And that explains – to take an extreme example – the astonishing erotic sculptures in some Hindu temples, which the Muslim, with his horror of idolatry, finds even more revolting than the Christian does. Marriage for the Hindu, as for some sorts of Christian, is a sacrament. For the Muslim (as also, rather surprisingly, for the Buddhist) it is only a contract. And a sophisticated Westernised Muslim would say that this is why the Muslim social system with all its faults, which he would admit, and probably be keen to correct, can never result in anything so tragically unjust – to choose another extreme instance – as the plight of the young childless widow in orthodox Hindu society, doomed to permanent degradation as a domestic drudge at her mother-in-law's bidding, simply because the mischance of her husband's death has deprived her existence of its religious basis.

In such society, a Hindu widow can never re-marry. And because of her sacramentally broken state, she is expected to avoid social frivolities, to wear dull clothes, to eat plain food. When callers come, she should politely hide away; it might distress them to have to behold so sorrowful a creature. On the other hand, re-marriage for a Muslim widow is easy. And a Muslim wife can divorce her husband, but her Hindu counterpart strictly never. The former, too, has always had well defined and fairly generous legal rights both to possess and to inherit property, her position here – in theory at any rate, though in practice she may be unaware of it – being much stronger than what, until recent years, it was in Hindu, and for that matter even in Christian society. And a Hindu wife may find herself one of an indefinitely expansible number of spouses, for polygamy among Hindus, though actually perhaps not frequent, has no fixed limits; whereas among Muslims, the Koran restricts the number to four. In all these ways, the Muslim woman's lot is nominally the better. Nevertheless, her condition in practice may be dismal, and a very proper object of solicitude by sophisticated Westernised Pakistanis, and particularly of recent years by ladies of the small but active Pakistani feminist movement, who are keen to make their country modern, and a match socially and industrially for the countries of the West.

Conventional Muslim society – not the sophisticated upper-class society which may be all that the Western visitor sees, but the immensely more numerous society of the simple villagers or, in the

cities, of the unobstrusive religiously orthodox folk – is very masculine in flavour. The male dominates; the woman's role is assumed
to be subordinate; centuries of adverse custom have so overlaid her
true Islamic rights, in matters such as divorce or property-ownership,
that she may not know they exist. And she suffers specific religious
disabilities. Tradition for instance debars her from praying at the
mosque even in her husband's or son's company. Some mosques
arrange separate enclosures for women; but in most, women simply
are not seen. Here, the contrast between Islam and other South
Asian faiths is very striking. Hindu and Buddhist women freely
wander with the crowds at the temples and viharas. Go to a Sikh
gurdwara, and you will find the men and women assembled in
orderly rows on either side of the aisle. But the huge Muslim con-
gregations so impressively lined up at the mosques on Fridays, or on
Id days and other great yearly festivals, are usually altogether male.
And although the Hindu woman, as woman, is devoid of all religious
and social significance – the childless widow's pitiable plight exempli-
fies this brutal truth vividly – she may nevertheless enjoy derivative
religious prestige via her accepted sexual role as mother or wife, and
indeed be worshipped in those capacities.

Probably worse however, from the practical aspect, is the Muslim
custom of purdah, or feminine seclusion. Though met with also in
Hindu society, particularly among Rajputs, it is comparatively rare
among Hindus, and has many bad effects : medically, educationally,
economically. Here again, the Western visitor may get a misleading
impression, because the Pakistani social circles he moves in are
mainly the upper-class ones. Ladies of aristocratic and wealthy
families began discarding the veil two generations or more ago. Most
of them probably are now 'out', and in conduct largely Westernised.
Many are supporters of the All-Pakistan Women's Association, the
lively feminist group founded by Begum Liaquat Ali Khan (wife of
the then Prime Minister) in 1949. Furthermore, the visitor may be
confused by what is normally discernible at the nethermost as well
as the uppermost rungs of the social ladder. Village women, except
before complete strangers, often go unveiled; they may be noticed
at work with their menfolk in the fields. Of the Pakistani women
classified under the latest census as 'workers' – less than 2 millions –
nearly 80 per cent were occupied in agriculture. And on the high-
ways, the handsome nomad women stride along, at their spring and
autumn migrations, free of the veil completely.[3]

[3] The closure of the Afghan-Pakistani frontier in 1961-2 diminished these
picturesque nomadic movements, but seasonal migrations between the plains and
Pakistan's own mountainous northern regions continue.

It is in the towns, among the middle and especially the lower-middle classes, that the grim custom of female seclusion prevails at its strictest. There, the unfortunate Muslim purdah-nasheen, tottering on the sidewalk, encased in her white burqa like a perambulating tent, is a startling, sorry spectacle that many a kind-hearted foreigner never gets used to. Plainly, a system which produces so dismal a phenomenon must be damaging, for body and mind. And indeed doctors ascribe much feminine illness to it, especially in families dwelling in cramped urban accommodation on tiny incomes : illness associated with lack of light and air and exercise, such as a osteomalacia, a softening of the bones very dangerous at childbirth; tuberculosis; anaemia; and an affliction of the eyes, said to be due to peering through the little slits in the burqa's headpiece. And mentally, whatever apologists for the system may say, the kind of life led by the average purdah woman year after year, if not suffocating, must at least be wretchedly narrow. Ignorance and apathy and superstition, the most baffling of the educationist's problems in the underdeveloped countries, can scarcely fail to linger, in a society where young mothers live under such conditions. And economically, of course, it walls off millions of the female population from productive activities outside the home, of the sort that the Western world, whether capitalist or Communist, nowadays gains so much wealth by.

Polygamy, which many Occidental commentators on Islamic institutions seize on avidly as the first thing to criticise, in fact matters much less. And here, apologists might find more logic on their side. They could point, as proof that there is something to be said for their system, to the evident sexual licence, the much-publicised marital infidelities, the broken homes, the divorces in the professedly monogamous West. The male mammal, they would suggest, is by nature more inclined to sexual variety than the female; Muslim social institutions, here, make reasonable allowance for a scientific fact. Western critics, too, often overlook how polygamy for Muslims started. Historically, it was restrictive. It was introduced, in Islam's very early days, into a previously pagan society where the permissible number of wives was limitless. The Prophet Mohammad fixed a maximum. Further, he enjoined that the husband – which must be a difficult feat – should treat each wife with equal fairness, or else marry no more than one.

The overriding practical fact however is that, in Pakistan as throughout the relatively poverty-ridden Muslim world of today, very little polygamy happens, because so few men have the money to afford it. Dependable statistics are hard to come by, but such as there are suggest that polygamous marriages in Pakistan amount to only about 2 per cent of the total. Anyway, they are rare. Nor should it be supposed that the women concerned always dislike such marriages. The possibility that her husband might legally take a second wife during her lifetime of course weakens a wife's matrimonial standing. But the idea is enshrined in her religious tradition; it comes as no shock; the Koran permits it. And circumstances may arise when such a marriage is positively wanted. This writer knows of a village wife, weakened by a gynaecological operation, who unremittingly nagged a reluctant husband to take a local girl as second wife, to help with the household chores and look after the children. But undeniably, in a society where the male dominates, brutal injustice may be done, not only by second marriages, but by divorce, which because of matrimony's contractual nature under the Islamic code can be put through easily. Pakistan's military régime grasped this awkward social nettle vigorously in March 1961, by means of the Muslim Family Laws Ordinance already referred to: an admirable humanitarian measure, which introduced very necessary safeguards and penalties. Under it, formal written approval by local councils must be got before a polygamous marriage can occur, and procedure for divorce by the man is stiffened up too. The aim is to protect the wife, as the weaker partner.

Enactments however can seldom quickly change a people's ingrained mental attitudes. To the unsophisticated Muslim villager, the root of these matters is simple, elementary. Men and women are unequal, whatever educated folk may say : God built them on a different bodily plan, for different purposes. And because the male is physically stronger, because he can never be incommoded by pregnancies or suckling, he takes first place. The practice in Western society, whereby at evening the ladies formally enter public rooms ahead of their husbands, gaily and variously clad, with the men tagging along behind in monotonous black uniforms makes him gape. He has seen it with his own eyes, on visits to the big city; and many of his own richer fellow-countrymen too, good Muslims, nowadays copy it. But in his village world, as in nature, it is the man who goes ahead, the man who on festival-days wears the bright colours and the finery, just as in the nearby forest the cock pheasant does. The woman follows after, looking dowdy – or, as he would say, modest. In the big city he has noticed the unveiled Westernised ladies' paint and powder, their veneered fingernails and perhaps toenails. Worse, he has noticed under the bright lights their sheath-like garments, so suggestively shaped, so scanty as coverage, the exposed white flesh, the naked shoulders and torsos; he has watched the men and women embraced, exchanging partners, dancing together to music two by two. All this, as he sees it, can indicate only one thing. Then give him his ancient Muslim customs, he might exclaim – if he could express himself in your sophisticated way; give him a world where the plain facts of nature and of inevitable masculine leadership are acknowledged. It is better and cleaner. An imported culture, based on a combination of make-believe and female sexual licence, can come to no good. It is at any rate a point of view.

But of all the social problems facing Pakistan, the biggest – though seldom even now fully seen as such – is population-growth. The figures are frightful. Polygamy seems to have nothing to do with them. Nearly every so-called 'developing' community is in the same plight. What the experts call the population-explosion, going on all over the globe, applies with maximum force in its most poverty-stricken parts. No evidence suggests any particular correlation between growth-rate and marriage-customs. The Muslim countries apparently do not fall into a coherent statistical group. Growth, generally, tends to be fastest simply where living-standards are low, and standards of illiteracy and ignorance high. Costa Rica, Venezuela and Brazil for instance, supposedly monogamous countries, had growth-rates according to the official estimates even higher during the 1950's and 1960's than India or Pakistan.

Basically, the trouble is due to the doctors, with their new drugs and devices for preventing people dying in the old ways; or, less crudely, to the extraordinary march of discovery by the medical profession, backed by biologists and chemists, during the last century and especially in the last forty years. Science may almost be said, now, to have put in mankind's hands the means (subject to the limits of normal longevity) for death-control; but to have failed in contriving birth-control where it is most needed : among the poor and ignorant. Until a really cheap, safe, simple oral contraceptive or mechanical device can be made available in vast amounts, and with convincing publicity throughout the world's 'developing' countries, the problem seems beyond remedy; only palliatives can be applied. Every inflow of well-intentioned capital and technological aid from the more developed Western countries and from Russia, organised in the hope of raising living standards, will be nullified by yet further increments of needy new mouths awaiting food.

At the Census of 1941, the sectors of the subcontinent which six years later became Pakistan were reckoned to have a population of about 70,000,000; and those which became the Indian Union, of nearly 315,000,000.[4] By the time of the Censuses of 1951, the figures

[4] Excluding Jammu and Kashmir, population about 4,000,000.

E

had gone up to 75,842,135 and 356,891,624, despite the casualties of 1947–8; and by the Censuses of 1961, to 93,720,000 and 436,424,429. That is to say, over the period 1941–61, Pakistan's population had increased by about 24,000,000 persons or 34·3 per cent, and India's by about 121,000,000 persons or 38·4 per cent. And unless some major catastrophe takes place, such as pestilence, famine, or nuclear war – or unless oral contraceptives can be introduced as indicated – the prospect of these fearful growth-rates being much diminished appears dim. Both the Indian and the Pakistani Governments have shown courage in trying to popularise 'family planning'. The Indian indeed the more so, because not only is this intimate subject, in that country as elsewhere, hedged about by ancient prejudice; among Hindus, a valid religious objection against it also exists, since it may be held to infringe the principle of ahimsa.[5] Muslims, with their more practical attitude to sex, do not feel this. But it would be fanciful to expect the present propaganda in either country to achieve much among illiterate multitudes scattered in countless villages thoroughout such huge areas, whether they hold ahimsa in respect or not. Many commentators on the social problems of South Asia refuse, really, to face the implications of this one, which is by far the gravest and most baffling of all.

[5] Non-violence; and by deduction therefrom, non-interference with the life-substance.

PART II

Chapter 4

Retrospect, 1857–1946

T
HIS chapter tries to sketch in some of the Pakistan movement's historical background. The first conspicuous item is the sepoy mutiny of 1857, which, for the Muslim community on the sub-continent, proved a shattering disaster. Actually their fortunes had been in steady decline for about ninety years; but the fact was not fully perceived. And now, suddenly, they found themselves plunged into unimagined humiliation and impoverishment. In dealings with the British so far, they had dealt with a trading Company; true, a very strange and strong one, which had possessed itself of huge territories, including – as far back as 1803 – Delhi itself. But the arrangement had let them keep some imperial pride, as well as per-quisites of past grandeur. All this, within a few blood-drenched months, was expunged. Not only were they ignominiously lumped together, with their former Hindu subjects, as denizens of a new, non-Muslim Empire; in their British rulers' eyes, they also bore most of the blame for the recent horrible upheaval and consequently had to bear the brunt of the reprisals.

From books on the mutiny, such as the several good ones brought out for its 1957 centenary, we now know that this apportionment of blame was lopsided and unjust. But the British believed it right at the time. Their victimisation of the Muslims was therefore harsh; they had had a bad fright, and were very conscious that the Muslims had not long ago been the country's rulers. And because of events quite unconnected with the mutiny, the Muslims were ill-placed to withstand the reprisals' economic impact. British influence had originally established itself in India around Madras, Bombay and Calcutta. Those happened to be Hindu-majority areas. So the Hindus had been the first to come into large-scale touch with the powerful foreigners, and accustom themselves to their ways. That gave them a lead economically; and during the 1780's Cornwallis's policies had the incidental effect of increasing this. And in 1835, Macaulay's famous minute resulted in the Moghuls' Court language, Persian, being displaced by English for administration of the Company's territories. Up-country Muslims in particular had fewer opportunities than Hindus for learning it, and this aggravated the community's difficulties in getting clerical employment in the changed conditions

69

of 1858. There were further items : widespread loss of lands, because
of measures which now required documentary proof of ownership;
loss, too, of former openings in the Army, because they were less
trusted; and loss of that intangible thing prestige, important the
world over, but especially so in Asia. It seems plain, retrospectively,
that the events of 1857–8 set the community back by at least fifteen
years in what, during the 1930's and 1940's, became its hazardous
belated race for independent nationhood.

The disaster's first effect was to press Muslims down sullenly into
their past. For solace their leading men turned to religious piety and
Urdu literature, largely refusing efforts to keep abreast with the
Westernising stream of affairs, or to collaborate with the infidel new
régime and the Hindu upstarts now flourishing in their place. Reactionary Muslim movements, such as that of the so-called Wahabis,
which had vexed the Company since the 1830's, got fresh sympathy.
This introverted mood persisted during the 1860's; and that it should
have changed, while time still remained for change to be of use,
was due mainly to two men : William Hunter and Syed Ahmad
Khan.

Though the latter's role was certainly the greater, Pakistanis perhaps rather overlook the former's – and indeed that of another
Englishman a decade or so afterwards, Wilfred Scawen Blunt. Hindu
historians readily recognise men of British stock, Dufferin and A. O.
Hume, Wedderburn and Robert Knight, as having been part-
founders of the Congress party in 1885, and thus of India's eventual
independence; Sikhs acknowledge the importance of J. D. Cunningham and Macauliffe in their renaissance; but neither Hunter's role
for the Muslims, nor Blunt's, seems to have been given due place.
The latter sympathiser got so far, while in Calcutta in 1883, as to
outline, pretty clearly, the Pakistan demand of the future. He said
the subcontinent should have two separate Governments, a Muslim
one in the north, a Hindu one in the south, and 'the whole civil
administration, legislation and finance (should be in) native hands',
only residual military power remaining with the British. Indeed as
Mr. Jinnah himself pointed out, the impossibility of unitary self-
government for the subcontinent had been suggested from an interesting British source long before: as far back as 1858, by John Bright.

Hunter's book came out in 1871, four years before Syed Ahmad
Khan's vastly influential first achievement, the founding of the
Aligarh Muslim College;[1] and its brilliant last chapter on 'The
Wrongs of the Muhammadans under British Rule', written with

[1] Later University.

intense sincerity, stirred British and Muslims alike, the more so because at the time he was a working civil servant. Syed Ahmad Khan's
achievements nevertheless were on a much broader front, more
specific, and more sustained. They included – besides Aligarh – his
success in winning recognition for the principle of separate electorates for Muslims on Ripon's municipal councils in 1882; and in
keeping Muslims uninvolved in the Congress party's renewed pleas,
in 1887, for quicker introduction of Western-style Parliamentary
bodies. His reason, both times, was the same: that representative
institutions of the British sort were unsuited to Indian realities, and
particularly to the Hindus' practice of caste. 'The system of election,
pure and simple, cannot be safely adopted; the larger community
would totally override the interests of the smaller.' His speech
during the 1887 controversy contained a well-known passage rich
with prophetic insight. 'Suppose that all the English were to leave
India,' he asked, 'who would be rulers? Is it possible that two nations
– the Mohammedan and Hindu – could sit on the same throne and
remain equal in power? Most certainly not. To hope that both
could remain equal is to desire the inconceivable.' Until his death
in 1898, his influence was still great. And 'when he was laid to rest
in Aligarh' – as Sir Theodore Morison recorded – it was fittingly
said of him that 'other men have written books and founded colleges;
but to arrest, as with a wall, the degeneration of a whole people, that
is the work of a prophet'.

The years 1871–87 stand out as a peak in the Muslim community's
evolution; as a period when decisive, concrete things happened. And
a historian can perhaps identify three further such peaks – prior to
Pakistan's creation of 1947 – between which lay periods of indecision
and fluidity. The next peak covers 1905–12; and in the preceding
trough – 1887–1905 – the most noteworthy happenings were the
effects of books, and the emergence of a movement. Outstanding
among the books was Ameer Ali's *Spirit of Islam*, published in 1891,
perhaps the most skilful feat of Muslim apologetics ever penned.
His purpose, like Syed Ahmad's – as we explained in Chapter 1 –
was modernist. Two others need mention : the poet Hali's moving
Musaddas; and – as an irritant – Bankim Chandra Chatterjee's
virulently anti-Muslim novel *Anandamath*. These came out before
1887; but the effects of thought-creating authorship take time to
show themselves, and both books were actively influential during
this period. Linked with Chatterjee's was the movement: the rapid
emergence, at this time, of an aggressive revivalist Hinduism, exemplified by Swami Dayananda's Arya Samaj in Northern India; by

Tilak's fanatical agitation during the 1890's in the Mahratta country; and by Swami Vivekananda's wonderfully persuasive overseas publicity for Hinduism at the Chicago 'Parliament of Religions' in 1893.

The peak-period 1905–12 opens with Curzon's partition of Bengal. and ends with Hardinge's annulment of it. Curzon's motive was primarily administrative: Bengal had become too populous, even then, for efficient management as one unit, and its outlying eastern areas, which happened to be Muslim-majority areas, were getting neglected. The second consideration in fact much resembled that which brought about the second partition in 1947; and as a result, local Muslims welcomed the change. Hindus, contrariwise, construed it as a premeditated attack on their interests, and an extraordinary clamour ensued, reinforced by terrorist outrages against British officials. These strained conditions continued throughout Minto's Viceroyalty, and as he ruefully remarked later,[2] 'we told the Musalmans that the partition was a settled fact, over and over again; there could have been scarcely a civil servant who had not declared that it would be impossible for the British Government to reverse the decision.' Thus, when in December 1911 reversal was announced, it appeared to many a surrender not merely to words, written or spoken, but to bombs and bullets. Before Muslims' eyes, the first big obvious crack in the British régime's moral structure had opened up.

However, during Minto's term of office their position had much improved in other ways. The Muslim League – potentially a rival to the Congress – was formed in 1906; and in the same year separate electorates, already accepted for municipalities, were extended to the new Legislative Councils which the Morley-Minto reforms created.

After the Bengal partition was annulled, four vague years of embitterment and confusion ensued, to be succeeded by the third peak, covering the years 1916–22; a unique one, because Hindus and Muslims drew closer together, during it, than ever before or since. And we may think it a striking paradox that, whereas World War I and its aftermath had this effect, World War II and the two ensuing years had precisely the opposite one, pushing the two communities apart. The reason lay in an external and, at first sight, completely irrelevant factor : the parlous plight, in the former period, of Turkey.

Italy in 1911 had started an onslaught against her; the Balkan States had followed suit; and now Britain – with others – was at war with her. All these were European, Christian countries. And Turkey, or the Ottoman Empire, was not only Asian; it was the heart of the

[2] In the Lords after return home, February 1912.

Muslim world, the home of the Caliph. And Britain and her ally Russia, not long before, had virtually partitioned Persia, a Muslim country, and done much the same with Afghanistan. On the other hand the Russo-Japanese war had excitingly shown that European or Christian Powers, after all, were not necessarily invincible when fighting Asian ones. And now they were fighting each other, locked in a vast fratricidal conflict which suggested a curious thought : that though at present certainly better than Indians at making machines, they might be morally much less superior than had been supposed.

The complex sentiments stirred up by all this influenced Hindus as well as Muslims, and in 1916 enabled the more liberal, un-theological wing of the Muslim League, represented by a rising young Bombay lawyer Mr. Jinnah, to reach the remarkable accord with the Congress about the country's constitutional future known as the Lucknow Pact. In this, the Congress for the only time in its career – persuaded by Tilak, now it seemed transformed from fanatic into statesman – agreed to Muslims having separate elec-torates. Essentially, the pact was a conference-room compromise, made between rational, well-balanced upper-class minds; and parts of it (including separate electorates) were taken over by the British for their next instalment of reforms, the Montagu-Chelmsford plan passed by Parliament late in 1919.

Meanwhile, however, conditions in India had much changed. To a general post-war malaise, and annoyance over rising prices, had been added in 1918 gusts of anger about what were considered pro-vocatively drastic Governmental measures to thwart subversion, the so-called Rowlatt Bills. Mr. Gandhi, fresh back from agitation in South Africa, organised hartals[3] against these, from which minor disorders ensued. The fact was that entirely new forces were being thrust into Indian politics at quite unfamiliar social and emotional levels; from the Hindu side by this new leader, a sort of religious demagogue apparently, and unlike Tilak (whom he seemed to be displacing) a man of low caste; and from the Muslim side by men far removed from Mr. Jinnah's coldly Westernised intellectual stand-point, popular theologians such as Maulanas Mohammad and Shaukat Ali, or Abul Kalam Azad, now because of the Turkish question all aglow with Islamic fervour, whose appeal by tongue or pen lay less to the Council-chamber than to the mob. By the spring of 1919, the resulting disorder or tension had become considerable in the Punjab. On April 10th, at Amritsar, four Europeans were killed by riotous crowds; and three days later occurred a catastrophe:

[3] Traditional one-day Indian strikes, vaguely infused with Hindu religious notions of grief or mourning.

troops under General Dyer's command fired sustainedly into a banned public meeting, killing at least 379 people and wounding over 1,000. Martial law was then imposed, and the local public for a while subjected to shocking indignities.

The horror caused by this affair might gradually have subsided, but for the arguments, stiff it seemed with racial prejudice, which were used in support of the firing, not only by witnesses before the inquiry-committee in India, but in the British Parliament and Press. And as the months of controversy dragged on, the smouldering sense of outrage in the Indian public mind increased, until in the spring of 1920 it found sudden opportunity for fusing with similar emotions set alight in another quarter : by the brutal terms of the Treaty of Sèvres imposed on Turkey, involving dismemberment of the Anatolian mainland, in clear breach, it was considered, of Allied pledges. This threw Muslim 'Khilafatists'[4] into partnership with Mr. Gandhi and his supporters, and together they launched a non-co-operation campaign against what he termed the 'Satanic' Government.

Though it caused the authorities great inconvenience and lasted until 1922, it never got near to bringing the Administration to a halt, as had been intended; and the first elections under the reforms were duly held. And by 1921 its inherent weaknesses were beginning to show. Talk by excited Muslims about jihad,[5] and about bringing the Afghans into India worried the Hindus; and in August, an anti-Government upheaval by the Muslim Moplahs of Malabar soon took a violently anti-Hindu turn, involving slaughter, rape, and forcible conversion. That knocked the backbone out of the campaign; and early next year, after twenty-one Indian policemen, mostly unarmed, had been killed by Congress volunteers at Chauri Chaura, Mr. Gandhi abruptly called it off, to the indignation of his extremer followers. The Muslims, for their part, soon had their main reason for agitation pulled from beneath them by the Turks themselves, whose startling secular renaissance, and victories over the intruding Greek forces culminated, two years later, in abolition of the Caliphate.

Hindu-Muslim relationships, thereafter, never regained the same friendliness. The intense, precariously-based enthusiasms of the 1920–2 non-co-operation campaign were followed by such disillusion that much of the sensible, cool-headed work done at Lucknow in 1916 was destroyed.

*   *   *   *   *

[4] Persons anxious for preservation of the Caliphate.
[5] Religious war.

The years 1922–37 may be dismissed briefly. From our point of view they are a trough. They began with much confused and futile Hindu-Muslim rioting in the cities, sorry evidence of the mutual exasperation that prevailed; and although they included several events which, from other angles, must be accounted very important, none of these, in themselves, decisively affected the Muslims' future. Among them were the visit to India in 1928 of the Simon Commission, coupled with the Hindus' and Muslims' failure to agree on any joint alternative to what the Commission might propose; the Round Table Conferences in London; Mr. Gandhi's two civil disobedience campaigns in the early 1930's, impressive affairs from which however Muslims generally held aloof; the Communal Award; and the passing by Parliament of Britain's last instalment of reforms before Independence – the Government of India Act of 1935.

One general point of Muslim interest however emerges : the way in which, between 1922 and 1937, the community's misgivings about self-government in a united India shifted from the provinces to the Centre. Whereas in the 1920's, Muslims were worried mainly about how dyarchy would work under the Montagu-Chelmsford system, in the 1930's their chief concern was to prevent a future Central or federal Government from getting too strong, from obtaining powers wide enough to put Muslims permanently at a Hindu majority's mercy. And there are two specific points also to record. At the session in 1930 of the Muslim League in Allahabad, a rough first sketch of what became the Pakistan-project was formally commended for attention, for the first time in the League's history – and by no less a figure than Sir Mohammad Iqbal, in his presidential address. And in 1933, at Cambridge, the word Pakistan was coined by a young Muslim, Choudri Rahmat Ali,[6] a historic achievement for which his name seems to have been insufficiently honoured by his countrymen.

The 1937–40 peak was due to an episode connected with provincial Ministry-making, particularly in the United Provinces.[7] At the time, no one quite grasped its far-reaching implications. Other provinces, such as Bombay, were involved too. The sequence of events needs recounting. In 1934 Mr. Jinnah had come back to India from a spell of law-practice in London, and he soon found

---

[6] In a pamphlet entitled *Now or Never*. Subsequently, he explained the term as follows: 'Pakistan is both a Persian and an Urdu word, composed of letters taken from the names of our homelands: that is, Punjab, Afghania (N.-W. Frontier Province), Kashmir, Iran, Sindh, Turkharistan, Afghanistan, and Balochistan. It means the land of the Paks, the spiritually pure and clean'.

[7] Later re-named Uttar Pradesh.

himself leader of the Muslim League. Like the Indian Liberal party, but unlike the Congress, it had as yet scarcely attempted 'mass contacts', and remained little more than a discussion-society for upper-class persons interested in a particular brand of politics. Three years later – and he had not had time then to improve it much organisationally – elections were held for the Legislatures under the new Government of India Act. He chose a temperate programme, conforming with his past record. A similarity between the League's and the Congress's ultimate nationalist ideals was stressed, and the Lucknow Pact of 1916 praised. And in some provinces – among them the U.P. – League candidates regarded themselves as campaigning jointly with the Congress, on the understanding that coalition Ministries would be formed afterwards; indeed, U.P. Leaguers evidently believed that two Cabinet posts had been promised them.

The Congress, now a very efficient political machine, did even better in the elections than its backers had hoped. Returns showed that unaided it could probably form Ministries in seven provinces out of eleven. The League, not yet being thus developed, fared no more than tolerably. The Congress leadership thereupon decided that U.P. Leaguers could only join the provincial Cabinet on terms unlikely to be accepted by any self-respecting party: namely that they must themselves become members of the Congress; and that the League's local parliamentary boards must be dissolved permanently.

The effect of this, simultaneously on many Muslim minds throughout India, was of a lightning-flash. What had before been but guessed at, now leapt forth in horridly clear outline. The Congress, a Hindu-dominated body, was bent on the Muslims' eventual absorption; Western-style majority-rule, in an undivided subcontinent, could only mean the smaller community being swallowed by the larger, as Syed Ahmad Khan had long ago pointed out; in the end, Muslims would find themselves just one of the lower Hindu castes, dissolved in a general grey idolatrous mush. Those were the opinions formed; and that British Parliamentary precedents might readily be found to support the kind of decision the Congress had made, after so big an electoral success – and assuming that no really firm promises had been broken – mattered not at all. For Britain was not India; conditions there were different; hers was a unitary society, not a plural or multi-racial one. And that the Congress's decision should actually have been announced by a Muslim, by Abul Kalam Azad, a Congress protégé now serving as the party's president, made the average Muslim's bitterness all the sharper. What – Leaguers asked themselves – could really have been such a man's private thoughts, when he came to sign such a statement?[8]

And after the Cabinets were formed, Congressmen did nothing whatever to sweeten things. No effort was made to show that the average Leaguer's reaction might be wrong. On the contrary Mr. Nehru – himself a U.P. man – was soon back in the province conducting a vigorous 'mass contact' campaign on his party's behalf among the Muslim poor, to swing their loyalties away from their allegedly 'feudal' co-religionists who controlled the League. Provincial Ministers in the U.P. and elsewhere did their daily business in a perceptible atmosphere of 'Ram raj',[9] repugnant to non-Hindus. And all sorts of petty pressures and harassments aimed against Muslims began to be alleged. Schoolchildren were instructed to worship Mr. Gandhi's portrait with folded hands in the Hindu manner, and to sing 'Bande Mataram', a nationalist ditty taken from Bankim Chatterjee's obnoxious novel. Beef-eating was actively discouraged; also the Urdu language and script; the best appointments always went to Hindus; the police sided with Hindus during riots; and so on. Details can be found in what was termed the Pirpur report, published in 1938 by an All-India committee set up by the League 'to inquire into Muslim grievances in Congress provinces'.

That some of the allegations were probably exaggerated or others untrue is irrelevant. What mattered was that most Muslims throughout the subcontinent believed them. Writers are now practically unanimous on the crucial importance of the U.P. Ministry-making episode in Hindu-Muslim relations; and it constitutes the fourth of our peaks. Thereafter, the impulse towards Partition acquired astonishing momentum. Mr. Jinnah's reorganisation of the League, his quick conversion of it from a debating society for elderly gentry into a mass-movement was obviously done with great skill; but part of the job just spontaneously did itself, on a wave of popular Muslim emotion. Spear, in a recent book, interestingly testifies to the pace of events, describing 'the changed atmosphere which greeted him on a return to Delhi in 1939, after an absence of two years; Pakistan was in the air'.

Not long after World War II broke out, in protest against the way in which India's participation in it had been officially decided on by Lord Linlithgow, the Congress Ministries in the provinces resigned. Some British officials in the provinces were genuinely sorry; unexpectedly pleasant daily working contacts had been gradually built

---

[8] Reproduced in Coupland, p. 294 (see Bibliography).
[9] A favourite phrase of Mr. Gandhi's, denoting a kingdom controlled by the Hindu Godhead.

up. But the League rejoiced, and arranged a 'day of deliverance' to celebrate the event, which was extensively observed. Affairs within the organisation then moved even faster. During the previous spring, a League committee had been appointed – few outsiders sensed the significance of it at the time – to report on 'draft schemes already propounded by those versed in the constitutional developments of India and other countries'; Mr. Jinnah was president, and Mr. Liaquat Ali Khan convener. Its observations apparently came under active scrutiny during the autumn and winter; Khalid Bin Sayeed's book gives details. And on March 23rd, 1940, at Lahore, the famous so-called Pakistan resolution[10] in favour of the subcontinent's Partition was put forward and passed.

The rest of the tale may be quickly told. The Congress, still blind to the decisive change in Muslim sentiment which its arrogance had brought about, took two further self-stultifying steps – after withdrawing its seven provincial Ministries in October 1939 – which for much of World War II left the political field almost completely open to the League; a state of affairs which Mr. Jinnah exploited to the full. The first was the 'individual' civil disobedience movement of 1940–1, which put several Congress leaders behind prison-bars for shortish periods; the next – much more serious – after the abortive Cripps mission of March 1942, was its 'open rebellion' of August.

Nearly three years of what its sympathisers called 'the deadlock' then followed; the last of this chapter's troughs. During this period, in the summer of 1944, talks took place near Bombay between Mr. Jinnah and Mr. Gandhi -- who had been prematurely let out of jail because of ill-health – in the hope of finding some way towards agreement. Their initiator had been Mr. Rajagopalachari, the only leading Congressman of his time wise enough to see what was happening to the Muslim community, and why, and to implore his party to do something big-hearted about it. But nothing resulted. And by the time the rest of the Congress Working Committee were released in June 1945, Mr. Jinnah had so strengthened his hold on the Muslims' allegiance, as to be able to impose his will on the conference held by Lord Wavell that month in Simla to discuss the country's future. Against the Congress's past proud unrealistic claim that it alone represented the Indian people, he re-emphasised his counter-claim: that the League alone represented the Muslims. Nothing would budge him from it; and on the rock of his refusal to allow either the Congress's nominee, Azad, or the head of the Punjab provincial

[10] In fact the word Pakistan was not used in it.

Unionist party, Sir Khizar Hayat Tiwana, to join a proposed new Interim Government at the Centre, the conference collapsed. And during the general elections of the following winter (1945–6) he convincingly proved the truth of his counter-claim, by victories as sweeping among his own community as the Congress, then and in 1937, achived among the Hindus. There were, in fact, two parties on the subcontinent, not one, and they were now heading straight for collision.

Chapter 5

Towards Civil War

TO define civil war may not be easy. And most people, if living in one, hesitate to admit it; just as they do if living in a slump, or nowadays a recession. Euphemisms are used, to conceal the nasty truth. They were used about living conditions on the Indo-Pakistani subcontinent in 1946–8. Yet if non-military carnage and commotion, estimated to have caused about 500,000 deaths, and the migration of about 14 million people, cannot be called civil war, it is hard to guess what could be. In fact, the human race has probably never experienced a civil war so big. Mr. Gandhi, far-sighted, and frank, recognised it for what it was a few days after it started, and gave it its right name. 'We are not yet in the midst of civil war,' he said in September 1946, 'but we are nearing it.'

The independent sovereign State of Pakistan was born into that carnage and commotion. It was her main first national experience. And to understand her problems, the attitudes of mind of her people, and the policies of her Governments is impossible unless the facts of her birth are recalled. They will therefore be considered closely in the rest of Part II. The previous chapter traced their remoter practical causes; this one will offer brief observations on the atmosphere surrounding events, immediately before the conflict began.

As has been stressed in Part I, the differences between Hindus and Muslims – historical and religious, cultural, social and legal, manifested in such everyday things as eating, dress, worship, marriage, personal hygiene, inheritance, and disposal of the dead – are big; bigger, to put it mildly, than those between most other groups of people living near one another on the earth's surface. Nevertheless, when in 1946 the end of the British rule in India appeared not only probable, but imminent, most of the leading Western-educated Hindus took it for granted that they would inherit the substance of British power, and that the Muslim minority would have to accept this fact. The ballot-box would see to it. They had been nurtured in the British political tradition, and felt sincere respect for it. And besides having a large majority over the Muslims, they were superior in wealth and education; so their right to the succession seemed plain. They therefore opposed with vigour any suggestion of the subcontinent's being partitioned, when this first came to be seriously bruited, preaching with conviction what may be termed the one-nation theory, or the theory of the single inheritance. And it was a theory with which British officials and politicians, whose forbears had given India both her existing administrative unity and her Parliamentary system, felt logically disposed to concur, even if admitting that Muslim objections had weight.

For the reasons explained in the last chapter, increasingly many Muslims however now objected very strongly. Even so, despite the Lahore resolution of March 1940, a proportion of them, in their hearts, were almost certainly not yet convinced that Partition, or the theory of the divided inheritance, was the right answer. Perhaps, they thought, a compromise might be reached; surely some acceptably loose federal arrangement, to relieve Muslim misgivings, could even now be worked out between reasonable men, which would avoid the need for a complete split? Real efforts at conciliation by the Hindus during 1946, such as Mr. Rajagopalachari had been urging since 1942, might have produced a useful response. But no such efforts were made. Insistence by the Hindus on the one-nation theory, unmodified, remained altogether rigid.

Looking back, we may feel surprised that the Hindus, or Congress politicians on their behalf, should have felt so sure, not perhaps of their right, but of their capacity to rule the subcontinent – an area as big as Europe minus Russia, and with a huge variegated population. Nearly a thousand years had passed since Hindus ruled it; and for two-thirds of that time, the Hindus had been under Muslim rule, not British. And as has been stressed in Chapter 1, the Muslim imprint on the subcontinent's affairs – in religion, in forms of Government, in architecture, in heredity – had been much deeper than the British. The subcontinent's Muslims now numbered 100 millions, certainly a big figure;[1] and during the last twenty-five years or so, since the enthusiasms of the Khilafatist agitation collapsed, Hindu-Muslim relations had been so uneasy that Ambedkar, leader of the Untouchables or Hindu outcastes, in a book issued in 1946, argued that between 1920 and 1940 there had in effect been 'a civil war, interrupted by brief periods of armed peace'. Of course the disorders then were trivial, compared with what ensued in 1947. Nevertheless, 'taking the period from February 1929 to April 1938,' he went on, 'the Hindus and Musalmans of the city of Bombay, alone, were engaged in sanguinary warfare for 210 days, during which 550 were killed and 4,500 wounded.'

[1] Estimate for 1946. In the 1941 Census it had been over 92 millions.

F

These were weighty considerations. Reasoned argument seemed needed, if the Hindus' ability to run the subcontinent in future by mere right of the ballot-box was to be accepted without question. Yet despite this, any hint that it might be wise to meet Muslims' demands half way, that in the interests of peace, recognition of the possibility of accepting something like Pakistan might help to show a way out of present perplexities, nearly always ran into unbending, indignant opposition. The suggestion was not only absurd, intellectually untenable; it was wicked.

This total resistance, this moral certitude that the Hindus through their main political party the Congress (which had a 3 per cent Muslim membership) must be the country's effective rulers from the Khyber to Chittagong was the outstanding fact of Indian public life in 1946. On it, all attemps at fending off what happened during the next terrible year broke down. And it would be wrong to ascribe it simply to the doctrinaire arrogance of a particular individual such as Mr. Nehru; or to the world-wide totalitarian trends of the last twenty years; or even to the average person's natural pleasure at the thought of bossing it over others. Deeper causes were at work. Good, unselfish, humble-minded men felt this certitude, this emotional inability to tolerate the very idea of Pakistan; men whom it was always a pleasure to meet. To them, the whole thing was nonsense, void of substance, a sin against the light, an outrage against the nationalist impulse, no more than a wretched, passing by-product of Imperialist Britain's self-interested policy of 'divide and rule'. Once independence had been got, all such bad notions as a need for partitioning the subcontinent would disappear.

Possible explanations for this extreme strength of feeling deserve a moment's thought. Originally, one factor may have been race; the question of brown versus white. Throughout Asia in the 1930's and 1940's – as throughout Africa in the 1950's and 1960's – fervent efforts were being made to throw off European colonialism. It could thus be argued that any separatist trend in India, such as the Pakistan agitation, risked letting down the anti-colonialist side. Up to about the end of World War II, this argument had some validity. But now that the British were almost certainly going, the validity shrivelled away.

Or secularism may have been a factor. The Muslim League said it wanted Pakistan as a place where the Muslim Faith could freely flourish (though doubtless some Muslims viewed it with an eye to getting better jobs, clear of Hindu competition). To Westernised secular-minded Hindus, the religious flavour of the Pakistan-project was objectionable. This doubtless in part explains Mr. Nehru's attitude. But does it explain it wholly? The objection after all was an intellectual one, which concerned mainly the academic few, and might have been expected to be put temperately. And the great majority of Hindus of course were by no means secular-minded; they were deeply religious. Why should the Pakistan-project have stirred such passionate indignation among the tiny, though influential, minority of Western-educated Hindus to whom religion, either way, mattered little?

We should perhaps consider whether these secular Congress leaders may not themselves, without realising it, have been swayed by latent religious motivation, conditioned into them by their upbringing. Consent to the creation of Pakistan meant that pieces would be lopped off the body of Bharat Mata, of holy Mother India. It would be hard for someone – however secular – whose childhood had been spent amidst the ceremonies and traditions of a Hindu family not to feel the distress of this. A book reissued in 1946 by Mr. Nehru's colleague Rajendra Prasad, subsequently President of India, which argues the case against Pakistan with skill, contains an interesting passage, relevant perhaps to this hypothesis. 'Every Hindu who performs his sandhya has to repeat a sloka in the sankalpa, in which he pictures the country as a whole, and imagines the waters of the Sindhu,[2] the Ganga, and the Cavery to be mingled together in the water of his small waterpot. And this has gone on, not only during the period of Hindu rule, but when Muslim Emperors ruled at Delhi. It is repeated even today, when British suzerainty spreads over the whole peninsula. It cannot be denied that, irrespective of who rules, and what were the administrative or political divisions of the country, the Hindus have never conceived of India as comprising anything less than what we regard as India today.'

Possibly the explanation lies here. At all events, by the spring of 1946, when the British Cabinet Mission arrived to discuss the transfer of power, resistance to the project of Partition, by secular-minded Congressmen as well as by the religiously orthodox Mahasabha, had come to contain an element of fanaticism. Thus the stage was set for tragedy.

Besides politics, military considerations were much in some men's minds during the winter of 1945–6. To a detached observer, the Empire in South Asia over which Britain presided now seemed very anachronistic. Early exit of the foreign rulers was made likely by

[2] i.e. the Indus, now a wholly Pakistani river (except for its highest reaches in mountainous Ladakh and Tibet). See footnote on p. 15.

their distant little country's weaknesses after the exhausting conflict it had just come through. Superficially, their rule might appear firm, in the first few months after victory; but underneath it could not be. A subcontinent of about $1\frac{1}{2}$ million square miles, and (then) of about 412 million inhabitants, some of them proud of their own imperial past, remained subject to an offshore European island, only about one-seventeenth as big and about 5,000 miles away, and with a population of only 49 millions. The thing was absurd. It had hinged on a quirk of history, clearly now ending : the island's possession of an almost global economic superiority over other countries through exercise of sea-power. Her wealth, it now seemed plain, must have been broken beyond repair by the second of two world wars waged within a generation; and sea-power, which in any case could not be upheld without wealth, was being jostled aside by a technical upstart, air-power, which had evidently made the crowded British Isles, behind the water-barrier that so long had proved their safeguard, one of the most dangerous spots on earth.

Observers in many lands, looking out over the hideously disordered scene, during that first dismal winter after a devastating struggle, and pondering on the big shift so manifest in the actualities of armed might, must have cast their thoughts uneasily back to the dissolution of other Empires during this self-same twentieth century : those of the Romanovs in Russia, the Habsburgs in Central Europe, the Ottomans; and particularly, perhaps, the Manchus in China. They may have wondered – as leading British officials in Whitehall and Delhi doubtless did, and as this writer remembers doing, in a Calcutta editorial chair – what strange new thing might emerge from the period of Chinese-style anarchy, lasting perhaps for decades,[3] which reason suggested might well soon set in throughout South Asia, as a result of the British régime's collapse.

Anarchy of that prolonged sort did not set in, as we know. There was a civil war, huge and horrible but (by Chinese standards) brief; a Partition; and then a recovery. And there can be no doubt now, when we peer back from our present vantage-point, that what prevented disaster was mainly just one thing, a rather brittle thing then, but which nevertheless held firm: undivided India's Armed Forces. They alone remained dependable, during the critical weeks after the British withdrawal; the sole remaining upholders, over large northern tracts of the subcontinent, of such shreds of 'law and order' as remained.

[3] From the date of the Boxer Rebellion to the establishment of the Communist régime in China was 50 years.

This factor in the events of 1946–8 has in the present writer's view never been properly brought out; books about Partition-time tend to pass it by, concentrating mainly on politics. Yet it is basic. What would have ensued had the indigenous Forces cracked? We have but to reflect on events in the Belgian Congo during the summer of 1960 to form some idea of the probable answer. And, as mentioned, those indigenous Forces happened already to be in rather a brittle state. It is a point sufficiently important to call for a chapter by itself, to explain why.

Chapter 6

Trouble in the Armed Forces

THE Armed Forces of undivided India actually came through the ordinary post-war stresses of demobilisation during the winter of 1945–6 very much better than some of the British Forces then on Indian soil. The events referred to in the last chapter were of different origin. They arose, dramatically, from two interconnected special affairs, whose emergence was doubtless difficult for the harassed authorities to foresee clearly – though it is a fact that, at the time, many considered that perspicacity in high places had been woefully lacking. These affairs were the so-called 'I.N.A.' trials; and the mutiny in the Royal Indian Navy.

During the few weeks when the excitement created by them was at its height – the spring of 1946, well before the Partition-time disturbances – observers found themselves faced with the grim question whether, if the Indian ship of State was destined to founder, as seemed quite likely, the particular rock she hit would prove not to be political at all, as most people assumed, but simply military. Would the timbers be burst asunder by soldiery casting off their bonds of allegiance? It had happened several times before in the subcontinent's chequered past, as Hindus and Muslims and Sikhs well knew; not merely in 1857, the date which always leapt to the British mind. If so, catastrophe lay nearer to hand than the darkest of previous forebodings had suggested.

As matters turned out, this rock was not the one struck. Yet the reasons for fearing it, during those agitated weeks of 1946, were strong. And it can be argued that what averted shipwreck was not so much wisdom at the bridge, as sheer luck, an accidental turn of fortune's wheel. The outcome, in any case, was crucial for the future stability, and indeed survival, of the successor-States to the British Raj; and even more for Pakistan than for India, because as the year 1958 showed, her destiny was linked with the quality of her Forces, and especially with that of the officers – mostly of about the status of major in 1946 – who, by 1958, had risen to high commands.

The I.N.A. trials, or more properly courts martial, were an offshoot of the biggest defeat in British military history: the loss in

February 1942 of Malaya and Singapore. About 130,000 officers and men were put behind Japanese barbed wire, a large proportion being from the Indian Army. During the weeks before and after the main disaster, Indian prisoners were also taken in Hongkong, Burma, and other places in East Asia. The total number of Indians in Japanese hands, by the end of May 1942, amounted to about 70,000.

At Singapore, after the surrender, the victors segregated their prisoners racially, the Indians being put in one set of detention-camps, the British and Australians in another. Why they did this soon became plain : they hoped to seduce the Indians from their allegiance, and get them to fight on the Japanese side. They worked first on some of the young captured officers; and before long, by this means, achieved a numerically much bigger success than war-time censorship allowed the public in Allied countries to realise. About 20,000 Indians were persuaded by blandishments, pressure or sheer terrorism to join a Japanese-sponsored 'Indian National Army', pledged to the overthrow of the Raj they had so recently served.

When in the spring and summer of 1945 the British Imperial Forces, instead, overthrew the Japanese, and regained all the lost territories, these 20,000 who had changed sides were a problem. Obviously most of them – the rank and file – were not gravely to blame. The surrender at Singapore had been an appalling débâcle; British prestige, they must have felt, had been altogether shattered. Many of them, arbitrarily cut off at the moment of surrender from their former British officers, and feeling forlorn, had chosen the path of nominal disloyalty and least resistance, merely because living con-ditions outside the barbed wire, on the terms offered, looked like being rather less wretched than within. And some – though doubtless fewer than later claimed it – had done so with the idea of abandon-ing the I.N.A. at the first good chance and rejoining the British side. To have punished such men, now, with the full rigour of military law would have been unjust; and because of their numbers, it would anyway not have been physically feasible.

But what about the few – officers in particular – who, soon after capture, had accepted the offer to change sides with alacrity, prose-lytising for the Japanese cause among their imprisoned compatriots? And what, even more, of those known to have helped in torturing of former comrades-in-arms for refusal to abandon their oath? The presumption, by those (still not many) who knew the facts, was that such individuals would be dealt with drastically and at once, on the spot, by recognised military means.

Not so however. The decision reached in Delhi was this. News of it first started trickling out from G.H.Q. towards the end of August 1945, and caused growing amazement. A few officers who had been ringleaders of the I.N.A. were to be brought to trial by court martial – in October perhaps, not before, because suitable arrangements could not be made. A series of such courts martial might be held. These would not be tucked away somewhere in Burma or Malaya – that would be unworthy, the public might think the accused were not getting fair trial. The accused officers would therefore be (or had been) brought to India. Further, the trials would take place in Delhi itself, the capital – the place, it may be recalled, which during Hardinge's Viceroyalty had been substituted for Calcutta as the seat of Government, largely because of its appeal to Indian nationalist feelings. As the authorities said, it was a communications-centre suitable for easy attendance by defence counsel, relations and so on. But it was also one where, obviously, every ingenuity in anti-Government propaganda that the Congress party possessed could be put to fullest use. And not only that; the trial would be held, the authorities announced, in – of all places – the Red Fort, which they considered 'the most convenient from nearly every point of view'.

Conceivably, among those points of view, was a notion that the Fort might serve as a taunt, for it had been the I.N.A.'s proclaimed objective in the hoped-for 'march on Delhi', heralded over the Japanese radio. If so, the authorities were not long-memoried enough. Even among the semi-literate, history on the Indo-Pakistani sub-continent, much of it transmitted orally from parent to child, can become a living thing, able to thrust itself startlingly out of the supposedly dead past into the thoughts and deeds of the present – as events in the Punjab during 1947 only too luridly showed. And for the subcontinent's peoples the Delhi Fort had significances far deeper than anything dished up by Far Eastern publicity-mongers during World War II. Muslims naturally recalled – which G.H.Q. apparently did not – that however suitable structurally it might be for staging a trial in, it had been built by the grandest of the several Muslim dynasties which ruled India before the British came, the Moghuls, and had been used by emperors not only as the hub of their administration, but as residence. And Hindus had tenderly in mind that it stood near the reputed site where, previously, a revered line of Hindu Kings had ruled, culminating in the gallant, tragic Prith-viraj; and that it was rich, as well, in Hindu mythological associations of much earlier date. Most vividly of all, Hindus and Muslims alike remembered that it was where the sepoy mutineers against the British had put up their last desperate stand in 1857.

And as if the misjudgement in choosing the Delhi Fort for the first trial was not enough, the three officers to be arraigned, it turned out, were not to include those understood to have committed the worst brutalities; and – more astoundingly still – they were to be from the country's three main communities simultaneously : Hindu, Muslim, and Sikh. If ever Machiavelli had inspired British policy in India, as Congressmen were wont to allege, he might have turned in his grave on learning this. 'G.H.Q. can't have gone mad, but it looks like it,' this writer remembers a stolid regimental officer remarking on the Calcutta-Delhi train. 'They must have some reason for what they're doing that we don't know of.'

Early in November 1945 the main trial began (various subsidiary ones were also now being organised). All the political ill-consequences which might have been foreseen from its staging quickly emerged. The publicity and excitement became tremendous. Mr Nehru, though he had not practised law for thirty years, made himself leading counsel for the defence. With him were Congress party lawyers of professional eminence : Mr. Bulabhai Desai, Dr. Katju, Mr. Asaf Ali; and Mr. Desai, in particular, excelled himself in extolling the three accused officers' patriotic virtues. Soon they became public heroes. Congress newspapers poured forth eulogies; demonstrations in their support were held all over the country. Nor could the Muslim League hold back. Though unenthusiastic, it had no choice, since one of the accused was a Muslim. So adverse a turn were matters taking, that before the end of November the Governor of the Frontier Province, Sir George Cunningham, observing from afar, felt impelled to write to the Viceroy – admitting that in broaching the subject he was 'going somewhat outside my proper sphere' – urging that the C.-in-C. should be persuaded 'to announce that, as Indian opinion is opposed to the trial, he wipes the whole thing out. I dislike saying this intensely,' he added; 'it is tantamount to surrendering to threats; the thing (however) is becoming Indian versus British. I am certain, from what I have heard from a wide variety of people here, that the only way of stopping the rot is by a clean cut, and at once.'

The affair dragged on however. Eventually, on January 3rd, sentences were pronounced, moderate in nature; and almost immediately G.H.Q. itself then proceeded to whittle even these away, in what seemed abject surrender to the storm of nationalist emotion which, by its own procedures, it had gone out of its way to arouse. An editorial in *The Statesman* newspaper observed: 'we wish we could record having seen any wisdom, Indian or British, in the handling of the I.N.A. trial now concluded in Delhi. We have watched the unfolding of this strange drama, one of the gravest in implication that modern India has experienced, in amazement and disgust. In our view, almost every imaginable blunder has been perpetrated from the outset by the military authorities, and by India's largest political organisation.'

This, naturally, is not the view held by all. Philip Mason, who was Joint Secretary to the War Department in Delhi at the time, and drafted the official communiqués on the trials, has said[1] it is difficult to believe that, when the original decision was taken a few weeks after Japan's surrender, 'any body of humane and responsible men, in that position at that time, would have decided on a different course of action. I defended it in the Assembly in Delhi in 1946, and I would defend it again today.' But he goes on to say that the course originally proposed was considerably modified, and he adds: 'if the way things would go had been foreseen, it would have been far wiser to adopt a different handling. It might have been done if anyone had thought of it. But no one did.'

That really seems the crux of the matter. Tuker, who was then G.O.C.-in-C., Eastern Command, has commented on the affair in terms of scathing condemnation. Here are some phrases culled at random from his book. 'This maladroit handling . . . An act of gaucherie which could not have been surpassed . . . Enough to make the ordinary European civilian refuse to credit his eyes or ears . . . It would be difficult for anyone to conceive of a more ill-advised procedure . . . The bewilderment of the regular officers can be imagined . . . Ineptitude had yet higher flights to make . . . Set to work to hew out the very roots of the Army. It is a wonder that the whole tree did not crash to the ground . . . To a man appalled at what was being done by their seniors; and from now onwards they turned away from Delhi. From that time dates the indifference of the British officer of the Indian Army towards his higher Command. Adjurations and defiances flowing from Delhi simply irritated him the more. He slogged along at his job for the sake of the regiment and its men.'

The mutiny of February 1946 in the Royal Indian Navy did not in fact cause grave trouble. But it well might have done. The G.O.C.-in-C. Southern Command, General Sir Rob Lockhart, has described it as 'a damn near thing'; and for four days it caused great and very proper anxiety. It was the fault, partly, of the I.N.A. trials – that is to say, of the senior British officers in G.H.Q. who rashly staged them and of the Congress politicians who exploited them; and partly of some of the rank-and-file of the British Forces on Indian soil then awaiting demobilisation, notably R.A.F. ground personnel at Cawn-

[1] In his Preface to Toye's book; see Bibliography.

pore and Dum Dum, who by organising 'strikes' – more correctly describable as non-violent mutinies – had set a flagrantly bad example. And the R.I.N., before the war, had been a tiny Service; of necessity it had expanded very fast; mistakes had been made, especially in choice of some officers, who lacked understanding of Indian conditions, or even knowledge of an Indian language. As a result, very genuine unredressed grievances had developed among the ratings. These facts came out afterwards, in the Enquiry Commission's report; they were not appreciated at the time. The mutiny was unforeseen and sudden. It began at Bombay.

On February 18th, ratings of H.M.I.S. *Talwar*, the main signal training establishment, started a 'strike', on the R.A.F. model, nominally over complaints about food. Next day, indiscipline quickly spread to other shore establishments, and to R.I.N. ships in the harbour, of which there were twenty-four. Thereupon, some hundreds of ratings broke loose into the European or 'Fort' area of the city, usually immune from the sort of street rioting for which Bombay was notorious. They smashed windows, hauled drivers of military vehicles from their seats, set upon British officers and other ranks walking on the pavements, and raised shouts of 'Jai Hind', the I.N.A. slogan. The American flag outside an office building was pulled down and burnt. And across the water, on several R.I.N. ships, the Congress party flag could now be seen, fluttering in the White Ensign's place.

By February 20th, every R.I.N. vessel at Bombay – they were all small craft, sloops, minesweepers, corvettes, but all were armed – was unquestionably mutinous, including the 1,700-ton flagship *Narbadda*. Officers had mostly been forced down the companionways and sent ashore. Along the waterfront, messages in morse or on the loud-hailer were being passed between the personnel aboard the ships and those on land, and once at least to political demonstrators in the city. Disaffected ratings could be seen moving about the harbour in launches. The occasional crack of small-arms fire was heard. British members of Bombay's leading social institution had a curious experience; Wilfrid Russell recounts it vividly. 'Five hundred yards to seaward, swinging at anchor in the harbour, the *Narbadda* was training her 4-inch forward gun-turret on the Yacht Club lawn. I took my turn at the telescope on the verandah, and watched the turret swing gently round in the direction of the Taj Mahal hotel, then back to the Empire's most famous club.'

Three tense and dangerous days ensued. On the Army's initiative, strong reinforcements were being brought in from Deolali and elsewhere in Southern Command: both Indian and British troops; artillery as well as infantry; Mahrattas, the Essex Regiment, Royal

Navy, Royal Marines. An armoured car regiment arrived from Ahmednagar, and drove ostentatiously through the city; R.A.F. fighter-bombers whizzed overhead. The arrival of the powerful British cruiser H.M.S. *Glasgow* from Colombo also had an important influence. Militarily, so far as Bombay was concerned, nothing very much happened before the mutineers' eventual surrender late on February 23rd, though there were nasty moments, notably around Castle Barracks on February 21st, when some of the mutineers within seized weapons from the armoury, and tried to rush Army pickets posted outside. In the resulting affray, ratings threw grenades, and were answered by machine-gun fire. On the same day, the dockyard was subjected to small-arms fire from some of the ships.

Two other things however had been happening meanwhile : an outbreak of fierce civilian rioting in Bombay city; and extension of the naval disaffection to other parts of the map. The first needs no describing here. Damage was heavy, and casualties amounted to 228 dead and 1,046 injured, vastly greater than from the mutiny itself. In nature, it differed little from any ordinary major Indian urban riot; Calcutta had two such outbreaks during the 1945-6 cold weather; but the fact that it synchronised with trouble in the Armed Forces of course made it much more perturbing. And as regards the second, it would be fair to say that, by February 21st, scarcely any of the R.I.N.'s 75 or so ships and 20 shore establishments scattered around the subcontinent remained unaffected, except H.M.I.S. *Godavari*, then at sea between Singapore and Madras; and from a military aspect, the mutiny took a distinctly graver turn at Karachi than at Bombay, since force had to be used to compel surrender.

After signing a letter to Delhi in which he remarked 'Politically there is nothing to report', the Governor of Sind Sir Francis Mudie was obliged on February 21st to add a hasty P.S. 'I have just seen Richardson,'[2] he wrote, 'who reported that a ship of the R.I.N. started firing its guns, first in the air and then all around it. One British soldier on patrol was badly wounded. A paratroop battalion is now moving in, and proposes to shell the ship with howitzers.' In fact, there had been some indiscipline on H.M.I.S. *Hindustan* the previous afternoon; and the Army, learning of this, and being aware that naval trouble had arisen in Bombay, took the precaution of sealing off Keamari port from Karachi city overnight. Local topography facilitated this; and as affairs turned out, it proved an excellent decision, since it prevented disorder spreading from the ships to the streets, as in Bombay. Next morning (February 21st) mutiny

[2] Major-General R. Richardson, Commander, Sind area.

broke out on *Himalaya*, the gunnery school. Ratings there shut up their officers, tore down the White Ensign, and then proceeded to cross the harbour in motor-boats to the *Hindustan*, which some of them boarded, soon acquiring virtual control of the vessel. Attempts had been made by the Army to head off the motor-boats by troops in other craft. This led to an exchange of fire, first by small-arms; but subsequently the ship opened up with its oerlikons on the B.O.A.C. terminal where troops were moving, and then started firing indiscriminately in all directions, some shells dropping in the Baluch lines beyond the Cantonment, and others away out at Clifton.

Throughout the day deadlock ensued, while reinforcements were brought up. Next morning, after repeated efforts to persuade the mutinous ratings to surrender had failed, the Army was ordered to seize the ship, and opened fire with 75 mm. guns, mortars, and automatic weapons. The ship replied with all she had, but was hit repeatedly, and after twenty minutes' action surrendered. Casualties aboard her were four killed and twenty-six wounded. In Bombay, the total military casualties on both sides had been three dead and thirty-two injured.

These two interconnected affairs, the I.N.A. trials and the naval mutiny, were clearly, in combination, bad enough to make far-sighted observers, during the spring of 1946, wonder how dependable undivided India's Armed Forces would henceforward be. And had such people, then, been miraculously granted a glimpse into the months ahead; had the curtain lifted, to show some of the extraordinary things that would happen in swift series before the end of 1947, their misgivings would have become acute. The outbreak, next August, of a sixteen-months' civil war between Hindus, Muslims and Sikhs, in curbing which troops would have to be much used; the complete and permanent withdrawal, by August 1947, of British Imperial authority; and the simultaneous hurried unpicking, for apportionment between two newly-independent and mutually unfriendly States, of the Forces themselves: these would have been what was beheld. And the subcontinent's abrupt descent into chaos would have been thought a virtual certainty.

How this was avoided is even now not easy to see, twenty years later, with the help of historical hindsight. The picture seems to include some sheerly irrational elements, products perhaps of the Indian sun, and the volatility of the Indian temperament. But some clear items can be picked out. First, the British military authorities' insistence, over many decades, on keeping troops and people apart. This policy bore rich fruit now; it was too firmly grounded to break or bend before the first intruding blasts of political agitation, tempest-like though those seemed at the time to city-dwellers during that bewildering winter of 1945–6. Tucked away in well-dispersed cantonments, remote from urban contacts, busy with their training and professional tasks, sheathed in tradition, officers and men carried steadily on, much less influenced by far-off trials and commotions than desk-users such as politicians, and generals, and newspaper editors might have supposed. It is likely, too, that those of us who lived on the subcontinent's eastern flank saw things in too sombre a light. Since the Japanese overran Burma in 1942, that flank had been near the fighting-zones; all the stresses and complications of war-time had been at their worst there; and compared with much of the subcontinent it was populous, and mingling between soldiers and the public therefore less easy to prevent. Throughout, the I.N.A. controversy was evidently looked on with a less worried eye by Northern and Southern Commands, from their tranquil almost pre-war surroundings in Rawalpindi and Poona, than by Eastern in Calcutta or Ranchi.

But there was something else; perhaps as big a factor as the aforegoing. From about the end of February 1946 people began noticing, with mild surprise, that the Congress party's propagandist activities for disrupting the Forces' discipline, so conspicuous in previous months, seemed getting less. These did not stop; but the impression conveyed was that the leaders had lost interest, and perhaps were toying with other ideas. And so, in fact, they were. This was mainly the doing of Sardar Patel, the 'party boss', the very practical Hindu – incidentally of strongly anti-Muslim bias – who controlled the levers that made the organisation work.

During talks between some of his colleagues and himself and the Viceroy Lord Wavell held in the previous December, he had formed the opinion that the British did at last – from the Congress's point of view – mean business. They were no longer pretending. They were getting ready to quit – for reasons, as they construed the changed post-war circumstances, of material self-interest. Himself a realist, he could respect such reasons; and he did not afterwards waver in his belief that he had judged their mood correctly – though he had a job, at first, in persuading his colleagues of this.

And if he was right, then some large conclusions followed. It meant that the very efficient military machine of undivided India, on which the British had lavished such care, would come, much sooner than anyone had expected, within the Congress's grasp. (That Pakistan would really be created, never at this stage entered his or other leading Congressmen's heads.) For nationalist India,

Hindu-dominated India, this would be splendid. Was not such an acquisition worth having – something big and solid, which shouldn't be fiddled with? – something that mattered much more than a fuss about a few young officers, weaklings possibly, who had changed sides during a war? Changing sides, or mutinying, could be wrong; it might not now be to India's benefit that her people should be encouraged in it.

It was with thoughts such as these, and with his colleagues in Delhi now half-converted to them, that in February 1946 he found himself in Bombay during the naval mutiny. And the evidence is strong that his influence helped to induce the mutineers towards their conveniently early, bloodless surrender. Quite what happened at the Congress's headquarters in the Bombay bazaars, during those critical days, is not on record; but clearly the party's Left-wingers, led by the fiery Mrs. Aruna Asaf Ali, suffered a sharp rebuff. The conservative group, which he headed – and which was locally represented by his near-namesake Mr. S. K. Patil – won a wordy battle very significant for the subcontinent's future, while armed mutineers and riotous civilian mobs roamed the streets. From then on, the Muslim League under Mr. Jinnah – which had never relished the I.N.A. agitation – and the Congress party's strongest group, though poles apart over other things, were tacitly together on one : that for practical reasons connected with their contrasted aims for the future, they both disfavoured fostering indiscipline in the Forces.

Chapter 7

The Cabinet Mission's Plan

NNOUNCEMENT from London that three British Cabinet Ministers would visit India,[1] to help solve her constitutional problems, was made on February 19th – oddly enough, the very day when the R.I.N. mutiny broke out; and some have suggested, perhaps not very convincingly, that the startling news from Bombay spurred on their work. At all events, after reaching India with their staff on March 24th, and entering on a busy round of interviews, they soon left almost no doubt that Sardar Patel's conviction was right : the British Government genuinely wanted to transfer power to Indian hands soon, and the Mission would press hard, and far, to achieve agreement on how to do this during their stay. All the news that filtered out from Delhi about the conversations went to confirm this.

Throughout April, the talks went on – as the weather got warmer. Early in May, it became clear that the Mission's efforts to bring about agreement between Congress and League were unavailing. They accordingly decided to put forward proposals of their own, their so-called Plan, or more properly Statement. It came out on May 16th. This is no place for describing its complicated details. In essence, however, it set forth methods for creating an ingenious three-tiered constitutional structure for a united India, which nevertheless did not totally prevent the eventual emergence of something like Pakistan if that was really desired; and, while such a Constitution was being worked out, for acceptance by a Constituent Assembly, the Plan proposed that a new 'Interim' Government should replace the existing one at the Centre, endowed with the widest possible powers, and including no British member except the Viceroy. Thus the Plan – though less obviously than the Cripps offer of 1942, for its mention of the Interim Government was brief – fell into two parts, a long-term one and a short; and these parts, it was later explicitly stated, formed an integrated whole which must be accepted or rejected together.

Rather to many people's surprise, since the provisions relating to a possible Pakistan seemed at first glance much too vague to square with the Lahore resolution of March 1940, the League on June 6th

[1] Lord Pethick-Lawrence, Sir Stafford Cripps, and Mr. A. M. (later Viscount) Alexander.

unequivocally accepted the proposals. The explanation for this lay in the provision, within the proposed three-tiered structure, for what were termed 'sections' and 'groups', and for withdrawal by individual provinces from groups, or (by implication) of groups themselves from the proposed All-India Union should they wish. This provision offered a sort of half-way house to Pakistan, and was in fact a typical British compromise, produced only after much heart-searching – for the British in general, and the Labour party in particular, clearly wanted to preserve India's unity if they could; a compromise which in the end, and in a hard-edged subtropical climate of extremes, quite lacking in England's convenient haziness, turned out to be tragically unworkable. It was evident even at the time, from the speeches made, that the League's decision to accept the Plan was made with misgiving, and only because a half-way house seemed in the circumstances better than nothing, and might well be exploited, before long, to achieve the desired end. However, the resolution as passed, besides being commendably prompt, was unqualified.

That could certainly not be said of the Congress party's resolution, which only emerged after what Lord Wavell later termed 'almost interminable haggling', despite the fact that on June 16th the Mission had issued a supplementary Statement about the Interim Government to help things along; and when it did emerge, on June 25th, it was clad in such involved language that the average person might well be excused for thinking it lacked any meaning. Scrutiny however disclosed two points : that the Mission's supplementary Statement of June 16th about the Interim Government was definitely turned down; and that while indicating, or more than indicating, that they accepted the long-term part of the May 16th Plan, Congressmen did so only subject to interpretations of their own about the sections and groups, which seemed in complete conflict with what was intended by the Plan's authors, that is to say by the British Ministers. Thus, to the eye of commonsense, the party's resolution amounted to a rejection. Moreover there had been disturbing rumours – later voiced publicly by Mr. Jinnah – about how, in last-moment confabulation between the anxious Mission and leading Congressmen, the Congress's eventual very qualified acceptance of the Plan's long-term aspect had been shakily arrived at.

This leads to the controversial affair of 'Clause 8'. The Mission's supplementary Statement of June 16th had included a clause which said that, 'in the event of the two major parties, or either of them, proving unwilling to join in the setting up of a Coalition Government on the above lines, it is the intention of the Viceroy to proceed

G

with the formation of the Interim Government, which will be as
representative as possible of those willing to accept the Statement of
May 16th.' To many, the Congress's resolution as formulated on
June 25th appeared to create the very contingency which this clause
– Clause 8 – had envisaged. More than awkward though it might
be to have the League in office while the Congress stayed out, especially when most of the provinces were still run by Congress Ministries,
there now seemed no escape from it, in morality or logic. For
whatever the Congress's resolution might mean as regards the long-
term part of the Plan, there could be no gainsaying that it had
turned down the short, that is, the part relevant to setting up an
Interim Government. Accordingly, astonishment was felt when on
June 27th the Mission stated that Clause 8 was not to be put into
effect, anyway for a time, and that administration at the Centre
would be carried on by a temporary 'caretaker' Government of
officials.

The present writer as newspaper editor was involved in this episode, and perhaps may emerge personally for a moment. Despite
much probing at the time, and subsequent cogitation and inquiry,
he has never understood it. For the only remaining wholly British-
owned newspaper in India, as *The Statesman* then was, to run into
collision with the Viceroy and three visiting British Cabinet Ministers
on such a big issue was not pleasant; however, an editorial came out,
which ended with some rough remarks. 'Politicians may do so,' the
editorial said, 'but it is not the business of statesmen to eat their
words. They should not risk bold, sweeping, unequivocal public
undertakings unless they mean them, and can be relied upon to fulfil
them. What was so emphatically considered needful and proper on
June 16th cannot well, within ten days, have radically transformed its
nature.' When, later, this writer discussed the affair with the Viceroy,
a standpoint of honest mutual incomprehension seemed soon to be
reached. The trouble evidently lay in some blurring or confusion,
beyond an inexpert person's grasp, between the Mission's two an-
nouncements : of May 16th, and of June 16th. Talking with him
there in his study, it was impossible to suppose him insincere; and
there was the further consideration that, besides daily collaboration
with the Mission, he had throughout been carrying the full administrative load of the Viceroyalty. Perhaps Sir Stafford Cripps had been
too nimble-witted. But possibly a truer explanation, kinder than that
pointed to in the editorial, is that four very overworked men, towards the end of those long weeks of confused negotiation in appalling heat – the summer temperatures of 1946 were even fiercer than
usual – had reached a state where they were genuinely unable to

interpret plain words like ordinary uninvolved mortals. The symptoms of hasty drafting, for example the alternation in Clause 8 between 'Coalition' and 'Interim', which most people had scarcely noticed at the time, may now be thought to confirm this thesis. Or perhaps the shift of words was deliberate, and meant to hint at the Mission's real intentions, as Lumby has suggested. But in that case the matter seems worse. It denotes that the Mission's striving after compromise had altogether overreached itself; that in their earnest efforts to be all things to all men, they had engaged in irreversible ambiguities, putting themselves in a moral as well as a verbal quagmire.

A storm of indignant protest against the decision of course burst forth from the League, Mr. Jinnah declaring that the British Ministers had been 'in honour bound to go ahead' on the basis of the Clause, and had revoked 'their plighted word and abandoned what was announced'. And the effects were far-reaching. From this time on, many Leaguers felt they had two opponents to deal with; the British, as well as the Congress. Some of them, especially perhaps Mr. Jinnah, who had lived in England for years during the early 1930's, had throughout felt suspicious of the Labour party; there had been a long history, dating back beyond the time of the London Round Table Conferences – indeed, to Tilak's London visit in 1919 – of close friendship between its supporters and the Congress. And now, because of the involvement in the Clause 8 affair of a high-principled soldier-Viceroy, supposed to be apart from politics, suspicion stretched forth to the British nation as a whole. In their weakened post-war state, Leaguers reckoned, these foreigners were bent merely on appeasing the Congress, regardless of the merits of a case; ethical considerations had gone overboard; what mattered was not whether an issue was right, but only that the Congress party, compared with the League, was the bigger and stronger, and the better able to cause trouble; and the more qualified, as well, to offer lucrative openings for British trade in the coming new era. Muslims, if they were not to be overwhelmed beneath the doubly inimical policies thus unfairly heaped upon them, could now only fight to preserve their rights and culture; negotiation was of little if any further use. That was the mood created. And looking back from our coign of vantage twenty years later, many would probably agree that the Clause 8 controversy must be labelled the first of three main factors which precipitated the civil war – now so near.

It may well be true, as Menon, Brecher, Moon and other writers consider, that the Cabinet Mission's Plan could never have worked; that it was too cumbrous, too papery, too much of a Crippsian intellectual feat; that the weakness of the federal Centre, and the strength given to the provinces or groups – meant to conciliate the League – would in practice have proved a fatal flaw; and that it took for granted an attitude of mind in those who would have had to use it, a British capacity for tolerant adjustment and mutual concession, which on the Indian subcontinent, with its quite un-British history and social conditions, simply did not exist, and whose existence moreover practical statesmen ought never to have assumed. Certainly from the standpoint of our knowledge now, we can see that, after the civil war started in August, the Plan was doomed, and that the repeated endeavours made during the following eight months to resuscitate it were mere beating the air; and Brecher perhaps identifies a basic defect when he says that the two 'grouping' clauses, out of which what he aptly terms 'the battle of interpretation' arose, really contradicted one another. If so, we may feel forced to conclude that the trouble about Clause 8 was no more than a by-product of something graver which lay further back, wrapped within the texture of the Plan itself, and deriving from a general well-intentioned doublefacedness on the plan-makers' part. On that reckoning, the Ministers, though so high-minded, had early stumbled into their ethical bog – with practical consequences in some ways very like those which, thirty years or so before on another part of the globe, resulted from the issue by British spokesmen, imbued perhaps with less lofty ideals, of conflicting offers to Arabs and Jews.

All this however was less discernible then, amidst the swirl and dust of contemporary controversy. And when on June 29th, two days after giving their decision about Clause 8, the Ministers withdrew to London, exhausted by all the heat, and talk, and confusion, they felt able to comfort themselves by reflecting that at least their hard work had averted total breakdown, which had more than once seemed imminent; that during the pause which would now ensue, the Viceroy in further palavers with the Congress and League might somehow hit on a way to make the May 16th Plan usable after all; and that, anyhow, their protracted three-months' visit and ceaseless efforts had convinced everyone on the subcontinent who mattered that Britain, or the Labour Government, really wanted to transfer power. On this last big point, whose importance must not be underrated, their confidence was indeed not misplaced; but for the rest, as we know, their hopes proved illusory, and within a fortnight of their exit a further event occurred, the second in our series, which as we can now see pointed straight to almost certain disaster.

This was a sequence of remarks in Bombay early in July by Mr.

Nehru, who during the intervening few days had succeeded Abul Kalam Azad as President of the Congress party. He was thus, if the British were really about to go, the person likeliest to become free India's first Prime Minister, and his utterances therefore were of outstanding significance. We are in good company in recognising them as historically crucial. Not only do most Western writers do so; Azad himself, his life-long partner, in a book published posthumously in 1959, unequivocally termed them 'one of those unfortunate events which change the course of history'. Doubtless they were in large part due to his intellectual standpoint as a Western-style Socialist and agnostic, as already mentioned, which led him to suppose that the Indian communal problem, since it was of religious origin, either did not exist, or at any rate was fundamentally much less important than most people imagined; that it had been artificially puffed up (which was partly true, but far from the whole truth) for self-interested purposes by foreign Imperialists and local 'feudalists'; that since it was 'medieval' and 'theocratic' – words he was fond of – its disappearance was 'inevitable'; and that it could in fact be blown clean off the political map now, by his own party under his presidentship, through a whirlwind of vigorous nationalist assertion. This led him to emit, at a singularly inopportune moment, what his biographer Brecher terms 'one of the most fiery and provocative statements in his forty years of public life'. And we may note that it was of a piece with what had happened, largely under his inspiration and now recognised as historically disastrous too, in his own province the U.P. nine years before, as described in Chapter 4: the fateful exclusion of Muslim Leaguers from the newly-formed local Ministry, and the Congress's attempted 'mass contact' campaign among the Muslim proletariat. It is ironic that, in the reflected light of these two sets of occurrences, Mr. Nehru, though so fervent an opponent of Pakistan, should without undue stretch of the imagination be displayed as one of its chief architects. Moon rightly remarks that it was almost as if a 'curse' had been laid on him and some of his colleagues, causing them 'to act in such a way as to bring about exactly the opposite result to that which they intended. They passionately desired to preserve the unity of India; they consistently acted so as to make its partition certain'.

Addressing the All-India Congress Committee at Bombay on July 7th about the outcome of the negotiations with the Cabinet Mission, he flatly declared, in his capacity as party president, that 'It is not a question of our accepting any Plan, long or short. It is only a question of our agreeing to go into the Constituent Assembly. That is all, and nothing more than that. We will remain in that Assembly

so long as we think it is good for India, and we will come out when
we think it is injuring our cause, and then offer our battle. We are
not bound by a single thing, except that we have decided for the
moment to go to the Constituent Assembly'. And at a Press conference three days later he went on to predict – which was even
more dangerous – that in all probability no 'grouping' of provinces
such as the Plan had provided for would occur, and that 'inevitably'
the federal Government would gain in strength at the provinces'
expense. The Congress, he reiterated, would enter the Constituent
Assembly 'completely unfettered by agreements, and free to meet all
situations as they arise' – an assertion which Azad, who had been
party president when the Congress's resolution on the Plan was
passed, sorrowfully recorded 'was wrong; it was not correct to say
that Congress was free to modify the Plan as it pleased. These matters
could not be changed unilaterally by Congress without the consent
of other parties'.

At all events, from the practical aspect Mr. Nehru's utterances of
early July revived in the strongest form all the fears of Hindu aspira-
tions for mastery via the ballot-box, which had been active in Muslim minds ever since Syed Ahmad Khan first began voicing them in
the late 1880's. The departed British Ministers had recognised the
strength, and by implication the validity of these fears, saying that
the mission had been 'greatly impressed by the very genuine and
acute anxiety of the Muslims lest they should find themselves subjected to a perpetual Hindu-majority rule', and that it would be
impossible to allay such anxiety 'by mere paper safeguards'. And
now, in Mr. Nehru's manifest determination to subvert the 'grouping' offered under the Mission's Plan, and to ensure the overriding
control of a strong federal Centre, Leaguers saw all their forebodings
confirmed. Mr. Jinnah forthwith announced that the Congress
President's statements necessitated the whole position being reviewed,
which would be done at a meeting of the Muslim League Council
due to be held towards the end of the month.

When the Council met on July 27th it was in thoroughly exasperated mood : exasperated against the British, as well as the Congress, because of the Clause 8 controversy. The session lasted three
days; and after truculent speeches a series of sweeping resolutions
was passed, which launched the organisation on entirely novel
courses. The Cabinet Mission's Plan, both parts of which as we have
seen it had accepted on June 6th, it now rejected totally. The League
would enter neither the proposed Interim Government, nor the
Constituent Assembly. Further, Muslims throughout the subcontinent were instructed, 'in token of their deep resentment of the atti-

tude of the British', to renounce all titles granted by the foreign Government. And they were urged, as well, to take or to support 'direct action' for attainment of Pakistan within the terms of the Lahore resolution of 1940, August 16th being fixed as 'Direct Action Day', and a committee of the League being asked to prepare a detailed programme. 'What we have done today,' Mr. Jinnah declared, 'is the most historic act in our history. Never (hitherto) have we in the League done anything except by constitutionalism. But now we are forced into this position. This day we bid goodbye to constitutional methods.' Neither the Congress nor the British had expected anything nearly so drastic, and the League's resolutions were received with surprise and dismay.

Meanwhile, on July 22nd, in the hope of getting things going, in spite of the acute differences between the two main parties, Lord Wavell had invited them to form an Interim Government at the Centre. This was meant as no more than a reiteration of the paragraph on the subject in the Mission's May 16th Plan; the Viceroy simply wanted to set up some representative and mutually acceptable stop-gap body, to run the country's affairs until solider arrangements could be made. But we can see now that the move was very ill-timed; it was made without fully realising the League's new mood, and in a form moreover which resulted in the League promptly rejecting it. The Viceregal invitation offered the League certain proportions of representation within the proposed new Government; but these differed somewhat from those offered during May and June. And they did not at all satisfy Mr. Jinnah, who forthwith flatly refused them, asserting that, to placate the Congress, the Viceroy had deviated from previous proposals on points vital to the League. According to Tuker, well meant though the offer was, it 'proved to be the spark which fired the charge in Bengal and India'; and from our present knowledge of what ensued this comment seems well based. The Viceregal invitation of July 22nd must thus be classed as the third item in our series.

The League's drastic decision on July 27th–30th put the Viceroy and the British Cabinet in a complete quandary. Quick choice between the two main contesting parties now seemed unavoidable, and either course held grave dangers. In making up their minds, they were however helped by the Congress, which on August 10th, realising no doubt how bad things had become, belatedly made what was perhaps its first sensible move of the summer, by passing a fresh resolution which, while maintaining its objections to 'grouping', nevertheless declared that its previous resolution had actually been meant to accept the Cabinet Mission's Plan 'in its entirety'. But with Mr. Jinnah, this cut no ice; it came too late. 'If Congress could change so many times, while the British were still in the country and power had not come to its hands, what assurance,' he asked, 'could the minorities have that once the British had left, Congress would not again change, and go back to the position taken up in Jawahar-lal's[2] statement?'

The Congress's motives at this juncture have been variously construed. Azad interprets the August 10th resolution as an embarrassed but genuine attempt, without openly repudiating Mr. Nehru's rash Bombay remarks, to smooth the way for a return by the League to constitutional courses. Leaguers, on the other hand, mostly regarded it as an unprincipled tactical device, aimed simply at getting the Congress well entrenched in office now that the League had backed away. Whatever the truth, the practical upshot was that, within a mere two days of the Congress's volte-face, the Viceroy, with the British Cabinet's approval – or perhaps at their prompting – asked Mr. Nehru to form the proposed Interim Government much on the terms already offered, but with an expressed hope that he would be generous in offering seats to the League.

Mr. Nehru promptly accepted. In the League's absence, he could in effect make himself Prime Minister, whatever the constitutional niceties might be; the Viceroy's powers of veto would be scarcely usable. He did indeed, in apparent magnanimity, forthwith offer seats to the League, as the Viceroy had asked; but Mr. Jinnah spurned this, as was predictable, since to have done otherwise would have meant the League deriving power from the Congress instead of from the Viceroy, in complete repudiation of its rigid stand hitherto. And in a statement soon after, he bitterly denounced 'the caste-Hindu Fascist Congress, and their few individual henchmen of other communities, who want to be installed in power, to rule over Musalmans with the aid of British bayonets'.

Except in one city, nothing of note except big meetings happened on 'Direct Action Day', August 16th; and such evidence as can be got does not show that the League's central leadership planned anything much to happen. Arrangements, owing to lack of time, had not yet been thought out. The 'Day', it was explained, was simply to be one when the League Council's resolution would be publicly explained. 'It is nothing but a statement,' said Mr. Jinnah, 'concerning the steps which we propose to take for our self-preservation and self-defence.' It was no 'declaration of war' on anybody. The meet-

[2] i.e. Mr. Nehru's.

ings would not in themselves be 'direct action'; and those who came were asked to behave peacefully.

How far the League Ministry then holding office in Bengal reciprocated these cautious ideas seems however very open to question. Except for its counterpart in Sind, it was the only League Ministry then existing; it declared the 'Day', in Bengal, a public holiday; and there was much to suggest that members of it thought 'a bit of a beat-up' to celebrate the occasion might be no bad thing. That, at any rate, was this writer's considered view, formed with a newspaper's means of information at his disposal. On the other hand, it is inconceivable that members of the Ministry could have wanted an outbreak such as happened, if only because there was no possibility of the Muslims winning. Though they enjoyed a majority in Bengal as a whole, they were heavily outnumbered in the province's capital, their proportion of the population there in 1946 probably being less than 25 per cent.

In the event, what happened in that one city, Calcutta, was utterly appalling. As mentioned, quite bad riots had occurred there not long before, during the preceding November and February; anti-Western racial riots, rather similar to the Bombay riot associated with the naval mutiny. But this was something unique; what a local commentator aptly termed 'a new order in disorder'; and no anti-Western riot but a communal one, of an intensity and size and savageness that no one had imagined possible. Away back in March 1931 at Cawnpore, when a communal riot caused about 400 deaths, everyone was so shocked that the Congress party decided to modify its whole policy, and the local British official's career was ruined. But now, in the so-called second city of the Empire, the deathroll was at least ten times bigger. The scenes of butchery and destruction, in what soon came to be called the 'Great Calcutta Killing', were indescribable. At the end of three dreadful days, corpses bestrewed the town. Borne everywhere on the warm moist monsoon breeze came the stink of human putrefaction. In Shampuker and such-like squalid outlying parts, on plots of waste ground, you could see mounds of decomposing, liquefying bodies, heaped as high as the second floors of the nearby houses because of lack of space elsewhere. A visit to the police morgue necessitated use of a respirator; unremoved rotting cadavers were stacked to the ceiling. If you wished to watch how a vulture opened up a dead man's abdomen, you could see it on the pavements of wealthy Park Street. During a three-hours' jeep-tour of the city with a pair of British N.C.O.'s of the military police, this writer reckoned (as they did) that we had seen more horrors than most modern soldiers ever do on the battlefield. Full nauseating details

of the conditions that prevailed, if wanted, can be found in Appendix
V of Tuker's book. About 100,000 people were rendered homeless,
mainly by arson. So great was the confusion, that all possibility of
a detailed numbering of the dead and injured was ruled out. According to some local newspapers' estimates, casualties ran to as many
as 50,000 – though that figure was certainly too high. Menon and
Lumby quote different official calculations : the former, 20,000
casualties including 5,000 dead, the latter, 14,000 including 4,000
dead. Woodruff chooses the smaller figure. *The Statesman*, using
its own sources, reached a figure for the total casualties (dead and injured) of 20,000 or somewhat more.

Even perhaps during the first day's fighting, and certainly during
the second and third, Muslim losses were the worst. Apparently local
Hindu organisations, hearing rumours that some sort of Muslim
attack was contemplated, had made formidable counter-preparations.
What decisively tipped the scales however was perhaps not the
massive retaliatory Hindu onslaughts but the intervention during
the second afternoon of the Sikhs, who had in the main held aloof
on August 16th. Something then bestirred these bearded warriors,
who incidentally enjoyed practically a monopoly of Calcutta's motor-
transport. The present writer recalls watching hordes of them that
evening, in vehicle after vehicle – taxis, lorries, buses – rushing
furiously up Chowringhee, from their suburb of Bhowanipore, to
join the fray on the Hindus' side in the city's smoke-shrouded
northern slums.

Quite why there should have been so complete and sudden an
administrative collapse in Calcutta has never been clear. The police,
as a result of the stresses of the time, and the general run-down of
the Services, had become less efficient. Nevertheless, according to
Tuker, who as G.O.C.-in-C. Eastern Command had access to much
official information, they did not lack self-confidence, and declared
themselves satisfied, until towards sundown on August 16th, that
they had things under control. This presumably is why the troops,
who proved remarkably effective when used, were not called in by
the civil power until much too late. The only possible underlying
explanation of so total a disaster, one may suppose, lay in the unique
degree to which the emotions of the two main communities, in a
very crowded city which had twice gone through serious rioting of a
different sort some months before, had been worked up by the political fears and hopes, and the inflammatory communal speeches of the
preceding few weeks.

On August 24th, while the afflicted city was still clearing up the
mess, and whiffs of putrefaction issued from hitherto unfound bodies

shoved down drains or trapped in burnt-out houses, the names of the members of Mr. Nehru's Interim Government at Delhi were announced. On September 2nd, it took office. And throughout India, that day, large numbers of Muslims hung up black flags on their houses in bitter protest.

These two events, the Calcutta killing, and the setting up of Mr. Nehru's first Government professedly in implementation of the British Cabinet Mission's Plan, in fact signalised the start of a sixteen-months' civil war; a conflict in which the estimated total death-roll, about 500,000 people, was roughly comparable to that of the entire British Commonwealth during the six years of World War II.[3]

---

[3] The official tally of Commonwealth deaths, civilian as well as military, between September 1939 and August 1945 is in round figures 540,000.

Chapter 8

Civil War – I

SOME days before Mr. Nehru's Government was installed on September 2nd, Lord Wavell managed to wrench himself from the exacting and (we may guess) at times uncongenial demands of politics in the capital, to see things in Calcutta for himself. He had made another such inspection-tour at a time of calamity previously, during the Bengal famine of 1943, just after becoming Viceroy; and much good had come of it. Scholar as well as soldier-administrator, it was doubtless his historical sense, as well as practical experience of big affairs, which enabled him to recognise at once that the Calcutta occurrence was one of those events that might well decide a whole series of others. Perhaps it had already brought India and her people almost to a 'point of no return'.

Menon's book gives fascinating glimpses of what ensued. 'A definite change in the Viceroy's attitude' was noticed after he got back to Delhi. He felt 'convinced that, if some sort of agreement between the two major communities was not brought about soon, the Calcutta happenings would be repeated'. He met Mr. Gandhi and Mr. Nehru on August 27th, and stressed that 'the only way to avoid similar trouble all over India was to set up Coalition Governments both in Bengal and at the Centre. The crux of the matter lay in the Congress interpretation of "grouping". The only chance of a peaceful transfer of power was that the Congress accepted the position that the provinces must remain in their sections, as intended by the (British Cabinet) Mission, until after the first elections under the new Constitution. He would not undertake the responsibility of summoning the Constituent Assembly until this point was settled'. And he handed them 'a formula which he thought might satisfy the Muslim League. The discussions, which now and then became rather heated, proved inconclusive'.

Menon then describes how Mr. Gandhi wrote to the Viceroy, saying that 'the Viceroy's language at their interview had been minatory'. On the other hand the Viceroy felt that, 'if Congress's intentions were as Gandhi's letter suggested, the result of its being in power could only be a state of virtual civil war in many parts of India'; and how Mr. Nehru was asked by the Viceroy to refer the matter to the Congress Working Committee; how the Committee 'were considerably surprised at the sudden change in the Viceroy's approach'; and how, eventually, after telegraphic exchanges with London, the Viceroy was in effect overruled, being told that 'His Majesty's Government felt that the Viceroy should not take any steps which were likely to result in a breach with the Congress'. Accordingly Mr. Nehru's Interim Government was sworn in; and it contained – which the League, as could have been foreseen, construed as a calculated affront – no fewer than three puppet or 'nationalist' Muslims whom the Congress had nominated.

It is tempting to speculate on what might have happened, during those few fateful days late in August, had the Congress leaders, like the Viceroy, been jolted into fresh lines of thought by reflecting on Calcutta's multitudinous dead; or had the British Cabinet not overruled the Viceroy. Here stands one of the big 'ifs' of Indian history. For if the Viceroy's reading of the lessons of Calcutta had prevailed, the civil war, then just started, might have stopped; and in that event Partition might have been unnecessary, some loosely federal arrangement on the lines of the Cabinet Mission's Plan perhaps proving acceptable after all. Or if, as seems rather more probable, Partition had occurred, then it need at any rate not have been accompanied by appalling bloodshed involving millions, nor have hardened afterwards into a 'cold war'.

But those are might-have-beens; for with the swearing in of Mr. Nehru's Government and the overruling of Lord Wavell's ideas the chance – if it was one – dropped. And now, across the 1,500 miles' length of the Indo-Gangetic plain, from Chittagong to Karachi, from Dibrugarh to Peshawar, a great gory tapestry of strife begins to unfold. After Calcutta, we must first turn further east, to a rather obscure place, Noakhali.

Noakhali's importance lies not in the amount of blood spilt there, but in the fact that, at the time, many people honestly believed that a catastrophic blood-spilling had happened. Moreover, trouble in the region had been foretold. As mentioned, the Muslims during the Calcutta killing had been worsted; and soon after, Hindus in West Bengal and up-country began whispering that a retaliatory killing was bound to follow in East Bengal, where Muslims had preponderant strength; the League Ministry in Calcutta, they believed, would fix it. The place mainly pointed to, for such an upheaval, was Comilla; and the Army did in fact send small precautionary drafts of troops there.

Accordingly, when reports reached Calcutta during the second week of October that disorders had started in the Noakhali and

ah districts not far from Comilla, Hindus at once assumed
ughter on a Calcutta-like scale was in progress. Excitement
great. Newspapers and agencies sent correspondents, who
sent back alarming despatches. It later however transpired that most
of these men never reached the trouble-zones, but had picked up
stories from refugees streaming out; and refugees in such circumstances are not good news-sources. To get to the trouble-zones was
indeed almost impossible during a short visit, for the disorders were
not concentrated as in Calcutta, but scattered over a vast countryside poor in communications. This was a phenomenon to recur elsewhere, and it made the authorities' job much harder.

What happened around Noakhali was indeed fairly bad in old-
fashioned terms – in the terms, for example, of Cawnpore in 1931;
but not in those of 1946. Gangs of Muslim hooligans roved the rural
areas, terrorising the Hindu minority, and threatening forcible conversion. Many Hindus seem to have escaped death or looting only
by consenting to this – a horrible thing to have to do. There was
large-scale arson. Panic-stricken fugitives fled westwards in thousands.
But later study of proven facts shows that most of the contemporary
casualty-reports were wild exaggerations; and that as part of the civil
war Noakhali was a small affair, falling into an altogether different
class from what happened before in Calcutta – and from what was
soon to follow in Bihar. According to statements in the British Parliament during November, the dead did not exceed 200. A subsequent
on-the-spot official tally, issued in Calcutta in May 1947, gave totals
for Noakhali itself of 220, and for Tipperah of sixty-five. Certainly
the upheaval was much exploited by influentially placed Hindus
for purposes of propaganda.

To some extent, too, its origins were not communal or religious
but economic. This point scarcely emerged at the time; but it
should not be ignored, because it also explains the course which
events took, much more gravely, during March and April 1947 at the
opposite end of the Indo-Gangetic plain; in Northern Punjab and
the Pathan country. There, as in East Bengal, though the Muslims
were the more numerous, the Hindus were the wealthier. They were
generally the landholding, mercantile and professional people,
whereas most of the Muslims were cultivators and artisans. And
such privileged classes as did exist among the East Bengal Muslims,
notably the aristocrats of Dacca, were still embittered by the annulment in 1912, because of Hindu hostility, of Curzon's partition of
Bengal. That partition, in 1905 – along lines not very different from
those in fact later taken by the 1947 frontiers – had been done, as
explained, partly for reasons of administrative convenience, but

also because Curzon believed that the East Bengal Muslims ought to be freed from the Hindus' economic stranglehold, exercised from Calcutta. And ever since the annulment — a pusillanimous surrender to terrorism, as many people then saw it, and the first clear sign since 1857 of the British régime's underlying weakness — local Muslims, whether of high class or low, sourly assumed that the rich men of that great city, British as well as Hindu, looked on East Bengal as a mere place to neglect, or to exploit. There was thus a strong sense of economic grievance — which incidentally goes far to explain why, since 1947, the East wing of Pakistan, despite its awkward distance from the West, has not let itself be gobbled up, Goa-like, by Mr. Nehru's India.

The communal slaughter in Bihar between October 30th and November 7th was a reprisal for the Noakhali affair — or for what, because of the propaganda, many normally decent and harmless Hindus supposed that affair had been. A 'Noakhali Day' sponsored by the provincial Congress Ministry started it, modelled on the Bengal League Ministry's 'Direct Action Day' before the Calcutta killing. And a new feature at once emerged: much of the butchery of hopelessly outnumbered Muslims bore every sign of careful prior planning, being the first of several such abominations to occur during the next twelve months. This, and the fact that (as at Noakhali, and unlike Calcutta) it was spread over a vast area of scattered villages, made it very difficult for the authorities to deal with; and the casualties were huge. A rough preliminary military estimate at the time put them — injured as well as dead — at 15,000. According to a subsequent statement in the British Parliament, the deathroll amounted to 5,000. *The Statesman*'s estimate was between 7,500 and 10,000; the Congress party admitted to 2,000; Mr. Jinnah claimed about 30,000.

A problem for the Army was serious initial shortage of troops, owing to units having been already sucked away to deal with the Bengal troubles. The Area Commander, Major-General Ekin, commented also on the complete lack of warning, despite the fact that the Intelligence Services were still good. (They had not yet fallen into the paralysis suddenly induced next February by Mr. Attlee's announcement that the British would soon be going, a grave administrative factor to be emphasised further in Chapter 12.) He stressed, too, that young and untried Hindu troops were so disgusted by the barbarities done by their co-religionists that, after an action against murderous mobs at Hilsa on November 4th, there was no doubt that they would be ruthless if required. Thus, 'by the time

Russell and his 5th Indian Division made their welcome appearance, and took over the trouble-spots in the Patna area, we had managed to deliver a dose of deterrent which put an end to the worst savageries'.[1] As in the Noakhali-Tipperah disorders, the efficiency and impartiality of the Army in very unpleasant conditions was later much praised. At one stage, as many as seven battalions were being used.

Retrospectively summarising his views on the outbreak Tuker, who as G.O.C.-in-C. Eastern Command had reports from the whole Gangetic plain before him, wrote that 'Of all the terrible doings of 1946, this was the most shocking. Great mobs of Hindus turned suddenly, but with every preparation for the deed, upon the few Muslims who had lived, and whose forefathers had lived, in amity and trust, all their lives, among these very Hindu neighbours. It has never been ascertained who was the organising brain of this well-laid, widely-planned plot of extirpation. All that we do know is that it went to a fixed plan and schedule. Had it not not been so, such large mobs, fully armed with prepared weapons, would never have collected in the time and moved with such obvious, fiendish intent from victim to victim. The number of Muslim dead – men, women and children – in this short, savage killing was about 7,000 to 8,000. Women and their babies were cut up, butchered, with an obscene devilry'.

Historians may reckon the Bihar calamity to have been decisive in its effects on the Partition-controversy. After so huge a slaughter, which bore signs of such cold-blooded preparing, possibilities of getting India's Hindu and Muslim populations to live together harmoniously under a single independent, post-British Government shrank towards zero. Admittedly, leading Congressmen in Delhi, when they realised what was happening, acquitted themselves admirably. Both Mr. Nehru and Rajendra Prasad went at once to Bihar, and were energetic in trying to get the killings stopped. Indeed, Mr. Nehru, for years assiduous in denouncing the occasional use of the R.A.F. for bombing recalcitrant Pathan tribal villages – in actuality a not ungentlemanly proceeding which involved due warnings, and withdrawal beforehand of the villagers behind ample rock-cover – now as India's Prime Minister (in Hindu eyes) threatened the roving Hindu mobs in the open Bihar fields with this very thing.

But the savageries had been too clearly a result of organisation, under Hindu communal leadership, for their effect on Muslim sentiment elsewhere throughout the subcontinent to be other than final. Newspaper reporting had been meagre : the riot-stricken areas were

[1] The reference is to Lt.-Gen. Sir Dudley Russell.

difficult to get about in; and the military authorities, with the Noakhali affair in mind, had managed to thwart most of the local Press representatives. But reports by word of mouth (which can have worse effects than print) were distributed far, supplemented sometimes by frightful photographs; and these, within a few weeks, began to shape events in places as distant as the Hazara hills above Mansehra, the villages of Rawalpindi district, and the Derajat country along the Waziristan borders. Thus the Bihar calamity, and the widespread popular knowledge of the appalling things done by a Hindu majority over hundreds of square miles within ten days or so, particularly to helpless women and children, brought to the surface such profound ancient fears and hatreds, such vivid historical recollection of former strife, as to make Partition practically unavoidable.

From now on, most of the upper half of the subcontinent between Afghanistan and Burma became to some degree involved. At about the centre, in the U.P., only a few days after the Bihar outbreak, there occurred the horrible rural slaughter at Garhmukteswar, where Hindu pilgrims, at the annual religious fair, set upon and exterminated Muslims, not only on the festival-grounds but in the adjacent town. And the police – this becomes a repetitive theme – stood complaisantly around doing little or nothing. The dead were estimated at between 1,000 and 2,000. The U.P. Ministry succeeded in wrapping a heavy blanket of silence round the whole business. Almost no authentic news got out on the civilian side; you will find scarcely a mention of the Garhmukteswar killing in the ordinary reference-books. But good military reports exist.[2] How far it was a planned butchery of the Bihar type must remain conjectural. And then there were the cities, particularly Calcutta, in which afflicted place, for twelve months, scarcely a day passed without 'incidents', from obscure stabbings and burnings in by-lanes to bomb-throwings and Sten-gunnings in the main streets. And despite all the local patrolling by troops and police, occasional heavier outbreaks kept occurring. For instance, during the six days October 25th–30th inclusive, 117 killed were counted and 456 injured. Pitched battles were being fought in parts of the city, and conflagrations raged for hours.

Woodruff, writing from experience as a District Officer in the U.P., describes conditions at this period in the following vivid passage. 'There was fear of the unknown on both sides; it would suddenly flare up when one side had the other at a disadvantage. It was

[2] e.g. in Tuker's book.

H

something against which all the old known precautions were useless. In the 1942 rebellion, communications and police-stations had been attacked; there were points to guard. In ordinary communal trouble there was usually some some point of focus, a mosque or a temple or a pipal tree. In a city, main thoroughfares could be patrolled. But this was unaccountable; no one could foretell where it would come next. In a village where Hindus and Muslims had lived peacefully side by side for centuries, sudden fear would blaze up, and the weaker would be slaughtered with every kind of barbarity, babies being killed before their mothers' eyes, women and children burnt in their huts. No District Officer could prevent it by force unless he could station a platoon in every village.'

Meanwhile, there had been a political change in Delhi. Half-way through October, the Muslim League decided to enter the Interim Government after all. Its right to do so had been formally held open, and it now agreed to take five seats as offered in July, not however from the Congress, but from the Viceroy. It regarded this as an important point gained. There had been a discussion on the matter between Lord Wavell and Mr. Jinnah on September 16th. On the other hand, it found itself obliged, in return, to drop its previous demand that the new Government should include no Congress-nominated 'nationalist' Muslims. Plainly, when standing out in August, it had put itself in a very awkward position on the fundamental matter of power. Refusing office might have short-term tactical advantages; but within a few weeks, Leaguers came to realise that it was enabling the Congress party to do much to their detriment on its own. What might be termed a forced compromise was thus reached.

As was to be expected, acrimonious dispute almost immediately broke out over the allotment of portfolios. The Viceroy, to get the new Government started, had urged the Congress to offer the League one of three so-called 'senior' portfolios : External Affairs, Defence, or Home : he thought the easiest to give up might be Home – Sardar Patel's portfolio. Backed by the Sardar Mr. Nehru emphatically declined, saying that to surrender any of these would unsettle the country. But the wrangle then took a surprising turn : the Congress leaders suddenly saw their way, with no very evident distaste, to surrender Finance – a portfolio which many would have thought even more worth keeping than the three they held. The story went around that they did so on the calculation that Muslims could not handle so difficult a subject, and would make fools of themselves.

For the League, the decision on Finance was a windfall; and

Azad in his book makes much of it, bitterly attributing to his Congress colleagues' bad judgement, at this juncture, the events within the Interim Government which eventually induced Sardar Patel to regard Partition as the lesser of two evils. We may discount some of this; Azad evidently disliked Patel; but there can be no gainsaying that, in letting the League get Finance, the Congress made a mistake, which the League – largely by giving free rein to the abilities of a senior Muslim civil servant, Chaudhuri Mohammad Ali – exploited to the utmost. As regards Defence, however, the League leaders themselves probably blundered. They had pressed for that portfolio as well as Home, thereby antagonising the Sikh leader Sardar Baldev Singh, who held it; and this may have contributed towards the Sikhs' political decision early in the following year – they were still uncommitted in 1946, except for temporary combatant purposes as in the Calcutta riots – to throw in their lot with the Congress.

Hoping against hope (as Menon puts it), many people started telling themselves after October 25th – the day when the allotment of portfolios was announced – that collaboration in the practical day-to-day tasks of governing would draw the two main parties together. This was still the view of the British Cabinet and the Viceroy, as was explained to this writer at the time; and he remembers working it into an editorial, not altogether with conviction. In fact, it soon became clear that Leaguers had entered the Administration without the slightest idea of a normal working partnership, or of accepting joint Cabinet responsibility. They meant (which after all was a well-tried Congress technique) simply to non-co-operate from within. 'We are going into the Interim Government to get a foothold to fight for our cherished goal of Pakistan,' declared Mr. Ghazanfar Ali Kahn, one of the League nominees; 'the Interim Government is one of the fronts of the direct action campaign.' Nor was this mere bombast or negativism. Policy soon began to be shaped by the League Ministries in almost total disconnection from the rest of the Government, greatly to Mr. Nehru's and even more to Sardar Patel's annoyance. Moreover, the League refused to budge from its decision against entering the Constituent Assembly. A year or so before, Mr. Jinnah had demanded two separate Constitution-making bodies, one for Hindustan[3] and another for Pakistan; and he stuck to this. Continuous bickering went on over the matter, and over the League's refusal to cancel its 'direct action' resolution of July 27th. The Congress held that, unless that was done, the League should

[3] The Indian Union's decision to call herself 'India', rather than Hindustan as had been assumed until a few weeks before Partition, still causes some confusion in Western countries, to Pakistan's detriment – perhaps intentionally so.

not be in the Government at all. The League retorted that the Congress's professed acceptance of the Cabinet Mission's Plan had been bogus throughout, adducing good arguments in support. Pressure was exerted on the unfortunate Viceroy to accept these rival claims, and there were several threats by the Congress members to resign; while, as background to the wordy strife, bloodshed and commotion proceeded over great tracts of the Indo-Gangetic plain.

During these lugubrious weeks of autumn, there were signs of growing anxiety in Whitehall. And towards the end of November, when affairs at Delhi seemed hopelessly deadlocked, the British Cabinet took the initiative once more. Four members of the Interim Government, together with the Viceroy and Mr. Jinnah, were requested to go to London for further discussions. Mr. Nehru was reluctant, saying that to accept would mean surrender to 'the League's intransigence and threats of violence'. There seemed signs, too, that the Viceroy was not keen, perhaps doubting such a visit's value. But early in December they all went, Mr. Nehru bringing himself to the point of departure only after a personal appeal from Mr. Attlee. Within a few days however, separately in ones or twos, the politicians were on their way back to India – Lord Wavell stayed behind for further talks – after the issue by the British Government of yet another Statement, to the effect that the members of the Cabinet Mission really had meant what they said, in their May 16th Plan, about the 'grouping' of provinces, and not what the Congress party had since kept saying that they meant, or that the words of the Plan could be construed as meaning. The Statement added (rather oddly) that the British Government had taken legal advice on the point. Morally, this was a feather in the League's cap; but from the practical aspect its utility was less clear. More important was the Statement's last paragraph, which read: 'There has never been any prospect of success for the Constituent Assembly except on the basis of an agreed procedure. Should a Constitution come to be framed by a Constituent Assembly in which a large section of the Indian population had not been represented, His Majesty's Government could not of course contemplate – as the Congress have stated they would not contemplate – forcing such a Constitution upon any unwilling parts of the country.' This has been described by Brecher, perhaps without exaggerating, as 'nothing less than a Pakistan Award'.

Lord Wavell's silences had long been famous, and according to the present writer's information they had a bearing on a decision made at about this time, but not immediately disclosed. He was not always conversationally difficult, however. In India the Congress leaders, after he released them from jail in 1945, had no particular trouble on this score. Most of them, including Sardar Patel, apparently found him more to their taste, more intelligible and congenial as a man, than Lord Linlithgow – to most people a rather stony, uninviting figure. Abul Kalam Azad, President of the Congress during most of Lord Wavell's Viceroyalty, developed a warm liking for him; the cordiality of the comments in his book is remarkable; and he does not mention the silences at all. But they certainly occurred, and were characteristic, and became the basis of some good stories – Bernard Fergusson's book is a source for them – and when they did, they could be baffling. And possibly mutual confidence between the British Cabinet and the Viceroy had already, amidst times so tense as these, become frayed by the divergence of views revealed during the latter part of August over the Calcutta tragedy.

The new year approached throughout a harassed subcontinent on a sombre note, as Tuker records. '1946 passed into 1947, with trouble everywhere in Eastern Command. In North Bihar, in the United Provinces, all over Bengal, and in the alleyways of Calcutta the minds of men were taut with fear, and benumbed with contemplation of the dreadful things that they and their brothers had done. The goonda population[4] fidgeted with the tools of their trade, still unslaked with carnage and looting.' The strain on those concerned with upholding order was becoming more severe. And there was industrial trouble too, including sabotage of collieries by flooding; at one time, as many as seventy-two manufacturing concerns in Bengal had actual or intended strikes on their hands. Most ominous of all, storm-signals began to be hoisted not only in Eastern Command but in Northern, as a result of sudden communal disorder in obscure hilly country along the borders of the Frontier Province and the Punjab.

This started during the second week of December, when so-called Nandihar tribesmen (non-Pathans) raided the hamlets of Battal and Oghi in the Hazara district of the Frontier Province. It quickly spread to neighbouring areas, the town of Mansehra being particularly affected, and then fanned out to Garhi Najibullah in the southern tahsil of Hazara. The adjacent tract of the Punjab near Murree was also involved. Loss of life and property among outnumbered Hindus and Sikhs, who were indiscriminately set upon, was considerable. Much of the terrain was mountainous, thinly populated, and difficult to reach, and it took the authorities days to get a clear idea of what was going on, and three weeks or more to master

[4] Goondas are roughs.

the trouble, after sending up a detachment of the Frontier Force Regiment to deal with it.

A factor in the upheaval, certainly, was increasing popular antagonism to the Frontier Province's 'Red Shirt' Ministry headed by Dr. Khan Sahib, as will be explained in Chapter 12. But the main causes were more elementary: realisation that the days of British rule were numbered, and that the forces of law and order must be weakening; resentment against profiteering by Hindus in times of war-created shortage; and a sudden upsurge of fury over the horrible incoming tales of anti-Muslim outrages in Bihar. Together, these constituted an ugly theme, and one destined for uglier repetition, before long, on the more populous nearby plains. The virus of civil war, which had first infected the body-politic on the flat Gangetic country, had now reached the turbulent North, more than 1,200 miles away, whose history and circumstances were very different, and where lay the chief recruiting-grounds for the Armed Forces.

In Delhi, throughout those weeks of winter, after the failure of the six-man V.I.P. visit to London, frustration became complete. On December 9th the Constituent Assembly had briefly met, as planned; but the Muslim League kept its word and ostentatiously stayed away. The heart-searchings caused by this among many of those present, including distinguished Liberals such as Dr. Jayakar, led to an adjournment till January, in hope that the difficulties might then be resolved. On December 21st and 23rd respectively Mr. Jinnah and the Congress Working Committee issued contrasting statements about the causes and effects of the London failure, neither of which advanced matters in the slightest. After its recess, the Constituent Assembly met again on January 20th; but once more no Leaguers attended. The contentious 'objectives resolution', which had caused misgivings in December, was thereupon passed, Mr. Nehru declaring that 'no work will be held up in future, whether anyone comes or not'.

On January 31st the League Working Committee met at Karachi, and described the Congress Working Committee's latest resolution (of January 5th) as 'no more than a dishonest trick and a jugglery of words', going on to denounce the Constituent Assembly's 'objectives resolution' as illegal, and to demand that body's dissolution, since the fundamentals of the British Cabinet Mission's Plan had been destroyed. Altogether it was markedly uncompromising. According to Lumby, 'that the League had no wish to be conciliatory, was evident from the fact that in none of its pronouncements was there any assurance of fair treatment for Assam, the Sikhs, or any other non-League element. (It) seemed to be claiming the right to enforce its will by means of the "brute majority" whose use by Congress in the Assembly as a whole it professed to fear so greatly.' A fortnight or so later came the inevitable counterblast on the Congress party's behalf from Sardar Patel at a Press conference. The Congress, he said, had decided that the British must either insist on the League's participation in the Constitution-making procedures, and on withdrawal of its latest Karachi statement, or expel it from the Cabinet. There was no third choice. If the British did not do this, the Congress would resign. And Menon discloses that this threat had been conveyed privately by letter to the Viceroy by Mr. Nehru two days before.

But in London, Mr. Attlee and his colleagues had been developing quite different ideas, and on February 20th, five days after Sardar Patel's ultimatum, these were startlingly disclosed, and for a while took the wind completely out of both Congress and League sails. They amounted to an unqualified double notice of quittance, and to the British Government's most drastic seizure of the initiative yet. At a date to be in no event later than June 1948, Britain would cease to rule India; and at a date not later than the end of the coming month, March, Lord Wavell would be replaced as Viceroy by Lord Mountbatten.

Chapter 9

Change of Viceroys

EVEN in the days of the East India Company, a civilian aristocrat had normally been head of the British administrative system in India. And after the régime became an Empire in 1858 the practice strengthened, this being shown early in the twentieth century when Kitchener, a known and keen aspirant for the post and a national hero, was passed over in favour of a not then very outstanding diplomatist, Hardinge. It is remarkable, therefore, that so tough a tradition should have cracked during the Viceroyalty's concluding troubled years. The last two men to hold the post, chosen respectively in 1943 and 1947, were men of war, taken direct from the Armed Forces. It was unprecedented.

Ordinary mortals in times of stress may turn instinctively to the military leader for aid, relying on his gifts of authority and quick decision. How far this is wise, or in the long run likely to justify itself by results may be disputed. In Britain, sentiment in high places has usually been much against it since Cromwell's day. But British ways of doing things are not necessarily best, at any rate for non-British people. Leaders such as Hindenburg, Eisenhower or de Gaulle, Nasser, Ne Win – or Ayub – may not, because of their Army training, have been less suitable than civilians for the great posts they held. At all events, this instinctive popular turning happens; and in the present context, it is relevant not only because the British Government acted so at variance with tradition in choice of their last two Viceroys, but because – as emphasised in Chapter 5 – the military factor was ultimately what fended off a Congolese or (pre-Mao) Chinese type of chaos for India in 1947. Had it not been for the Armed Forces' discipline and cohesion, the ship of State which the British had built there could never have got across the storm-swept seas of those exceptional times; it would have foundered.

Apart from the interesting circumstance that they were both war-leaders, Lord Wavell and Lord Mountbatten had little in common. Indeed, perhaps only one other common attribute can be named – brains; real mental distinction, and many people's ignorance that they possessed it. Behind his rugged but otherwise unremarkable bodily exterior, and his prestige as a soldier, Lord Wavell was both

120

scholar and poet. As a boy, he had been 'in College' at Winchester; which meant that he had passed what was then, and probably still is, about the stiffest intellectual test for thirteen-year-olds in the world. And throughout life and in odd places he had maintained his love for poetry and history and the classics, sometimes to the stupefaction of those he worked with.

Lord Mountbatten was not scholarly in his teachers' view; at Osborne and Dartmouth his attainments had been mediocre. But no one brought in contact with him in later years could doubt that he had a mind altogether exceptional in quality; of great breadth and speed, questing and retentive. He also had intuitive gifts, which Lord Wavell probably lacked. In a previous book,[1] describing his arrival in Delhi as 'Supremo' of the newly-formed South-East Asia Command in 1943, this writer noted that 'some commentators, echoing the gossip-columnists of past years, had termed him a "playboy". It was exasperating nonsense. (There was) a party at that time, given to enable him to meet war correspondents. He made a most engaging speech. I think nearly all of us were captivated, and supposed we had heard something of solid value. Only afterwards (did we realise) with what extreme skill – quite rightly in the circumstances – he had in fact told us practically nothing.' And I proceeded : 'Very different, except for the great ability displayed, was his famous Press Conference as Viceroy in 1947, when he expounded the Plan of June 3rd to about 300 critical questioners in the Princes' Chamber. For sheer intellectual range and vigour, for assured grasp of minutiae, yet brilliant marshalling of the main lines of a long, difficult argument, it was an extraordinary performance.'

However, in almost everything but those two items, the differences between India's last two Viceroys were conspicuous and even startling. Lord Wavell was reticent, enigmatic; some would also say grim. He had no particular liking for social events and wholly lacked interest in or capacity for self-display. His Viceroyalty ended on a characteristic mute question-mark. Lord Mountbatten, a controversial figure, extrovert and sociable, very handsome and considered a showman by some, functioned by contrast in a blaze of publicity. Lord Wavell came of a good old Hampshire family which included some fairly distinguished men – mayors of Winchester and major-generals. But it was not aristocratic; most people would have termed it upper-middle class. Lord Mountbatten was more than an aristocrat; there had been nothing like him in lineage among Viceroys before. A great-grandson of Queen Victoria, he was linked ancestrally with about half the Royal Houses of Europe, present and past. And

[1] *Horned Moon*, pp. 106, 107, condensed. (See Bibliography.)

by comparison he was young still, only 46 and full of go, with much of his future yet to make. Lord Wavell on the other hand, at 63 and perhaps a bit battered, was obviously near the end of a career which had raised him to heights unforeseeable at the start. As Viceroy, he had perforce dealt with politics; but it was not evident that he liked them, nor could it be guessed where his party preferences if any lay. Lord Mountbatten's interest in them however, even while he was 'Supremo' in Delhi or Kandy, was frank and lively; and from his conversation and his wife's, few could doubt that their sentiments lay towards radicalism and the Left. Lord Wavell, again, was a man of firm moral or religious convictions; the signs of this could not be misread. What his successor's convictions rested on was less clear; some regarded him as a typical product of that rootless, empty era, the early 1920's, who had been impelled, by sheer energy and ability, towards an ambitious dynamism.

As mentioned, Lord Wavell's Viceroyalty ended on a question-mark; and that understates it. There is a mystery here, which has given rise not merely to gossip, but to honest speculation and misgiving. The impression remains that he and the British Government came into fundamental disagreement on policy; that they could not see eye to eye over the method, and in particular the timing, of the end of British rule. Hints are heard that he put forward a 'Wavell Plan', politically and militarily clear-cut, whereby British authority would have been withdrawn from the subcontinent much more gradually; that this was turned down; and that, had it not been, much of the appalling slaughter at Partition-time, and the resulting ill-will between the two successor-States, might have been avoided.

For the uneasiness on the subject which lingers, the British Government of those days had largely itself to blame. The times were extraordinary; demands on Ministers' energies and wisdom were many; lapses from customary politeness were sometimes inevitable, and could be understood. But the way in which Lord Wavell's loss of office was explained to Parliament and the public was undeniably very graceless and strange. A Viceroy's term lasted five years; Lord Wavell, at this time, had been at his post less than three-and-a-half. His predecessor Lord Linlithgow, a civilian – a formidably able and industrious man but few would say a great one – had for war-time reasons been pressed to stay on for what eventually became about thirty months beyond the normal term. Lord Wavell's early exit was accounted for, in the policy-statement of February 20th, by his appointment in 1943 having been of a special war-time sort. Doubtless strictly speaking that was so; and had he been succeeded by a civilian, in reversion to the usual practice which, until he was chosen, had prevailed over the whole eighty-five years of the Viceregal office's existence, such an explanation might have served. But it looked thin when his successor was to be another war-leader. Besides, he was to be almost hustled out; it emerged that he would have only about five weeks in which to pack up and go. According to Campbell-Johnson, who was in the gallery of Parliament at the time, Mr. Attlee's reference to him on February 20th had seemed 'cold and perfunctory'. On top of this Sir Stafford Cripps, throughout the long, able speech with which he opened the two-day debate on Indian affairs on March 5th, made no mention of him whatever. The omission was thought extraordinary, enabling Mr. Churchill, next day, to say that Lord Wavell had 'been dismissed', and to press pertinaciously for more information, and for a public statement from him after his return. Mr. Attlee, in replying, was averse from such ideas, and appealed to the ethics of cricket as a way out, claiming that 'if a change of bowling is desired, it is not always necessary that there should be an elaborate explanation'.

A few facts have come out since, which elucidate somewhat, though without full access to Lord Wavell's papers – on which the late John Connell had been working – much must remain obscure. But the date when Lord Mountbatten was first asked to become Viceroy is interesting. Campbell-Johnson records that Mr. Attlee offered him the post on December 18th; and Wheeler-Bennett's account, based on the Royal Archives, seems to tally. That is to say, the offer was made about nine weeks before the change was announced, and while Lord Wavell was still in England. The conference which he and the political leaders from India had in London with the British Cabinet had lasted a mere four days, from December 2nd to 6th; but he himself stayed on 'for consultations' after they left, and did not emplane for Delhi until December 22nd. At what stage he became aware of the approach made to Lord Mountbatten does not emerge. But it seems virtually certain that the Prime Minister or the Cabinet decided in principle on a change of Viceroys during the first half of December, and probably during its second week.

Mr. Attlee, it also seems clear, was the initiator. His autobiography indeed as good as says so. From the time of his membership of the Simon Commission in the late 1920's he had been interested in Indian affairs, and many still regarded him as the Labour party's chief expert in them, though in fact, by 1947, his first-hand knowledge must have got rather rusty. Years later, during an interview to celebrate his 76th birthday, which caused surprise by its indiscretions, his comments on Lord Wavell, though of a passing sort, were disparaging. Asked about the change of Viceroys, he said the idea 'came to me, quite as an inspiration, one day', that Lord Mountbatten was 'the man for this'; he had 'just the qualities'. Lord Wavell on the other hand, 'a silent bird', lacked 'the quickness of mind to settle a situation' – strange comments, surely, from a Prime Minister whose own silences, or reticences, had notoriously irked some of his colleagues, and against a soldier whom the Germans, in 1939, had reckoned the ablest in the British Army, and who as recently as 1941, in Africa, had been winning brilliant victories. No one has suggested that, during his last Viceregal months, Lord Wavell was on the edge of a breakdown. Mr. Attlee's three fellow Ministers, when they and Lord Wavell were in daily association during those hot strenuous weeks in Delhi earlier in 1946, had certainly not indicated that they would have endorsed any such adverse view; and on getting back to England they were enthusiastic in his praise. In the Commons, on July 18th, Sir Stafford Cripps spoke of 'the amazing way in which the Viceroy carried the load of these negotiations throughout all these months, during which he had all his many day-to-day duties in the Government of India as well'; Lord Pethick-Lawrence was equally eulogistic in the Lords; and Lord Wavell himself wrote to the King in glowing terms about the Ministers. The scene, at that time, was thus apparently one of complete amity; and although, as we have remarked, at least one fairly serious difference of opinion arose between Cabinet and Viceroy not long after the Ministers left Delhi for home on June 29th – such conflicts were part of the system, all Viceroys found themselves involved in them – it would seem that at any rate nothing went irreparably wrong until the latter part of 1946, probably during that London visit.

What was it? Did it come from a basic cleavage on policy, and especially on the timing of the British withdrawal; or from something more personal? The material available strongly suggests the latter. The idea that there ever existed a specific and fully prepared 'Wavell Plan' for winding up the British Raj in a slower and (inferably) less bloody way than the one adopted, and that the Cabinet overthrew this, seems a myth, or at most a half-truth. During the autumn of 1946 there was indeed much talk that the British might give up India not in one piece, but sectionally, proceeding from the south northwards. Thereunder tranquil Madras, for example, would have soon become completely free, while Armed Forces still under British control (including British troops) stayed on in the Punjab as a buffer against communal strife. How far the kernel of this idea was supposed to be secret is not known to the present author; but variants of it were freely debated by those then in touch with officials and politicians; it pervaded the mental atmosphere, as books such as Tuker's show. Lord Montgomery indeed describes it as having come up conversationally in Delhi as early as June, during his few days' visit there before he became C.I.G.S. And Lord Wavell certainly for a while not only regarded it with favour; he commended it to the British Cabinet. But that seems about all.

The legal or constitutional objections at the British end, in terms of Parliamentary procedure, allotment of time and so on, as Whitehall pointed out, were formidable; and according to information supplied from several sources, Lord Wavell himself, during the winter of 1946–7, at no stage seriousy contemplated a date for the final British withdrawal (whatever the procedure for withdrawal might be) remoter than that towards which the Cabinet's thoughts were at that time also moving, namely towards the end of 1948. In fact, at any rate during that crucial December of 1946, his thoughts were evidently more progressive on this point than the Cabinet's. During his London visit, he advocated a final British withdrawal by March 31st, 1948, that is, three months earlier than the date which Ministers themselves, in February 1947, after weeks of evident hesitation and apparently on Lord Mountbatten's urgings, decided to announce. Whether at that period he favoured an actual public announcement of a date is not clear; some evidence can be brought to the contrary. But on the main question of what the approximate date should be, it is on the face of it highly unlikely that his views and those of the Cabinet can have been in sharp conflict; for the pressing realities about the 'run-down' of the British element in the Services, on which Sir Stafford Cripps dwelt so cogently in Parliament on March 5th, were even more starkly manifest to him and his Government in Delhi than to the authorities in London; and it is known that he pressed them repeatedly and with vigour on Whitehall's attention.

The gist of these realities was that, during the twelve months beginning in April 1947, the number of British officers in the Indian Army – an Army still swollen because of the war, and already much 'Indianised' – would drop from 11,400 to 4,000. And in the upper tiers of the Civil Services, to which recruitment had ceased in war-time, the shortfall was even worse; whereas in 1935 those Services had had over 2,900 British officials, they now, early in 1947, had only about 1,600. Such depleted personnel, military and civilian, obviously would not do for the unusually exacting tasks on hand. Thus the Raj was under administrative compulsion to end itself soon, unless the far-off British nation could be persuaded to accept a complete reversal of affairs, involving substantial fresh British recruitment, and an unflinching determination to rule India from strength for, say, another ten years (it was impossible to imagine fresh recruitment of quality being got for a shorter period). No evidence can be found to show that Lord Wavell wanted any such reversal, or supposed that, in Britain's enfeebled post-war condition, it was feasible. Of course none exists, either, to suggest that he would have approved the date of quittance being pulled ruthlessly forward, as it was, from June 1948 – the date announced by the Cabinet in their statement of February 20th – to August 1947. This is often brought up in argument; but it is beside the point, for during the winter of 1946–7, when the change of Viceroys was decided on, no one had in mind the likelihood of a quittance during 1947. That idea only came seriously forward next May, after Lord Mountbatten had been in office some weeks.

How, then, if there was no major divergence on policy, are we to account for what, it seems, Mr. Churchill rightly called a dismissal? As has been mentioned, there were signs that Lord Wavell was not keen on that December sortie; he doubtless reckoned (prophetically, as events showed) that not much could come out of it; he went because the British Government insisted. And, as stated, while in London he was at his most disconcertingly gruff or taciturn. Cabinet Ministers were baffled; being themselves at a loss to know what to do, they had hoped he might offer some important new ideas. From the letter which he wrote weeks later to the King, which Wheeler-Bennett reproduces, it is unmistakable that at this stage serious disharmony did exist. The Viceroy thought the Ministers indecisive, and his comments as recorded were tart. 'I failed, after many hours of conference, to get any definite policy from Your Majesty's Government.' They, on the other hand, apparently considered his recommendations insufficiently political in content, a fact which doubtless explains Mr. Attlee's contemptuous reference, mentioned by Campbell-Johnson, to the Viceroy having had nothing better to offer than 'a military evacuation plan'.

Perhaps we may reasonably infer that, by this time, Lord Wavell was in the Service slang of those days almost browned-off. During the previous wearing months of difficult, shifting negotiations, he had made practically every conceivable political move open to him; yet the crux of the Indian problem – how to bring about a Hindu-Muslim settlement, and to effect a smooth transfer of power – still eluded reach. He had lived under almost continuous strain since

1939. Possibly he did not find the Labour Ministers very congenial; their ways of thought, and their careers, had in most respects differed markedly from his; and he had been chosen not by them, but by the previous Coalition Ministry. Though honoured to be Viceroy, he had never aspired to the job, nor did he much enjoy some of the duties involved. He had simply been doing his best as a soldier, in the position his King and country put him in. From such of his letters as this writer has seen – not many – the impression shapes itself of a man who shied away from politics whenever he decently could, seeking relief in administrative problems more to his taste: food-supply, public health, use of aircraft for getting officials quickly over India's big distances, and so on.

Like Lord Linlithgow, though perhaps for dissimilar reasons, he seems to have found human relationships difficult, in complete contrast with his uninhibited successor. Or it might be truer to say he often just underrated or forgot their importance. Mr. Attlee said he knew that Lord Mountbatten 'got on astonishingly well with the Indians', but that he doubted whether they and Lord Wavell 'could really understand each other'. On balance, most informed persons would probably agree that this contains truth. But it is not wholly true. Evidence exists that, in his discussions with the leading Indian figures who most mattered, his unruffled fairmindedness, his direct practical approach to a problem, his lack of political or communal prepossessions, and his indomitable perseverance amidst unique difficulties earned him more liking, indeed affection, than was at the time publicly known. The profound effect which these qualities had on Abul Kalam Azad, when President of the Congress party, has already been alluded to. It amounted almost to a conversion, and was further revealed in Azad's moving and courageous public statement when Lord Wavell left office. There are indications that Lord Wavell did not find that he and Mr. Nehru had much in common; nevertheless Mr. Nehru's valedictory statement was generous. And he certainly at times got on well with Sardar Patel. Moreover his relations with the future creator of Pakistan, Mr. Jinnah, if not warm, were at any rate better than his successor's. Whereas to many Indians (and indeed British people too) his predecessor Lord Linlithgow had seemed pompous and chilling, such epithets would not apply to Lord Wavell. Nor was he a bloodless abstraction to the multitude; Spear remarks that, by his handling of the Bengal famine – a calamity which his predecessor had appeared almost to ignore – he 'came nearer to the hearts of the people than anyone since Lord Irwin'. The same writer terms him 'the least obtrusive of rulers'. He could in fact almost, at times, be humble; and he had an engaging readiness, very rare in leading British personages, to admit mistakes publicly. Some of the leaders of the Congress party indeed resembled him in that – though in their case, observers might wonder whether it was not apt to be used insincerely as a tactical device, a form of psychological warfare whereby an opponent might find himself subtly disarmed.

All these items could be weighed in his favour. Yet his famous silences, his complete uninterest, often, in the social trivialities which can soothe and please, did undeniably amount to a drawback; lunch-parties are told of, at which ladies were present, when his incapacity for small-talk dumbfounded all. India is an emotional land; and on the political plane his seeming inability to respond to emotional situations in an emotional way led occasionally to awkward moments, both during the conference in Simla, and afterwards in the Interim Government. His inarticulateness sometimes also misled visiting British politicians. Woodrow Wyatt, who was attached to the Cabinet Mission, records (perhaps rather naïvely) that whereas 'Stafford Cripps was sharp, quick and incisive, Wavell's mind appeared slow and a little woolly; where Stafford Cripps was never at a loss for words, Wavell was silent for long stretches'; though we may note that, to Abul Kalam Azad, the two men's qualities appeared in a different light, wholly unfavourable to the visiting Minister. However, some Members of Lord Wavell's Executive Council (before the Interim Government was formed in August 1946) seem also to have been to a serious extent bewildered. It was an unwieldy body, composed mainly of senior British civil servants and nominated Indian public men, much enlarged to meet war-time needs, and it is on record that at least one British Member found the Viceroy baffling to work with; it almost seemed 'as if he could not bring himself to trust civilians'. Another British official, not then a Member, but who as a Secretary to Government saw things at close range, chose an equestrian simile to explain the sometimes puzzling atmosphere. Lord Wavell, he believed, sat uneasily in the Viceregal saddle; his hand never had quite the right touch on the reins. Whereas nearly every previous Viceroy either came from a family where entry into politics and Parliament was almost second nature, or else had acquired political experience of his own, with Lord Wavell that was not so; and he was perhaps himself, as a result, unhappily conscious of lacking the instinctive awareness of how politicians in Delhi and (more important) in distant Westminster might react.

The aforegoing, if the analysis is correct, tots up to something a good deal simpler and less sinister than is often supposed. Lord

Wavell's services may have been ended in an uncouth and graceless way; indeed almost everyone, looking back, would agree on that. But this does not mean that ending them, at that time, was wrong. Evidently in the Cabinet's view he had outlasted his utility. Circumstances had changed much since his appointment; and for that, in any case, the Labour party as such had not been responsible. Though he had done all he could, it had not proved enough; nor, apparently, had it now much chance of doing so. 'I did not think,' wrote Mr. Attlee, 'that he was likely to find a solution.' Something was lacking; the only hope for extrication from deadlock seemed to lie in a change. 'New men,' in the Prime Minister's opinion, 'were needed for a new policy.' Soldiers, professionally, were liable to abrupt transfers and retirements; so formalities proper for a civilian Viceroy were not obligatory in this case. Civil war or its equivalent was going on; the tide of affairs was flowing very fast; irreversibly dangerous positions, affecting the fate of millions, might suddenly be reached before anyone fully realised it. Such gigantic hazards mattered more than the observance of punctilio towards one man. That seems to have been the line of the Government's reasoning; and a responsible commentator, surveying the confused scene as it then was with a historian's hindsight, must hesitate to say with certainty that such reasoning was bad.

It is perhaps easy for people to forget quite how grave things had become, politically and administratively, during the last phase of Lord Wavell's tenure. Menon's book offers sharp reminder; and few who lived amidst these things would call it overdrawn. During those early weeks of 1947, he wrote, 'The situation was so bleak, that it looked as if the country was heading for certain disaster. With the Muslim League conducting a civil disobedience campaign against two Provincial Ministries, and its representatives in the Central Government openly preaching "direct action", Hindu-Muslim differences were further accentuated. Even some members of the Services, at least in the upper levels, had given up their traditional loyalty and impartiality, and had begun openly to take sides in the political controversy. The precarious food position, the steadily deteriorating economic situation, and widespread labour unrest added to the threatening symptoms of a general collapse.'

If we may venture a guess, it might be that Lord Wavell in his heart was not altogether sorry to go. He had held a great post, in uniquely perplexing and strenuous times, and by now had probably had about enough. No doubt, with good reason, he felt riled by a minor item : the clumsy way in which his exit from office had been brought about – as indeed he admitted to his former A.D.C. Bernard

I

Fergusson. During the last weeks, there is reason for saying that Ministers in London scarcely bothered to answer his letters. But such feelings as he had on these points were kept for a few. Campbell-Johnson, describing the day in Delhi when the Viceroys changed place, wrote that he found himself at lunch placed next to Lord Wavell, 'who looked very bronzed and fit, (and) was most affable. The A.D.C.s seemed relieved. Usually, to be next to him is to be placed in a silent corner next to a non-conductor. Not so today.' And Tuker, who as G.O.C.-in-C. Eastern Command attended the handing-over ceremonies, recorded how he 'went to Delhi to say goodbye to Lord Wavell, who was as usual quite imperturbable and without any rancour'. He added : 'there, too, we met the incoming Viceroy, sparkling as a new Rolls-Royce. The still serviceable tractor trundled out.'

Chapter 10

The Sikh Problem

BETWEEN Mr. Attlee's announcement on February 20th that Lord Wavell would be leaving office, and the latter's departure as described, was however nearly five weeks; and in those pregnant times, burdened with such a big weight of history in the making, many important things could happen in so short a while. These things have yet to be described; and they are best approached via the Sikhs who, from March onwards, played a crucial part in the catastrophic events of 1947. Had it not been for the existence of this distinctive community, and – from the aspect of the subcontinent's Partition – for its awkward position on the map, the whole process of Pakistan's birth and early existence would certainly have run a different, simpler, and happier course. The Sikhs, accordingly, need a short chapter to themselves.

Many otherwise well-informed people know little or nothing about them, and their unusual history. This is true of Indians and Pakistanis, as well as of foreigners. It seems to have been largely true of Mr. Jinnah, Mr. Liaquat Ali Khan, and other important men in the Muslim League – as well as of most leading Congressmen. During that fateful winter of 1946–7 it was a dangerous kind of ignorance.

Doubtless a reason for it is that the Sikhs amount to only about 6 million people; a tiny figure, when set against those for other communities in South Asia. Hindus, or Muslims, or Buddhists have consequently been the people who first interested Western students of Asian affairs and comparative religion. Only two British writers of standing have made any comprehensive study of the Sikhs: J. D. Cunningham and Macauliffe. It is noteworthy that a fairly modern book which offers Westerners a distillate of Eastern religious wisdom, Aldous Huxley's *Perennial Philosophy*, contains not a single index-reference to the Sikh gurus or their scriptures, though some of the writings attributed to Nanak or Arjun Dev are of high quality, fit probably to rank with those of Muslims such as Jalal-ud-Din Rumi or the Hindu and Buddhist mystics.

Yet small communities, after all, can have great influence on events; as for instance the Jews. Hasty modern-minded men, such as Lord Mountbatten and some of his staff, who in June 1947 brushed

131

aside the possibly disastrous significance of the Sikh factor in the perplexities of Partition, might well have recalled this, or remembered that Sikhs are rather more numerous than Scots,[1] whose contribution to the world's doings has not been negligible.

At first glance, anyway to a Western eye, Sikhs in their religious beliefs, and in practical details of daily life, seem to have much more in common with Muslims than with Hindus. They profess belief in one God; in an inspired book; and in a prophet (or in their case a succession of ten prophets) who offered humanity revelation. Unlike Hindus – and unlike Catholic Christians – they reject and despise images or idols, sacred rivers or grottoes or mountains, spectacular austerities, and celibacy. Their prophets or gurus were not other-worldly men; they did business or farmed, were married and raised families. And (like the Prophet of Islam) they insisted that they were human; they were never to be worshipped as incarnations of the Deity. Sikhs have no priests – the granthis are merely scripture-readers – and no caste system; indeed, their religion started as a revolt against caste, and against the complexities and superstitions fostered by the Brahmin priesthood. Like Islam, it was a simplifying, cleansing movement. Thus before God and amidst their fellows, Sikhs (in theory) are equal; their religion enjoins them to eat together, to work together, to share the necessities of daily life on a level. In practice, being realistic people, they are on the average readier perhaps than Muslims or Christians to acknowledge frankly that equality seldom works; but the theory is there. Similarly, so far as eating goes, like Muslims they take meat; Hindu vegetarianism and ahimsa are not for them.

Furthermore and above all, again like Muslims, Sikhs are men of war; their Faith and their history are entwined with valorous feats of arms; Gandhian pacifism finds no place at all in Sikhism, as consolidated by their tenth and last guru, Gobind Singh. It was this fact that enabled them, welded together as a militant theocracy under Ranjit Singh during the latter part of the eighteenth century, to make themselves masters of the Punjab, and in the 1830's, of much of the Pathan country and Kashmir as well. 'The Sikhs,' observed J. D. Cunningham on his first page, written about 1844, 'have now become a nation; they occupy, or have extended their influence, from Delhi to Peshawar, and from the plains of Sind to the Karakoram mountains. If a base of 450 miles be drawn from Panipat to the Khaibar Pass,[2] two triangles almost equilateral may be described

[1] About 5 million Scots, as against 6 million Sikhs, in their respective homelands. Both Sikhs and Scots however are energetic travellers, and proportionately large numbers of them live and work abroad.

[2] Normally spelt Khyber; but Khaibar is more correct.

upon it, which include the conquests of Ranjit Singh and the fixed
colonies of the Sikh people.' It is a description which emphasises the
Sikhs' status as Imperialists.

Thus, outwardly, in particular perhaps to a Western Protestant
eye, the resemblances in matters religious, social, and martial between Sikhs and Muslims are close. And during the decades of the
British Raj, most influential eyes in fact were Protestant. To that
circumstance must probably be ascribed some misunderstandings. For
a vigorous sense of estrangement between Muslims and Sikhs –
something which the less perceptive kind of Westerner, steeped in
another historical tradition, remained scarcely aware of – springs on
the one hand from the very fact of those Sikh conquests, of that Sikh
dominance early in the nineteenth century between Panipat and the
Khyber, and on the other, of the many gory happenings which befell
Sikhs during the previous century-and-a-half at Muslim hands.
History, particularly if recent and bloody, counts for more with
ordinary folk than culture or religious doctrine; tales of persecution,
of death and cruelty, of battles, triumphs, and the ignominies of defeat, unfortunately hold the common man's attention more than
the sayings of saints. Few Muslims can avoid feeling indignant that,
after more than seven centuries in which the only dynasties ruling
between Delhi and Kabul were Islamic, Sikh Raj should have set
itself up not only over the Punjab, but over much of the Pathan
plains and Kashmir as well; that it was able to inflict ruthless exactions and physical violence almost with impunity on a predominantly
Muslim populace; that Ranjit Singh at Lahore became as mighty
a potentate as many an earlier Sultan of Delhi; that there were
Sikh-occupied forts commanding a Muslim countryside from places
as far apart as Multan and Attock; that Hari Singh Nalwar held
the spectacular stronghold Jamrud in the mouth of the Khyber,
the pass through which successive Muslim invaders had emerged
triumphantly out of Central Asia in the past; and that these horrible
things, so humbling to Muslim pride, were happening less than one-
hundred-and-fifty years ago. As Caroe remarks, among Muslims of
all that north-westerly country 'the name of the Sikhashahi – the
Sikh Rule – is a synonym for misgovernment and oppression in the
mouths of teachers and children to this day'.

In the same way, no Sikh can forget the death after torture at
Lahore in 1606 of the fifth guru, Arjun Dev, a helpless prisoner of
the Moghul Emperor Jehangir; or the decapitation of the ninth,
Tegh Bahadur, at Delhi early in Aurangzeb's reign; or the fearful
harassments from the same monarch suffered by the tenth and last,
Gobind Singh, and the burial alive of his two boy-sons at Sirhind;

or the almost inconceivable barbarities undergone by Sikhs in the
reign of Ferrukh-Siyar, as described by Barstow, when Gobind's
disciple Bairagi was 'torn in pieces by red-hot pincers after having
been compelled to take the life of his own son', and when 'a hundred
Sikhs were put to death daily, contending among themselves for
priority of martyrdom'. These calamities befell the Sikhs at the
hands of the Moghul rulers of Delhi to the east. They also suffered
harassments and humiliations from the Durranis of Kandahar and
Kabul to the west, notably the deliberate despoiling by Ahmad
Shah's invading forces, twice within the decade 1757–67, of their
holy place at Amritsar. Such things, endured during the later con-
solidating phase in the growth of the Sikh Faith, and during the early
days of Sikh temporal power, bulk large in the remembrance of a
numerically small people, and do not make for any love towards
Muslims, despite the many practical ways in which Sikhism and
Islam, as religions, imbued as both are by a sense of tauhid, of the
One-ness of God, seem almost to mingle.

And on the other flank stands Hinduism, placidly awaiting the
Sikhs' return; oblivious or disdainful of all the heretical past movements away from her; prepared to include practically anything in
her vast vague embrace. Sikhs, despite their supposed exit from her
fold as indignant reformers, have never ceased to be Hindus – in the
Hindu view. Schismatics may break away, as again and again they
have done down the centuries – Buddhists, Jains, Vaishnavites, what
you will – in vigorous revolt against what they regard as Brahminical
shortcomings or malpractices. It does not really matter, they remain
Hindus still – even extremist Sikhs do, such as Akalis and Nihangs –
as an inquirer will be told at any ancient Hindu village shrine, or as
you may learn from the sophisticated guardian of some new-built
temple such as the huge Birla Mandir at New Delhi. There has never
been any bar against marriage between Hindus and Sikhs – such as
there is between Hindus and Muslims, or Hindus and Christians.
They were one in olden times, so they are still. The path for a Sikh
contemplating reversion to Hinduism is therefore easy: a rite or two
in expiation, some holy words from a Brahmin's lips, the chink of
coins; and the deed is done. He is back once more in the world of
his distant ancestors; that unique paradoxical world, attractive yet
repellent, so broadly tolerant yet so narrowly hedged about, in which
good and evil, idolaters and iconoclasts, the pantheist and the believer
in one God become the same; in which all hard-edged contrasts
merge, the black and the white melting into an undifferentiated grey
mush, to be calmly reabsorbed, at leisure.

Thus, in the winter of 1946–7, the Sikhs approached the great political changes impending in a divided state of mind. So far, despite certain incidents, as in Calcutta, they were uncommitted in the civil war. There had been no real occasion to get fully involved; the Sikh population in the Noakhali area, in North Bihar, and around Garmukteswar had been negligibly small. So far as they understood what was happening – which was not much, even the Khatri Sikhs are seldom politically wise, though much given to intrigue – they mostly felt pulled both ways. Two-and-a-half grim centuries of history disposed them towards an unhesitatingly anti-Muslim attitude, as had indeed been evident from their main political organisations' immediate antagonism, in May 1946, to the 'grouping' proposed in the Cabinet Mission's Plan. But they could see the practical resemblances between the Sikh and Muslim ways of life, and knew that on important points the two religions tallied. And though in general they had no particular quarrel with Hinduism, some of them, especially the influential Akalis, mistrusted its motives. These would have agreed with Barstow that, at heart, Hinduism has 'always been hostile to Sikhism', because the Sikh gurus had 'successfully attacked the principle of caste'; and that it therefore necessarily strives for Sikhism's overthrow, 'both by preventing the children of Sikh fathers from taking the "pahul", and by seducing professed Sikhs from allegiance to their faith. Hinduism has strangled Buddhism, once a formidable rival; it (is now making) serious inroads on Sikhism'. A proportion of leading Sikhs would concur.

Schizophrenia[3] or split-personality is a dangerous state, for the patient and for others, especially if he is bodily strong, and by temperament slow to anger but capable of appalling barbarities when roused; and the Sikhs were rather in that state, as the great changes of 1947 drew nigh. Unfortunately, too, the pulled-both-ways standpoint from which they found themselves watching the growing conflict between Hindus and Muslims was complicated by other factors. The Sikhs are by temperament or tradition individualists and democrats; a people responsive to leadership by other and greater individualists, Sikh or non-Sikh, men of the mettle of Ranjit Singh or Henry Lawrence. But in modern times their political leadership has often been poor, partly because their numbers are small, but also because their talents are of a markedly practical, go-getting sort. As a result of this second factor, their ablest men, the cream of the community, are continually being skimmed off into lucrative activities outside politics. Thus when, in 1947, they were faced with the need for great decisions calling for the utmost sagacity, most of these able men were not available; they were fully preoccupied else-

[3] The term is used here in its popular sense; medical men might not approve.

where, in Government service, military or civilian, or in prosperous businesses in India or abroad. Politics among Sikhs has in recent years been a profession which got not much more than the leavings.

Further, though Sikhs throughout the centuries have often shown remarkable cohesion, they have seemed to achieve this in some intuitive way. As Spear puts it, their rise to power during the middle of the eighteenth century 'was rapid but disorderly; no strong chief existed to check them, but no accepted leader directed their movements'. Even Ranjit Singh 'did not claim the despotic sway of a traditional monarch; to the end, though taking the title of Maharajah, he claimed to be no more than the general of the Khalsa; he was, in some sense, its elected chief'. When formal decisions have to be taken, Sikhs in theory at least take them democratically. Compromises must be reached; other men besides the knowledgeable or eminent must get their say. Western theorists have sometimes enthused over the Jat Sikh peasant on his flat Punjab fields – or, for that matter, the tribal Pathan, fingering a trigger on a Frontier precipice-edge – finding them, in their rough respective ways, fine democrats; embodiments of a Greek ideal. But healthy democratic feeling among ploughmen or goatherds perhaps has not assisted the Sikh or Pathan people, any more than it did ancient Greeks in their little city-States, in deciding big, urgent problems wisely.

Chapter 11

Civil War – II

THE outstanding fact of the last phase of Lord Wavell's Vice-royalty – from about January 1st until March 22nd, 1947 – was the gradual, steady spread of grave communal disorder, from the areas of the Gangetic plain east of Delhi already heavily infected, on into the Punjab, and out beyond to the Pathan country. It pushed not merely into the cities, such as Amritsar and Lahore, but deep into the rural areas. Nothing seemed able to stop it. Like an old-fashioned attack of septicaemia before the days of sulfanilamides, it travelled from the eastern limb of the Indian body-politic, without pause, towards the more vital warlike parts; and forebodings of the grimmest sort grew, in the Army, and among administrators and others who understood the Punjab's special significance – as emerges clearly in books such as Tuker's, or Moon's.

The reason for this lay in the fact that more than a quarter of the Armed Forces' manpower came from this one province; and recruitment from the smaller, less populous Pathan country beyond was at a high level too. In 1939, proportions had been higher: in the Punjab, as much as 48 per cent of the total. However during the war, the Forces' huge increase had thrust recruitment out to parts of the subcontinent previously considered unmartial, such as South India; and the Punjab's proportion therefore temporarily shrank – though by no means of course its numbers, which became even bigger. And now, in January 1947, the proportion was rising again; it went up by 3 per cent in less than a year. Exceptionally many simple sepoys, therefore, had their homes and families in these rural Punjabi and Pathan tracts; many ex-soldiers on pension lived there too; local knowledge of how to use arms was widespread; and quantities of unlicensed weapons were believed to have been hoarded after the war. So if large-scale communal rioting once started in such country, bringing death or rape or maiming to the wives and children of serving soldiers or damaging their crops and houses, and if these things became widely known, or even rumoured, the Forces' morale and cohesion throughout the subcontinent would come under extreme strain. And behind this would lurk another, incalculable factor : the tensions, latent now, but probably still existing, caused by the I.N.A. and R.I.N. affairs of a year before. Thus the outcome, it was reckoned, could be catastrophic.

Already the Punjab was in an unhealthy state politically. No grave communal clashes had occurred – a fact on which civilian administrators, when they compared it with what had been happening to the south-east, much prided themselves. But since the cold weather of 1945-6, the Ministerial set-up had been very weak and shaky. As Chapter 4 mentioned, general elections had been held then throughout British India; and the results, in the Punjab, could scarcely have been more awkward. For years before, the province had been run by the Unionists, a non-communal party peculiar to the Punjab, and composed of Muslim, Hindu and Sikh groups mainly representing the countryside against the towns. It had been much respected : it safeguarded landlord and peasant alike against the formerly rapacious money-lending, mercantile class; and it kept the peace between the three communities. However, its Muslim group – much the biggest – proved unable to withstand the communal emotions stirred up by the novel post-war Pakistan agitation elsewhere on the subcontinent, and in the elections it was utterly routed by the Muslim League, winning a mere seven of the Muslim-reserved seats out of a possible 86, in a House of 175. The League's triumph was also great in the other provinces. Altogether it won 428 out of a possible total of 492 provincial Muslim seats – as against only 109 in the previous election; and at the Centre it captured the entire bunch of the Muslim seats – 30 in all. Thus its position throughout the country was immensely strengthened; and in the Punjab Legislature it became the biggest single party, with unprecedentedly high prestige.

But the electoral system built up by the British in India had been deliberately weighted, province-wise, in favour of minorities – largely, which was ironic, at the League's own request. Thus whereas in Hindu-majority provinces, such as the U.P., Muslims got more seats than their population-strength warranted, in the Punjab the opposite happened; though Muslims there constituted 57 per cent of the population, they got only 51 per cent of the seats. This had the disconcerting result that, at the end of the 1945-6 elections, the League in the Punjab, despite sweeping success, just failed to obtain the absolute majority which would have enabled it forthwith to form a Ministry; and thereupon, to most people's astonishment, the much-weakened Unionists – residual Muslims, plus Hindus and 'Khalsa National' Sikhs – in hasty coalition with extraneous Congress and Akali Sikh members, persuaded the Governor Sir Bertrand Glancy that they were in a position to take office. And the Unionist party's leader, Sir Khizar Hayat Tiwana, a Muslim, again became Premier.

The Leaguers of course were furious. To be thus balked of victory, and at so historically critical a time, when great constitutional decisions were imminent, and in the Punjab of all places – regarded as the hub of the Pakistan-project – was galling in the extreme; and indignation based on a sense of bafflement, of Muslims having somehow once more been diddled by people cleverer but less deserving than themselves, led to a steady worsening of communal relations. In retrospect, it seems surprising that disorder did not break out several months sooner. Mathematically, the Governor's decision had been just sustainable; 88 seats appeared to have been collected, against 87. But it exposed itself to sharp criticism, from British observers uninvolved in the controversy, as well as from Leaguers, on two counts : that he had had close personal associations previously with the Unionists; and that the new coalition was so obviously heterogeneous and hastily contrived. Looking back, it can clearly be seen as an error, which contributed heavily to the eventual disaster. Moon considers it 'amazing that the Governor acquiesced, without the slightest struggle, in a Ministry so harmful to the public interests'.

Even so, the tentative efforts which had been in progress for some while to bring about an understanding between the Muslims and the Akali Sikhs for the Punjab's future salvation – in which Moon incidentally took part – did not wholly peter out. It was felt that, if this could be achieved, the province's problems would be almost solved. And during the following winter (1946–7), private talks between Akali and League representatives took place, on the former's initiative. At that time, scarcely anyone imagined that, if Partition happened, the Punjab (or Bengal) would be divided. The assumption was that, in such an event – which most Hindus and Sikhs still thought unlikely – the split would be by complete provinces; which meant that the Sikhs' homeland the Punjab, being in a Muslim-majority province, would become part of Pakistan. And the Akalis wanted to discover whether the Leaguers had any ideas worth listening to about the Sikhs' status in the proposed new-fangled country.

For reasons of prestige, such a move on their part cannot have been easy. The hostile resolution passed by the Sikh community's Panthic Board on June 10th about the Cabinet Mission's proposed 'grouping' was an obstacle; and the League, on its side, seems to have made no gesture whatever of interest in the Sikhs since April, when some

Sikh leaders including Giani Kartar Singh were invited to, and actually did attend – a fact seldom now remembered – the impressive gathering in Delhi of most of the 428 League legislators who had won seats in the recent elections. The Akalis' move however – according to this writer's information – was unavailing. They failed to get what they considered a clear response. Their inquiries were referred to the topmost levels of the League, but the answer came back merely that the Sikhs would receive fair treatment in Pakistan, and should rely on the Muslim leaders' good sense when the time came. This, they felt, was not nearly enough. They could get better from the Congress, which was bigger and stronger, and with which their affinities were probably closer. And they construed the League's attitude as a studied rebuff – though it may not have been so meant. Perhaps Mr. Jinnah and Mr. Liaquat Ali Khan, neither of them well acquainted with Sikh affairs, had not yet fully applied their minds to the problem, and thus felt unable to make promises. Looked at in the light of after-events however, the episode – whatever its explanation – seems a turning-point in those fateful twelve months.

It is easy, now, to criticise the League leadership on aspects of its conduct during the few years preceding Partition. Need Mr. Jinnah have been so unbending? Might not a more conciliatory stance over this obviously very big question of the Sikhs' destinies – as over others hinging on more personal relations, such as the political futures of Sheikh Abdullah of Kashmir, or of the Khan brothers of the Frontier – have proved useful? The matter can be argued both ways. On the one hand, it could be said that nothing less than utter rigidity, than an undeflected concentration on a single aim, could have brought to birth a project so conjectural, then, as Pakistan seemed to be – even to many Leaguers; that the situation's uncertainties were such that the slightest weakness, or inconsistency, or leaning towards compromise, would have toppled the whole thing over. On the other, in this particular affair of the Akalis' approach, we may consider that a great opportunity was let slip; that a less empty answer would have spared the Punjab carnage and partition; and moreover would have brought into existence a Pakistan geographically bigger, and militarily and economically much stronger than in fact emerged. And memories of former bitter strife – critics might add – need not invariably prevent effective partnership. Nations and peoples do forget. For instance, only nine years after the end of the second of two wars of devastating ferocity, fought within a generation, Britain and Germany became allies within Nato. Is it not remarkable? Or to take a smaller example, and one which directly bears on Muslim-Sikh relations: what about the Bengal riots in the spring of 1950, when India and Pakistan stood on the brink of war? The Sikhs of Calcutta then repeatedly went out of their way to help outnumbered Muslims who were the victims of Hindu mob-violence, risking their lives and treasured motor-vehicles in doing so. The anti-Muslim spirit of the 'great killing' of August 1946 had evaporated; Bengali Hindus were evidently now the people whom the Sikhs disliked. On the subcontinent as elsewhere, memories may not always be long.

For what it may be worth, this writer's view however is that if, in the winter of 1946-7, the League leadership let an opportunity slip, it was not, by that time, one of much substance; that no firm Muslim-Sikh rapprochement was feasible. Admittedly, this is based more on instinct than reason; on a flesh-and-blood remembrance of what were the public's swaying moods. But other observers who were on the subcontinent might agree. Certainly Pakistan would have been a very different State, had the Sikhs been embodied within her. But they have since proved, on occasions, quite troublesome for independent India; might they not have been even more so for Pakistan, the smaller and brittler country?

To speculate on the possible course of events, had the League leaders paid more attention to the Sikh problem while it was still fluid, and perhaps made some magnanimous gesture during those crucial winter weeks of 1946-7 before calamity came to the Punjab, is nevertheless a legitimate historical exercise. Our knowledge, now, of what happened so soon after, throws into lurid relief how big were the issues at stake.

By the late autumn of 1946, with semi-repressed civil war going on over many eastern parts of the Gangetic plain – in the Noakhali area, around Calcutta, in Bihar, and in tracts of the U.P. – India had become full of private 'armies', excitable volunteer bodies created to foster the interests of the competing communities; and it was this fact, in the Punjab, which eventually precipitated disaster. The Hindus had their Rashtriya Swayam Sevak Sangh (R.S.S.S.) and milder Congress Seva Dal; the Muslims their League National Guards; the Sikhs their Akal Fauj and Shahidi Jathas; and there were subsidiary bodies such as the Red Shirts, Khaksars and so forth. Early in 1947, the Punjab coalition Ministry under Sir Khizar Hayat, aware that the existence of such bodies spelt danger, suspecting that communal tensions in their own province had nearly reached snapping-point, and recognising, as well, that breakdown in the Punjab might for military reasons plunge the whole country into chaos, decided to ban all such 'armies', together with political meetings and street-processions. They announced this on January 24th.

It was an orthodox administrative move, but a rash one, for it flew in the face of realities. The Ministry lacked the strength to implement it fully, and it gave the League a wonderful opportunity to retaliate – just the kind of thing that perhaps it had been waiting for. Forthwith its leaders announced, in effect, that in the context of contemporary Punjab affairs such a ban could have only one target, itself, the party which, but for an ignoble intrigue between Hindus and Sikhs and local British officialdom, would be holding office now; that such an assault on democratic liberties by a minority-régime was intolerable; and that they would accordingly start 'an all-out non-violent mass struggle' aimed at putting the Ministry out of power. The intention, in fact, was to make the Punjab the first formal testing-ground for the League's 'direct action' resolution, passed during the previous July.

The struggle proved well organised. With mocking exactitude it mirrored the techniques used by the Congress party for its recurrent 'civil disobedience' campaigns waged against the British since the 1920's. Thousands of enthusiastic Muslim demonstrators had to be arrested, women as well as men, who offered themselves for imprisonment willingly, seeking martyrdom. Jails quickly became over-full. Resort was had to the device of arresting leading persons only, and removing the rest in lorries to distant places and decanting them there to find their way home as best they could; this perhaps attracted attention to the movement all the more. Soon, a Ministry which contained a Congress element, and towards which Congress leaders in Delhi showed lively sympathy, became subjected, from Muslim popular sources, to all the embarrassments which foreign administrators had experienced at Congressmen's hands in the recent past.

The campaign lasted about five weeks, and as we shall see, was supported, latterly, by one launched in the Frontier Province in protest against a similar Ministerial ban there. And by now, a Muslim disobedience movement against a Congress Ministry was developing in far-off Assam, over the eviction of Bengali Muslim immigrants. On the whole, the demonstrators in the Punjab and the Frontier maintained the discipline of 'non-violence' well, if we allow for the turbulent nature of the human material involved, and the unlicensed arms which both provinces were believed to contain. But inevitably, as during the Congress party's campaigns earlier, there were blood-bespattering 'incidents', notably at Lahore, Amritsar, Jullundur and Gujrat. Tension in the Punjab was now so extreme as to be near a break.

On February 20th came Mr. Attlee's big announcement in the British Parliament. Five days later, Sir Khizar reached an arrangement with the League. Political prisoners were to be released, and the ban on public meetings lifted; the League, for its part, would stop civil disobedience. And then on March 2nd, to many people's surprise, he resigned. Realism in Punjab affairs, he explained, was now imperative, because the British were going; and realism was impossible while a few Unionist Muslims served as buffer between Hindus and Sikhs on the one hand, and the League on the other. He thought the political field should be left clear for the League, who represented most Muslims in a Muslim-majority province. It was a dignified statement.

The mathematical conundrum in the Legislature however remained much as before. The League, committed to its unqualified Pakistan policy, could get no Hindu or Sikh backers; and once again, disadvantaged by 'weightage', it just failed, despite appearances of vigorous effort, to collect enough seats to form a Ministry. Perhaps however the local League leadership was hampered by internal disagreements, for though the Governor Sir Evan Jenkins invited the Nawab of Mamdot as titular leader to submit the names of prospective colleagues, it seems he never did so. Faced by a riddle resembling that which had confounded Sir Bertrand Glancy a year before, Sir Evan after a few days' probing resorted – as Sir Bertrand might have done – to personal rule under the 'breakdown' procedure of the Government of India Act.[1]

This was made the more unavoidable because on March 4th, while the talks were going on, what had so long been feared had happened; communal tensions in India's 'model province' had snapped. Savage rioting had started in the streets of Lahore, and the news was spreading fast. The startling arrangement between Sir Khizar and his League opponents; the release of jubilant resisters from jail; the coalition Ministry's downfall; and then the attempts to form a League one in its stead had together brought about excited counter-demonstrations by Hindus and Sikhs. And the latters' leader Master Tara Singh, according to reports current at the time, impetuously drew his sword in a street-procession outside the Legislature, urging his co-religionists to 'overthrow the Muslims'. Whether this really happened seems uncertain; some British officials say it was only rumour. But it was widely believed by Muslims and Sikhs

[1] Section 93.

alike, which is what mattered. Both communities construed it as an act of the gravest purport, for the sword with Sikhs is one of the five symbols of the Faith, and its ceremonial unsheathing gives religious sanction to war.

Within a few hours, Multan, 200 miles to the south-west, was involved; and by March 6th large parts of it, and of Amritsar – where there had been suppressed trouble on February 24th – were in flames. Damage in these cities proved even worse than in Lahore : 750 houses were destroyed in Multan, and in Amritsar, 40,000 people became homeless. Next day there was rioting in Gujranwala, Sialkot, Jullundur and Ferozepur; and during the night of March 7th–8th, the hill-station of Murree away in the north, and at that season half-empty, was set upon by Muslim marauders mainly from Hazara district, who freely looted and burnt much of the best Hindu and Sikh house-property. Almost simultaneously, rioting broke out in Rawalpindi city, but was in part curbed by the British battalion on duty (the Norfolks). A feature of the urban disorders everywhere was the systematic arson. And in the Central Punjab, firearms were often used, in the countryside as well as the towns, though in the Rawalpindi area officers of the 7th Indian Division reported that the chief weapons were still spears and other primitive things.

And that brings us to the worst aspect of the affair : the astonishing way in which the disorders fanned out into the villages, where (as the Noakhali and Bihar outbreaks had shown) communal strife was peculiarly difficult for a weakening Administration to deal with. A clear picture of what was going on in much of rural Punjab became for a while impossible to get; and in the three northernmost districts and adjacent Hazara (part of the Frontier Province) 'law and order' for a while practically collapsed. According to a Government statement on March 20th, the deathroll throughout the Punjab by then amounted to 2,049, but estimates by non-officials of standing were much higher; and about 20,000 troops were engaged in restoring control.

Shocking barbarities were done by all three communities, though not of course comparable with what were to follow at Partition-time. Hindus and Sikhs were the main aggressors in the cities of Central and Eastern Punjab. But in the villages of the north, where conditions came nearest to anarchy, and where Muslims were in a large majority, hopelessly outnumbered Hindus and Sikhs – especially Sikhs – were set upon with a fury which amazed British and other uninvolved witnesses. It might be said that this was just part of communal warfare's horrible chain-reaction; the sequence had been Calcutta, Noakhali, Bihar, Garmukteswar, Lahore, Rawalpindi.

1 Jute worker of East Pakistan, wearing wide-brimmed hat, washing raw jute in knee-deep muddy water

2   A fine mountain landscape in the upper
part of the Swat valley, West Pakistan

3   A modern mosque at Islamabad, Pakistan's
federal capital, parts of the new city's lay-out
visible behind it

4 The road to Hunza, cleaving its way through
the Karakoram range; parts of snowy Rakaposhi
(25,550 ft.) soar in the background

5 The new Rawal dam near Rawalpindi, built
to augment the water-supply of that city and of
nearby Islamabad, Pakistan's federal capital

6 A tranquil scene. The Karnafuli river,
Chittagong area, East Pakistan

7   Evening on the Buhri Ganga river, upstream
from Dacca, East Pakistan; boatmen returning
from work

8   A busy time at the Narayanganj jetty, about
nine miles south of Dacca, East Pakistan

9　The Military Cadet College, Chittagong,
East Pakistan

10　View of the large fertilizer factory at Fenchu-
ganj, East Pakistan

11   Part of the handsome new building of the
Faculty of Arts, Dacca University

12   The renowned and exceptional old Star
Mosque at Dacca

13 Elegant gateway to the splendid old Moghul
fort at Lahore, built in Aurangzeb's reign
(seventeenth century)

14 Styles in modern Pakistani urban architecture;
the Inter-Continental Hotel, Karachi

15 Busy young artisan in the Street of the
Coppersmiths, Peshawar

16 Worker in a tailor's shop, Peshawar
(typically, a rug of good Central Asian
design hangs on the wall)

17 A nomad youth in the crowded alleys of Parachinar, near the Afghan border

18   Postgraduate students of Peshawar University,
in lively discussion at the cafeteria

19   Tribal Pathans dancing, Kurram valley,
West Pakistan

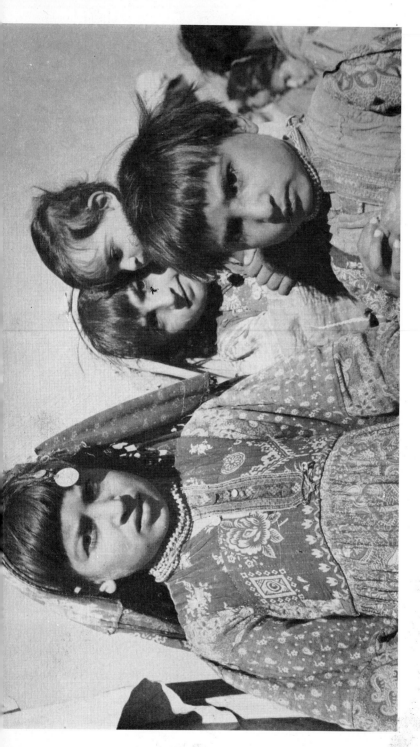

20 Tribal Pathan children in the Khyber area, West Pakistan

22 Frontier Corps sepoys, Kurram Militia. It is spring, and the nearer one wears a wild tulip he has plucked in the rocky waste

21 Strong-faced but handsome; a Mahsud tribesman from South Waziristan

24 An unusual view of the Khyber pass, looking down on the Afghan frontier-post from a salient of Pakistani territory. Pakistan lies to the left (east); Afghanistan to the right (west)

23 A Frontier Corps fort near the Afghan border; the Pakistani flag flies a-top; a wild cloudscape and landscape lurk behind

26 Punjabi peasant, Gujranwala, West Pakistan

25 Playtime for Punjabi children on a canal-bank near Lahore

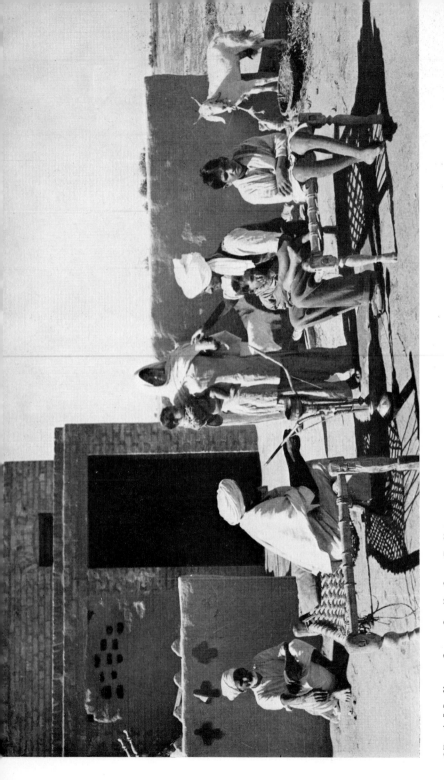

27 A Muslim refugee family from India, now resettled in the Thal land-reclamation area near

But the singling out of the Sikhs was irrational on that reckoning, because the previous anti-Muslim outrages further east, in Bihar and elsewhere, had been almost entirely the work of Hindus. With their turbans and long hair, Sikhs of course are noticeable in a fracas and easier than Hindus to identify; and to the Muslim peasant-mind at a time of excitement, both kinds may equally seem infidels, the many affinities between Sikhism and Islam being ignored. But almost certainly another factor was strongly at work. History, a century or more old, had become active again; traditions of bitter resentment against the injustices and humiliations of the 'Sikhashahi' of Ranjit Singh's time. As Caroe remarks, an Englishman in this northern country sometimes has 'a feeling of wonder, that the deeds and words of the past should be so close to the minds of men today'. And on top of this, the Sikhs in these northern parts were mainly of the not very tough Khatri or mercantile class, and their comparative wealth had become a cause for envy.

Gen. Sir Frank Messervy, who was then G.O.C.-in-C. Northern Command, has described the events of that troubled March as he saw them from his Rawalpindi H.Q. and in tours of the rural areas; and his account vividly brings out this sudden phenomenon of strong anti-Sikh feeling in a predominantly Muslim countryside. 'The main attack, if you can call it that,' he writes, 'took place on a night – I think March 7th – when unfortunately I had a sort of "coming-out" party for my daughter in Command House. There had been little warning, though some small preliminary rioting had led us to have the British battalion in 'Pindi[2] at short notice. It was a concerted attack, and very widespread throughout the rural areas, which suggested that it had been planned, and made it very difficult to deal with – entirely different from the normal communal riots in large cities. I flew in a small plane low over villages in the 'Pindi District, where there was a mixture of Muslim and Sikh population. It was a horrible sight. You could see corpses laid out in the fields just outside a village, like rabbits after a shoot. As many reliable people said, the attacks seemed to be almost entirely anti-Sikh. I remember one of my staff, a G.2, who went down to 'Pindi station to get a ticket on a warrant, coming back very white-faced, to say that while he was at the ticket-office he had felt a weight against his back, and turned to find it was a Sikh stabbed in the back and dead, but not a soul would say they had seen anybody do it. Also, I remember an officer's wife arriving by train. The train had been stopped outside Chaklala and she heard shrieks and groans (the time was just about dawn). She lowered a shutter, and looked out,

[2] i.e. Rawalpindi.

K

to find Sikhs being dragged out of the carriages and hacked to pieces by the side of the line. She was horrified and screamed, whereupon one of the band came up to her carriage and said "Don't be frightened, Memsahib, nobody will harm you. We've just got this job to do, and then the train will go on." The reasons for the attacks being mostly against Sikhs were almost certainly historical : traditions of Ranjit Singh's oppression and so on; also economic to some extent. I remember inquiring about how the Mohiyal Brahmins had fared in the Salt Range, where they had several villages; the Guides Cavalry at one time had a squadron of them, and we had a few in Hodson's Horse. I think they got off almost unscathed.'

Whatever the explanation of the disorders' markedly anti-Sikh bias in the three northernmost districts, it was an occurrence of far-reaching, dire significance for the year 1947 and gave rise at the time to a confident prediction. This fact is brought out with special clarity in Moon's book. Experts in Punjab affairs such as himself at once began forecasting that, after what had so brutally happened to outnumbered Sikhs mainly of the rather soft commercial classes in these remoter Muslim-majority parts, and after the taunts for being less virile than had been thought, which Muslims – and Hindus – had forthwith raised against the Sikh community in general, Sikhs would inevitably retaliate in a region of their own choosing, doubtless eastwards of Lahore. Numbers there would be more in their favour, particularly in the rural areas; it was the traditional heart of the Sikh country, inhabited in the main by the formidable Jat Sikh peasantry, a people slow to wrath but amply capable of appalling cruelties. The only question was when. According to Tuker, Northern Command in Rawalpindi, as early as April, was 'forecasting two months for the Sikhs before they started on their war of revenge'.

Chapter 12

Civil War-III

LORD Mountbatten started his Viceroyalty with great advantages. He seemed to have almost every quality needed for his toweringly important post : outstanding aptitude for leadership, coupled with all the social graces; good brains, good looks, a fine physique, the prestige of Royal birth. Further, there was his spirit of adventurous radicalism, which suited the prevailing Indian realities.

And apart from gifts of nature and ancestry, he had something else, given by the British Government – or perhaps extracted from them; something his predecessor never had: a clear policy-directive set within a fixed framework of time. The gain here was immense. It lent his task the sharp-edged definiteness of a military operation. Both he, and Lord Wavell, had been war-leaders; and a historian might some time speculate interestingly on what Lord Wavell as Viceroy would have done with such a thing – had he been granted it. It put the initiative wholly into Lord Mountbatten's hands, throughout his short term of office. Some might wryly say that to use the initiative in order to destroy is relatively easy; the new Viceroy was about to knock down and tear apart what a long line of his predecessors had built up – an Empire. But they would probably agree that initiative was something no Viceroy had really enjoyed since Curzon's time, if then. 'In almost everything (that Britain) had so far done in India during my seventeen years there, she had lagged behind events. If, under his impetuous spurring, she now got some steps ahead of them, that at least would be a mistake in the right direction.'[1]

The reasons for this lagging were several and intricate. Woodruff well describes the sort of hamstrung balancing-feat, increasingly difficult, which twentieth-century Viceroys, till the spring of 1947, found themselves obliged to perform before effective movement became possible. 'It was out of the question,' he observed, 'to fight for the subjugation of India, and just as unthinkable to force Muslims to submit to Hindus. On the other hand, we (the British) had given India political unity, and we wished to preserve our handiwork.

[1] Quoted from an earlier book by the present writer: *Horned Moon*, p. 106. (This chapter's opening paragraph echoes it also.)

147

Nor could we lightly abandon interests which had on the whole supported British rule : the Princes, the depressed classes, the aboriginals, the planters. And we wanted to hand over power to someone who could keep the country stable. These considerations made a complex position from which to bargain. In any kind of settlement, whether you are buying a house or handing over an Empire, it is of immense advantage to be unhampered – to know just what you want and what you are prepared to pay. In all these respects the Viceroy was hampered, until 1947.'

Lord Mountbatten had something yet more, which his predecessor lacked: not merely the flair for contemporary publicity indicated already, but able would-be chroniclers on his own staff.[2] Thus, whereas an inquirer still gropes in darkness for explanations of much in Lord Wavell's Viceroyalty – awaiting something authoritative, such as the book Connell is said to have begun – he finds that Lord Mountbatten, by contrast, conducted his affairs in daylight; and a wealth of graphic, well-authenticated information is available from important books since published.

Immediately after arrival on March 22nd he got busy with a round of interviews; indeed, so enthusiastic was he that before the swearing-in ceremonies, while Lord Wavell was still Viceroy and in the house, he sent off notes to Mr. Gandhi and Mr. Jinnah, suggesting that they should meet him. And it soon became clear that the freshness and informality of his approach, his vigour and intelligence and charm, his comparative youth, his liberality and transparent lack of race-consciousness (perhaps a result of his cosmopolitan upbringing in the palaces of European Royalty, listening to complex international talk) were putting him on very cordial terms with leading members of the Congress party, especially Mr. Nehru. Less was known about his contacts with the League. And we can now see that it might have been salutary had Leaguers themselves, as well as uncommitted onlookers, given more attention at the time to this item, an ominous one.

The change of Viceroys had no particular effect on the civil war. There were occasional pauses. One had been noticeable just after the policy-statement from London on February 20th; another towards the end of March. And about three weeks after Lord Mountbatten took over, he achieved what seemed might with luck prove a major success, by getting Mr. Gandhi and Mr. Jinnah to appeal jointly to the public to stop violence. But its effects were ephemeral. As has been suggested in Chapter 8, the conflict probably became

[2] Campbell-Johnson, Menon, Ismay.

irreversible at the time of the Bihar calamity; and only Partition now – this was the basic though still unacknowledged truth – could stop it.

The whole Indo-Gangetic belt was in some measure involved, from Shillong to the Khyber, including much difficult foothill-country as well as the open plains; and had not military strength been at hand, to buttress up a police force which, over much of eastern India, was becoming increasingly communal or demoralised – and part of which staged an ineffective mutiny in Bihar during March – the Administration might already have slithered into chaos. Sporadic strife was also occurring elsewhere; Bombay, several times, had fairly heavy casualties. One got used to it all. Bicycling one day along a Calcutta street, thinking out what to put into an urgently-needed editorial, I barely noticed that people were rushing about shouting; excitements had become so frequent. At a traffic-block further on my annoyed orderly, coming up behind, told me I had pedalled vaguely through a riot, which I later learnt caused several deaths; what I had half-supposed to be motor-vehicles backfiring were bombs and bullets. Tuker refers to the state of affairs in that city between March 29th and April 7th. 'Lawlessness had hardly broken the surface this time; yet our records showed (within a week) a total of over 800 known casualties. How many never came to light one cannot say; it is fair to assume that about 1,200 people were killed or maimed in those few days. Yet one cannot describe any particular incidents. Little crowds, little affairs in little streets; leaving behind them on the ground two or three dead with a few injured staggering away, or being borne off by one side or the other.' What a contrast to the time, not long before, when it had been the pride of the British Raj to ensure, as Woodruff puts it, that 'as near as could be, in a country with some four hundred million inhabitants, no one should fall to the ground by violence without an inquiry and a report to Government' !

The extraordinary condition that the subcontinent had reached, by the time of the change of Viceroys, is illustrated by the fact that, of the eleven provincial Governments, nine were now ruling not by orthodox peace-time means but by ordinance or decree, empowering them arbitrarily to ban meetings and processions, and to inflict drastic punishments. Yet the strife went on. The main change, to-wards the end of March, was its spread from the still badly disturbed northernmost districts of the Punjab – Rawalpindi and Attock – and from the Hazara district of the Frontier Province, into the Pathan country proper. There, in Peshawar, an anomalous Ministry was in

office, from causes originating in peculiarities of Frontier history
fifteen or twenty years before. Although 92 per cent of the province's
inhabitants were Muslims, the Ministry was a pro-Congress one,
headed by Dr. Khan Sahib, the elder of the previously-mentioned
Khan brothers, creators of the local 'Red Shirt' party.

How this curious state of affairs arose needs explaining. Caroe
is the best modern authority on the subject. Pathans are fiercely
freedom-loving people, and British rule had reached their country
later than any other part of the subcontinent, doing so moreover
for reasons mainly strategic, rather than mercantile as elsewhere. And
it never appeared very stable there. At first, in 1849, Pathans found
themselves lumped together administratively by the British rulers
with Punjabis. But in 1900, during Curzon's Viceroyalty, a separate
province was carved out for them, the North-West Frontier Province,[3]
consisting of the five settled Pathan districts of the plains, to which
was loosely tagged on, under a Chief Commissioner's (or later a
Governor's) political tutelage, the unadministered, hilly tribal belt
along the Afghan frontier.

When however the Montagu-Chelmsford reforms of 1919 were
introduced, the measure of self-rule which they conferred on the
other provinces was withheld from the Frontier – again, for strategic
reasons mainly, though also because of the region's poor revenues.
This discrimination against a people in fact more independent-
spirited than any on the subcontinent aroused wrath; and the resultant banding together of local Muslim leaders and members of the
Hindu-dominated All-India Congress party, in joint antagonism to
British authority, brought about very serious disorders in and around
Peshawar during Mr. Gandhi's civil disobedience campaign in 1930.
The discrimination ceased in 1932; the reforms were then extended
to the Frontier, which also, not long after, participated in the further
instalment under the Act of 1935. But it was then too late. Enjoying
as they did a huge numerical preponderance in their homeland,
most Frontier Muslims felt none of that mistrust of Hindu intentions characteristic of Muslims elsewhere; and the fortuitous alliance
of the 1920's between Pathans and Mr. Gandhi's followers thus
survived the vicissitudes of two decades. In provincial elections which,
for special reasons, occurred in March 1945, Dr. Khan Sahib and
his 'Red Shirt' party overthrew the Muslim League Ministry which
(in the self-imposed absence of the Congress) had held power for
most of the war, and confirmed this success in the country-wide
general elections during the winter of 1945–6.

Within a few months, however, it began to seem unlikely that he

[3] Generally called the Frontier Province for short.

and his colleagues any longer represented majority opinion. Reports indicated a swift swing of sentiment away from the Congress. 'The actual position in 1946,' wrote Abul Kalam Azad years later — he had been Congress President at the time — 'was that the Khan brothers did not enjoy as much support in the Frontier as we in Delhi thought.' Dislike of British rule was coming to matter less to Pathans than misgiving about what might come after. Would it, in effect, be Hindu (or Hindu-Sikh) rule? With astonishment, they were realising that this was a contingency impossible to exclude. Even uneducated Pathans take lively interest in current politics — more so than the Punjabi peasant does — besides having long historical memories. They recalled, now, the disastrous quarrels within their own Durrani dynasty which had brought them, by the 1830's, under an indigenous régime from India, the aforementioned hated Sikhashahi. They would have no more of that. 'Raghe Hari Singh!' Pathan mothers will shout even nowadays to troublesome children, 'Here comes Hari Singh!', and the warning works;[4] much as, last century, 'Boney's after you!' worked in English nurseries.

By the autumn of 1946, the Peshawar bazaars were full of blood-curdling tales of conditions in riot-torn eastern India. Nor were the settled districts of the plains, linked with the rest of the world by their roads and railways, the only Pathan tracts affected by resurgence of historical and communal feeling. In remote fortress-like hamlets overlooked by watchtowers in the unadministered hills up above, dwelt people not merely predatory and tough, but well-informed to an extent that city-dwellers often failed to realise : the tribesmen; and these had begun to look towards the fertile lands below and to their weapons, as their forbears had done, evolving happy projects for jihad and for loot.

That was how matters stood when in October 1946 Mr. Nehru, as head of the Interim Government at Delhi, pluckily but against the advice of Caroe, the provincial Governor — as also that of Azad — decided to visit the Frontier, urged on by Dr. Khan Sahib's brother the so-called 'Frontier Gandhi'. On reaching Peshawar airport, according to Azad's account, 'he found thousands of Pathans massed there, carrying black flags and shouting (sic) anti-slogans; Dr. Khan Sahib and other Ministers who had come to receive (him) were themselves under police protection, and proved completely ineffective.' And during the few subsequent days of his official tour, Pathans had before them visible proof of what the political changes in Delhi might mean; changes which had coincided with unprecedented communal

---

[4] They mean the famous Sikh general Hari Singh Nalwar, who administered the Peshawar area on Ranjit Singh's behalf. (See Chapter 10, p. 133.)

slaughter in Bengal. A Hindu politician stood in their midst, a
Brahmin, no puppet of the British as they could see, but almost the
subcontinent's ruler. Their reaction was plain. The visitor received
verbal insult at a tribal jirga (assembly) convened in his honour up at
Razmak; and elsewhere, as Azad records, 'his car was stoned, and
(he) was once hit on the forehead; Dr. Khan Sahib and his colleagues
seemed so completely helpless that Jawaharlal[5] took the situation
into his own hand.' Throughout the tour, Mr. Nehru showed characteristic courage; but it proved a fiasco, weakening the Congress
party's prestige and imperilling the minorities. 'A step which was
unnecessary', Azad in retrospect termed the visit, and one 'which I
opposed'. Soon afterwards, appalling photographs began to circulate
of the things done to outnumbered Muslims in Bihar, supplemented
perhaps by charred or blood-stained pages of the Koran, and soon
followed by reports about the horrors at Garmukteswar. Anti-Hindu
sentiment, smouldering already, was fanned to a glow.

But the local Ministry, relying on money and propaganda from
Congress headquarters in Delhi, remained unbudged, and fended
off collapse with notable skill. Dr. Khan Sahib was a largely selfless
administrator, much less obstinate and narrow-minded than his
brother; and his Hindu colleague, the Finance Minister Mr. Mehr
Chand Khanna, had pluck as well as brains. In February 1947 however the Muslim League, after launching its 'all-out non-violent
mass struggle' against Sir Khizar Hayat's precarious coalition in
Lahore, extended this to the Frontier Province, whose pro-Congress
Ministry thereupon became exposed to the embarrassments of a
type of activity which the Congress itself had invented to vex the
British. Local officials, as well as the Ministers, were surprised by
the ingenuity with which it was maintained; and this was needed,
because as affairs turned out it had to continue until June. Dr.
Khan Sahib and his colleagues seemed unshaken by the downfall
within five weeks of the nearby Khizar régime. Theirs, they believed,
was no hastily-devised makeshift, but well rooted in local political
feeling. Soon, nearly all the local League leaders headed by Khan
Abdul Qayyum Khan (once a Congressman) had been arrested,
and the jails were filled with their supporters. Yet outside, processions of League enthusiasts kept going out, regardless of the ban.
Effigies of Dr. Khan Sahib on donkeys were paraded through the
streets, beaten, and publicly burnt. Lawcourts, police stations, octroi
posts were picketed; and trouble was caused on the railways, not
only by picketing ticket-offices, but by issuing bogus 'Pakistan'
tickets, pulling the alarm-cord, or lying on the track. As in the Pun-

[5] i.e. Mr Nehru.

jab, feminist activity was in evidence, which startled those knowing how strict purdah had been on the Frontier till very recently. Ladies of upper-middle-class families more than once scaled ladders propped against the walls of jails which housed political prisoners, and brandished League flags aloft. The rural areas were also affected. This writer recalls how, touring the Frontier as late as May, he watched tonga-load after tonga-load[6] of hefty Pathan peasants, handcuffed to constables, being borne off stolid but determined down the Mardan-Peshawar road to prison, after attending village demonstrations for the League. Clearly the campaign had good discipline and substantial public backing.

Nevertheless bloody minor scuffles did occur, these adding to the risk that – as eventually happened – the outnumbered Hindu and Sikh minorities would be subjected to hot-tempered attack. Incidents of some awkwardness took place in or near Peshawar on March 10th, and April 1st and 14th, and in Abbottabad on April 4th. Moreover towards the end of March, fresh communal trouble broke out in the Hazara district as an offshoot from the Punjab rioting. As background to it all, was bureaucracy's worried knowledge that the province was full of weapons, largely unlicensed.

Disorder reached what we can now see was its peak during the third week of April, in the province's previously quieter southern part, the Derajat. Fierce rioting then occurred – partly anti-Hindu, but partly from mere zest for loot and destruction – in and around Dera Ismail Khan, a district headquarters, and at Tank, a market town frequented by tribesmen. At D.I.K.,[7] the jail had become packed with imprisoned Leaguers; and starting from that, trouble arose inside on April 15th, quickly spreading to the town, and for some hours got quite out of hand. There was much looting and arson. Troops hastily arrived from Manzai, and helped the police; but sniping and attempts at incendiarism went on for days. And it is curious to read, in an official report, how two members of Dr. Khan Sahib's Ministry, politicians in theory linked to Gandhian pacifism, arrived from Peshawar and pressed for 'more ruthless measures', including use by tanks of 37-mm. guns against towers being used by snipers. The Army dubiously obliged, and one such tower was knocked down by gunfire. During six days of disorder, 900 shops were officially stated to have been destroyed, and the strain on the police was increased by knowledge that the trouble had spread to nearby villages, those involved including Gomal Bazar, Paharpur, Kotla, Musa Zai, and Jatta Jalwa.

[6] A tonga is a pony-trap.
[7] The customary abbreviation, because of the full name's clumsy length.

And as mentioned it spread to Tank, where an alarming state of affairs developed on April 17th, and was notable for the fact that, owing to local difficulties in getting Army reinforcements, five platoons and some mounted infantry from the South Waziristan Scouts, a unit of the Frontier Corps, were brought down from the hills. This was one of the very rare occasions when a riot in the plains was dealt with by this famous Corps, a mobile militia distinct from the Army, whose proper functions lay up in unadministered tribal territory.[8]

The trouble in Tank started from some trivial bazaar fracas; and soon much of the town's resident Muslim population, supplemented by tribesmen in transit, was looting Hindu shops and house-property. There was much burning and sniping, and the night was officially described as 'highly confused'. Incendiaries could be glimpsed through the smoke, darting over rooftops, and conflagrations raged for three days, intensified on April 19th by a high wind, and by the success at one stage of Bhittani tribesmen, outside the town, in diverting the water-supply for their own purposes, namely irrigation of their fields. Much of the sniping came paradoxically from the biggest Hindu houses, whose owners, it was afterwards learned, had hired tribesmen to protect them – mainly Mahsuds, the wildest of all – a situation which appealed to these characters' sense of humour and of business acumen. Their payment having been agreed to on a time-basis, every hour that the Government forces could be kept at bay meant additions to the wads of cash already stuffed in tribal pockets. The authorities' main problems were to control the fires, to protect the mercantile Hindus and Sikhs numbering several thousands, and to thwart the growing mobs of excited tribesmen milling about just beyond the town's perimeter, seeking to get in and plunder. Casualties were few; but heavy material damage was done, much to the inconvenience of the local Muslim townsmen afterwards.

At Tank is a hospital, then run by British ladies of the Church of England Zenana Mission, mainly for tribespeople travelling to and from the hills; and from notes by the doctor in charge, Miss Shearburn, two points of broad significance emerge : that (as mentioned already) reports of the anti-Muslim pogrom in Bihar during November precipitated the riots, but that, though they were thus in a sense religious, sheer economic injustice also played a part. 'Communal resentment,' she writes, 'which had been smouldering, was fanned during the winter by reports from India. It had been the custom for Muslim merchants from Kulachi, twenty-six miles

[8] See also Chapter 14, p. 189.

from Tank, to go there for trade. Before the riots in D.I.K. and Tank, a party of them was returning from Bihar. The train was halted in a lonely part, where Hindus were lying in wait. Many Muslims were slaughtered; and such as escaped returned to Kulachi, bringing with them tales of killing and terror. These stories went around the district.' And she goes on : 'When food and clothing were rationed during the war, we here in Tank became aware that relations between Hindus and Muslims were getting strained. Hindus controlled nearly all the trade; and although the monthly ration of 1½ yards of cloth was not enough to make a garment for one person, and even this was often unobtainable, yet the Hindus seldom lacked for clothing. The same was true of food. Among our patients, Hindus never seemed short of anything. During the riots in April 1947, there was a continuous stream of villagers passing our property, making their way to the city for loot. Many, I think, regarded this as a heaven-sent opportunity to get back some of those things they had been kept short of for so long, and had seen Hindus enjoying. We remembered well how village Pathans used to come to hospital, saying that someone else at home was also ill, but could not come that day for treatment, because there was only one suit; she would come tomorrow, when today's patient could lend her the clothes !'

Recognising, at the start of his tenure, that the Frontier temporarily at least was the most explosive spot on the Indian map, Lord Mountbatten extricated himself in April from the political whirl at Delhi for a few days' inspection; and Campbell-Johnson and others have vividly described the subsequent excitements. In Peshawar, a crowd of League supporters, estimated at between 70,000 and 100,000 strong, gathered near the Fort − there had been another large one outside the aerodrome − determined to press their views on the Viceregal party; and if the local authorities including Caroe the Governor, and the Viceroy himself, had not dealt with the situation imaginatively and with speed, bloodshed would almost certainly have ensued. How much good the visit did in reducing political tensions is hard to say. Historical hindsight now shows that, with the suppression of the riots at D.I.K. and Tank about ten days before, the main crisis was over. But at the time the only certainty, not only on the Frontier but all across the Indo-Gangetic plain, was that affairs had passed beyond normal administrative prediction, and almost anything could happen anywhere. It is clear that, from the start of the Muslim League's civil disobedience in February, right up to the announcement in the British Government's plan of June 3rd that Frontier people would be allowed a referendum on whether to join Pakistan, this traditionally turbulent corner of the subcontinent remained in a highly dangerous state.

Thus winter had passed into the Pathan country's swift and beautiful spring, and spring into blazing May and June, with an anomalous pro-Congress régime at Peshawar still clinging to the shreds of power, surrounded with much popular antagonism and disorder. Harassed officials must have cast envious glances at their colleagues in the Punjab, who since the collapse of the Khizar Ministry had been using authoritarian procedures under Section 93.[9] Looking back, and considering the Frontier's peculiarities – its strategic and diplomatic importance, its formidable restless tribes up in unadministered territory, and the fact that this whole trans-Indus region, in history and culture and sentiment, had an ambivalence of outlook, a tendency to turn west from India towards Iran or Afghanistan, similar to Burma's eastward leanings towards Thailand and China – we may feel amazed that, during those tense weeks of 1947, something within the civilian Administration did not crack.

A factor in preventing this, which may be overlooked, was the skill with which, up in the hills, officers of the Political Service and the Frontier Corps, under the Governor's directions, tactfully influenced the tribes towards restraint. And in the settled districts the police (unlike some of those in eastern India) remained efficient. And, as well, there was the reality of the Army, proportionately thicker on the ground here than in other provinces – four brigades were available around Peshawar alone – and now being more freely used to support the civil power than at any time in the last three decades. That fact, and awareness of it among a population familiar with fighting and firearms, was perhaps what, in the last analysis, fended off disaster.

During May, in the riot-torn Punjab, despite Governor's rule, and the subsequent availability of 20,000 troops, trouble flared up again, particularly in the crowded alleys of Amritsar and Lahore. Expert incendiaries were more active than ever. All over the subcontinent, there were increasingly valid reasons now for deterioration. Such authority as British officials wielded was shrivelling, for power was due to pass, in any event, to indigenous hands not later than the summer of 1948: that aspect of Mr. Attlee's February announcement had become clear even to the ignorant poor. Until June 3rd, however, no one knew exactly to what or whom it would pass: whether to one new régime; to two; or to several. Consequently – after the short pause in February – it almost seemed that fixing a

[9] i.e. the 'breakdown' clause of the Government of India Act of 1935.

time-limit, by giving fresh spurs to uncertainty, had merely increased the civil war's momentum. Rival parties felt the more compelled to stake out their claims and face one another with accomplished facts, before the hand-over.

A more specialised point of great importance – touched on in Chapter 8 – is the February announcement's destructive effects on the Administration's sources of intelligence. And in the Punjab, India's 'model province', which had not suffered the decline in standards which provinces farther east, near the fighting-zones, had been obliged to acquiesce in during World War II, the change seemed specially abrupt. Here, we have not just an impalpable ebbing of British authority, but a physical loss. Police informers suddenly realised that work for an avowedly moribund régime involved appalling danger; they must stop it, unless they and their families were to suffer nameless future evils. A former official of the province, in a memorandum to the author, has roundly said that the February announcement caused 'the complete collapse, almost instantaneously, of the highly efficient Punjab C.I.D. Up to that date,' he proceeds, 'we were amazingly well informed about everything said and done by Muslims, Sikhs, and Hindus alike. But when it was known that the British were going, all sources just dried up.' This sudden wilting of previously dependable means of information must have been a big cause of the swift administrative decline so evident over Northern India during the spring of 1947.

Late that May, approaching Lahore by air from Peshawar, and pondering on Pathan problems recently under study, this writer was aroused to Punjab actualities by what he saw ahead. On the horizon, under the bright blue dome, billowed up a dense dun smoke-mass; and flickering at the base of it, red even through the dazzle of an Indian hot-weather afternoon, were little tongues of flame. Much of the bazaar-area in the old walled city was ablaze. Nor was disorder confined to the Punjab cities. This was the month when little-reported events began in the province's remote dusty borderland with the U.P. and (as it was then called) Rajputana, a country of stone and low hills about sixty miles south of Delhi: the first incidents of the horrible struggle called the Meo revolt, which dragged on through the summer, culminating during August in organised butcheries of the Muslim peasantry.

Trouble continued also at the subcontinent's other end. Conditions in Calcutta have been mentioned : for twelve months, scarcely a day without 'incidents'. And in Assam, where the League had championed the 'squatter' claims of Muslim immigrants from Bengal, civil disobedience went on – as on the Frontier – against a Congress

Ministry. Rightly, as events showed, Eastern Command never re-garded this very seriously – most of Tuker's references to it are cheerfully contemptuous – and troop-dispositions from the weakening reserves were made accordingly. But it was impossible to be sure. Worried officials up there pleaded for reinforcements. The one safe rule now – the point is well made by Ismay – was to expect the unexpected. 'There was no knowing when a new outbreak would start, or where, or when and where it would end.' As the editor of a paper issuing simultaneously in two cities over 800 miles apart,[10] the present writer can confirm this, from experience. Several times I misplaced myself on the map, having reckoned, from the apparent trend of affairs, that at a particular date I would be more needed in Calcutta than Delhi, or vice versa – whereas in fact the contrary happened.

Meanwhile, in the Interim Government at Delhi, relations be-tween Congressmen and Leaguers had been no whit sweetened by the change of Viceroys. In March, before Lord Wavell left, the startling Budget presented by Mr. Liaquat Ali Khan as Finance Minister, imposing a punitive tax on company profits, a capital gains tax, a lowering of the surtax level, and in other respects 'soak-ing the rich', had at once been construed by Congressmen, rightly we may guess, as aimed at the wealthy Hindus from whom their party got funds; and the controversy about this – during which Mr. Nehru's Socialism did not prevent his taking the capitalist side – spilt over into the new Viceroyalty's opening weeks. It had become unmistakable by now, not only that consultation between Ministers in the rival wings of Government was non-existent, but that the British Government's hopes during the previous autumn, that con-tact in practical day-to-day tasks would bring about mutual under-standing, were based on a fallacy, and had not the slightest chance of fulfilment. Bitter quarrels within the Cabinet kept flaring out in speeches and Press statements, Ministers publicly reviling one another. 'Pandit Nehru, in the External Affairs Department,' writes Lumby, giving instances, 'made diplomatic or consular appointments some of which – such as the appointment of Mr. Asaf Ali, a Congress Muslim, as Ambassador to the United States – were highly distasteful to the League; while Mr. Chundrigar, the League Commerce Member, sent abroad trade representatives – some of them vigorous propa-gandists for Pakistan – responsible only to his own Department.' A

[10] Calcutta and Delhi. The distance is about the same as between London and (say) Danzig, or Toledo; an absurd problem – in European terms – for an editor to face.

striking passage in the Indian chapter of Ismay's book describes his astonishment, after reaching Delhi with the new Viceroy – he was one of two eminent men specially brought out to assist him – at the state of affairs that prevailed. His previous experience of India had been in the 1920's and 1930's, concluding under the Willingdon régime. He found that 'communal bitterness had grown to incredible proportions'. Within a week of arrival, he was placed at dinner between two Ministers, a Congressman and a Leaguer. 'Throughout the meal these cultured men, who normally had impeccable manners, spoke to me unceasingly, in loud voices, about the iniquities of the opposing community.' As to the Interim Government as a whole, 'I doubt,' he remarks, 'whether there has ever been a coalition whose members were so determined not to co-operate with each other.'

During April and May, Lord Mountbatten's exploratory talks with the political leaders went on about how soon, and to whom the British could part with power. Opinion in the Congress party's upper ranks seemed on the point of recognising – though in a most grudging way – that the Pakistan-project must be conceded; that the continuing civil war now precluded any other course. But it was plain, as well, that the new State's dimensions would be shrunken ones. In no circumstances would Hindus and Sikhs let her consist of five undivided provinces, as the project presupposed.[11] For months, Congressmen had been persistently objecting to Assam being initially 'grouped' with Bengal, as required by the Cabinet Mission's Plan; and they had now got Mr. Gandhi's support in this. That implied the loss, for Pakistan, of one entire province, unless something could be done about transfer of Sylhet district. And in Bengal and the Punjab – much the largest provinces of the project – local non-Muslims, as early as January, had begun to raise a partition-clamour of their own; to say that, if the subcontinent had really to be divided, then there must be a division of their provinces as well, since the over-all Muslim majority in both was small; and that to include a mass of recalcitrant non-Muslim citizens permanently in Pakistan would be an impossibility. Thus, much of Bengal and the Punjab, perhaps almost half of each, would be lopped off. And by March, when civil war had engulfed the Punjab, and the Sikhs had joined the Hindus, this demand naturally got more strident. Nevertheless, there was probably still a bargaining element in it. As Lumby notes, some reckoned that, if 'faced with the certainty of getting only part of the Punjab and part of Bengal, (Mr. Jinnah) would back down,

---

[11] Bengal, the Punjab, Assam, Sind and the Frontier Province. Baluchistan was sometimes brought in as a sixth, but as yet it lacked comparable self-governing institutions.

and induce the League to renew its acceptance of the Mission's
Plan; for there was at this time', he goes on, 'a widespread impression, shared by non-partisan observers and even by sympathisers
with the League, that a truncated Pakistan would be neither viable
economically, nor capable of self-defence.'

But towards the end of April, expectations among leading Congressmen of any backing-down by Mr. Jinnah had faded. Addressing
the Constituent Assembly as its President when it met (again without
Leaguers) on the 28th, Rajendra Prasad surprised uninitiated hearers
by seeming almost resigned to Partition. 'It may be,' he sombrely
observed, 'that the (Indian) Union may not comprise all provinces.
If that unfortunately comes to pass, we shall have to be content with
a Constitution for part of it.' And in the same week Mr. Nehru more
roughly said 'the Muslim League can have Pakistan if they want
it, but on the condition that they do not take away other parts of
India which do not wish to join Pakistan'. Menon's and Azad's books
offer illuminating glimpses of what had been happening in Congressmen's minds to bring this change about. The main consideration evidently was that, as circumstances had developed, Partition offered
the only realistic way whereby independent India – even if in the
process she lost much good territory – could be reasonably sure of
establishing a strong Central Government.

On May 2nd Ismay left for London; and it was indicated that he
had taken with him a draft 'plan'. This was indeed quick going, for
the Viceroy had been in office less than six weeks; and on May 10th
a communiqué announced that on May 17th the Viceroy would
meet representative political leaders in Delhi 'to present to them the
plan which His Majesty's Government has now made for the transfer
of power'. Immediately afterwards however confusion followed.
Another communiqué came out next day, putting the meeting off
till June 2nd. And on May 15th emerged the fact that Lord Mountbatten would himself be flying to London.

We know now, from the inside accounts by Campbell-Johnson,
Menon, and Ismay himself, what was going on; and an exciting
story it is. The impression outwardly conveyed at the time however
was of sorry fumbling. It looked as if the initiative, which the
February 20th announcement had given the British, and which the
new Viceroy had so vigorously taken up, had somehow been let
slip. And indeed – for a few days – this was the case. The draft that
Ismay took to London, which meant transfer of power by the British
to individual provincial Governments entitled thereafter to recom-
bine into two new States if they wished, had apparently been chopped

about by Whitehall, in ways which increased the misgivings already felt about it by some at the Indian end. And we are told that Lord Mountbatten – up in Simla for a few days – then suddenly got 'a hunch' that the whole thing simply would not do; that he thereupon – Mr. Nehru being his guest at the time – rather against his staff's advice 'gave (Mr.) Nehru the chance of reading' it (but not, we may note, Mr. Jinnah); that Mr. Nehru's reaction was very adverse; and that a new draft was then rapidly evolved, largely based on ideas put forward earlier by Menon as Constitutional Adviser.

Quite how big the difference was between the two drafts is not clear. Ismay's account indicates a much smaller gap than Campbell-Johnson's and Menon's. At all events, the new version evidently hinged on three main things : first, that power would go, not initially to individual provinces as required by the first one, but direct to two relatively strong Central Governments – the plural of course denoting acceptance of the Pakistan-project; next, that the transfer would be done through the existing constitutional machinery for achieving Dominion Status – which, besides other advantages, would be specially useful for retaining indispensably-needed British officers in the Armed Forces; and last, that the timing would be pulled right up from June 1948 to some much nearer date, to be fixed by the Viceroy during the visit he was about to make to London. Even if the difference between the drafts was not so big as Menon has suggested, few officials can have had a more thrilling experience than his, in those frantically busy days, as he watched the change unfold, largely under his pen, and in fulfilment of ideas which, as he explains, had taken shape five months or so before during talks he had with Sardar Patel.

The question has naturally since been much asked, whether that final acceleration, that sudden cutting off of corners on the last swift lap of the British régime's journey, resulting from those fresh thoughts in Simla, was really necessary; whether methods less hasty might not have been as effective – and much more humane. Hundreds of thousands of lives, critics suggest, might have been spared had something different been decided on during those crucial days of May. Was such 'dynamism' justified, such ruthless impetuous pressure, which as events turned out meant advancing the transfer-date by nearly ten months? Could no better course possibly have been found?

The problem is a huge one. To deal properly with it would need a whole book. Here, we can no more than skirt its edges. Anyone who did a job of some prominence in the India of those days is used

L

to such questions being put. And he may have difficulty, still, in answering. He may indeed never have made up his mind. Perhaps he suspects, but is not sure, that any of the several conceivable courses other than that chosen – all of them, presumably, involving either a slower pace of British withdrawal, or attempts to resume ruling 'from strength' – would have led, in the end, to results even grislier than occurred. And he may, as well, be uncomfortably aware that the opinions he inclines to now, based on reflection or after-knowledge, clash with those he held earlier. Possibly he carries self-mistrust one stage more, and wonders how valid present after-knowledge on such a matter can be. For historically, we still stand close to those huge events of 1947; and besides mere size, they were very complex, rapid, and hard to follow; and Whitehall's rules keep many of the important Government papers necessary for fair judge-ment locked away and inaccessible.

Further, he may feel uneasy about his questioners' motives. Some of them will be open-minded seekers after truth. But others will be prejudiced; they will hope to extract a particular answer. And this, probably, will be 'No!'. They will want to be told that that sudden last acceleration in British moves towards quitting India was a terrible, unnecessary mistake; that some better, practicable choice lay to hand. Nor will such people always be politically of the Right. Others, sentimental and politically pinkish perhaps, humanitarians anyway, may prove more perplexing to him, especially if they were actually working in the Punjab in those days. They would be British people of the sort who had willingly let themselves get integrated with the lives of their Indian fellow-beings, who had developed more than average affection for the country they lived in, a warm sense of inclusion in it, and who thus had close personal knowledge, through their Hindu and Muslim and Sikh friendships, of what those suffer-ings of 1947 amounted to. Such people, it can be understood, feel vulnerable to the sort of taunt that this writer recalls hearing during the winter of 1947–8 from an American lady; an incident trivial, no doubt, but revealing. The British during the previous August, she said, 'just had to go, because they weren't strong enough to stay. They couldn't afford the cash, or the Tommies' lives. And my! they're clever! You should have seen the slick get-away they made of it.'

This writer ranks himself among those who, in this great affair, would attach more weight to opinions formed at the time – at any rate when, as in his case, remembrance of them can be verified by things written at the time – than to opinions formed at leisure in a different land twenty years later. He suspects that twenty years are not enough. Sixty might do, the more so because they would require release of the official documents. So he now – for what it may be worth – sets forth those 1947 opinions of his, mentioning however that they must have been influenced, to some extent, by geography. They were formed in Delhi; and federal capitals are notoriously misleading places – Washington, Ottawa, Canberra, Karachi or Rawalpindi are all the same in this. Perhaps Delhi's tense, extraordinary atmosphere, that May, distorted many people's sense of realities. Nevertheless, it is a fact that, to an observer looking out from a newspaper office there at the political and administrative scene spread around, the conclusion seemed inescapable, then, that swift, drastic action of some kind, almost of any kind, had become imperative.

Signs of imminent disintegration showed up everywhere. 'Law and order', over great tracts of the subcontinent, had become practically non-existent and the established structure of civilian Government was visibly crumbling. The Armed Forces remained outwardly dependable and solid; but even they, because ferocious communal strife had broken out near the Punjab homes of so many soldiers, might at any moment crack. And ahead of the Forces, inevitably, if Partition were decided on – this had now to be faced – lay a splitting; perhaps not at the moment of Partition, its date was as yet uncertain, but within at most a year or so; and no one in authority seemed able yet to explain how the dividing of so well-integrated a military organism would be arranged, or what fresh perils might arise when it was, or by what means these could be forestalled. Indian history, before the British period, was full of ugly episodes revealing what bands of undisciplined, unpaid troops roving the countryside might do.

Communism was active; a glance at news from the industrial centres showed much unrest. And the war-time semblance of amity between Russia and the Western Powers had broken down; what new intrigues therefore might not Soviet agents be up to in the big cities? It had to be remembered that, for three years or so from 1941, the Indian Communists, because they supported the war-effort and the Congress party did not, had received encouragement from the British Raj. Famine was another possibility. As the catastrophic events of 1943 in Bengal had shown,[12] Indian agricultural statistics, or official forecasts based on them, could prove hopelessly unreliable; so any unlucky climatic twist or executive muddle might cause fresh shortages. Nothing whatever had yet been settled about the future of the princely States, whose combined area covered well over a

[12] 1,873,749 people were officially admitted to have died of starvation.

third of the subcontinent; and the rulers of some large or populous ones – Hyderabad, perhaps Kashmir, Bhopal, Travancore – evidently had thoughts of proclaiming themselves independent. How viable they were was a matter of opinion; some certainly had an impressive weight of tradition behind them; at the time, most people reckoned them tougher than they proved.

Other would-be separatisms were sprouting up, some of them palpably bogus, others not : demands such as those by the Adibasi tribesmen of Orissa for a separate State of Jharkhand; comparable ones by the fiercer Nagas on the Assam-Burma border (who in fact gave independent India much subsequent bother); demands, fostered apparently from Nepal, for separation from Bengal of the Mongoloid hill tracts of the Darjeeling area; demands for an autonomous Muslim pocket or corridor in Western U.P., where the later Moghul culture had been strong, and Afghan Rohillas lived; for a distinctive Dravidian set-up in the far south, where remembrance lingered of ancient Tamil kingdoms, and the continuing arrogance of northern enthusiasts for the Hindi language was disliked; for Pakhtoonistan, a separate Pathan State, now clamoured for by the Red Shirt party as counterblast to the Muslim League's civil disobedience, and favoured, though for different motives, both by Mr. Gandhi and the Afghan Government; and of course for Khalistan, a separate State or homeland for the Sikhs, rulers of the Punjab a century or so before; and, most surprising of all, demands suddenly raised by the local Muslim League Premier Mr. Suhrawardy in partnership with Mr. Sarat Bose, a dissident Congressman, for a 'sovereign, independent, undivided Bengal in a divided India'. Unless something decisive was done, to check all this, general disruption seemed assured.

Woodruff's book contains a vivid passage, which correctly mirrors the attitude of mind of many in Delhi at the time. 'For years,' he says, 'the problem of handing over power had been clogged by detail; the assumption of the Services – set out with such admirable clarity and perception in the Simon Report – had been that everyone must be protected. The Princes, the Untouchables, the Muslims, and a great many more – all must be guarded; unity must be preserved, and life must not be lost. It was on these assumptions that the Services had been brought up, and it was because those assumptions were unquestioned that England had a wolf by the ears. It required great courage to simplify and falsify the problem, to ignore those complications, to disregard the snapping jaws and quietly let go of the ears. It was dangerous and courageous; it was the right thing to do. The price grew with delay. It is only necessary to count the dead, month by month, to see how true this was. It had to be done quickly.'

At any rate, as we know, it was. Campbell-Johnson, Menon, Ismay, and Abul Kalam Azad from his different viewpoint, offer illuminating details of what went on behind the scenes in Delhi and London, and why, during that second fortnight of May; and on June 2nd the publicly decisive moment arrived. Seven political leaders representing the Congress, the League, and (so it was assumed) the Sikhs went by invitation to the Viceroy's House to be told 'the plan', as now finalised with the British Government's consent. Throughout previous weeks, their private talks with him had kept them in intimate touch with its shaping at nearly every stage. Next evening, three of them – Mr. Nehru, Mr. Jinnah, and Sardar Baldev Singh for the Sikhs – broadcast about it, indicating, with whatever reluctance, their consent; and on June 4th Lord Mountbatten expounded it to the outside world at his remarkable Press Conference.[13]

So here, at last, was an end to uncertainty. The British would quit almost forthwith; not next year, but in the startlingly, perhaps alarmingly short time of about eleven weeks. Unqualified political independence throughout the subcontinent was at hand. And unless voting by the agreed procedure in the provincial Legislatures went altogether contrary to expectation, Pakistan, a new nation, after very bitter dispute and struggle, would be born. And so, as well – to quote Moon, who takes a standpoint contrary to his fellow-member of the I.C.S. Woodruff,[14] but who served in the Punjab, whereas Woodruff did not – 'with a quite unprecedented unanimity, all set forth together, on a path leading straight to mass slaughter. In Bengal, this was a dangerous possibility; in the Punjab, an absolute certainty. Fortunately for the peace of mind of those who led the way, none of them except Baldev Singh knew much about the Punjab, so they did not realise what was coming. British officials of the Punjab were not in that happy position'.

---

[13] He, too, had of course broadcast the previous evening.
[14] Philip Woodruff was a pseudonym for Philip Mason, author of the Preface to Toye's book, see p. 90.

PART III

Chapter 13

Birth of a Nation – I

THOUGH it is only too true, as the next chapter will bring out, that Pakistan was born into what Moon terms mass slaughter, it is true, besides, that the first result of the June 3rd decision was a short but marked lessening in the civil war. Menon goes so far as to say that 'only in parts of the Punjab, and in Calcutta', were there 'sporadic disturbances'. That exaggerates what at best was but an ephemeral thing. For example a Punjab Government report for the first half of June declares that, in Lahore and Amritsar, 'the exhortations of India's leaders have gone unheeded, and community sanity is completely lacking; arson, murder and bomb-throwing continue to be everyday occurrences, and damage is great, both for life and property'. And the rustic communal savageries between Muslims, Meos, and Hindu Ahirs and Jats, in the Punjab's south-easternmost district, only about sixty miles from Delhi, went on as if the utterances by eminent personages there had never been made. And 'incidents' were frequent farther east, in towns and villages strung across the U.P., Bihar, and Bengal out to Dacca. Sometimes 'order' was propped up only by displays of armed strength. Describing Calcutta early in June, Tuker writes that 'throughout the city, and Howrah, the roads were carpeted with police and military, on foot, on picket and on patrol, and moving ceaselessly round in jeeps and trucks, their rifles and automatics at the ready. It was virtually military government – if not so in name – with the Governor as commander, and all under him a part of his forces'.

But certainly, for three weeks or so after June 3rd, there was everywhere a lessening of strife and casualties – the biggest yet. Presumably the local organisers whose brains had been behind many outbreaks found themselves outpaced by events, and compelled to cast their thoughts hurriedly into the future. What did the June 3rd plan portend for them, and their co-religionists? Complete transfer of power by the British was much nearer than anyone had supposed. How could they exploit this? It cannot have been easy, at first, to feel sure.

And there were other favourable factors. After the plan was announced, the Muslim League called off its civil disobedience in the Frontier Province and Assam. That eased things in those areas –

besides paving the way, usefully for the League, towards smooth working of the local referenda which the plan provided for.[1] And Mr. Gandhi helped. As late as May 31st, undeterred by the changed climate of ideas about Partition among his Congress colleagues in the Interim Government, he had continued to declaim passionately against it. 'Even if the whole of India burns, we shall not concede Pakistan, no, not if the Muslims demand it at the point of the sword.' But by June 4th he had begun to swing round. Partition, he then decided, would be no fault of the British, but of Hindus and Muslims for failing to agree; and by June 7th, his views had so altered that he felt able to advise the All-India Congress Committee to approve the plan. This it did on June 14th, the Council of the Muslim League having in effect done so on June 10th. Excellent progress was also being made already by the hard-worked officials towards setting up the technical bodies to deal with the huge administrative tasks ahead: the Partition Council, the Joint Defence Council, the Boundary Commissions and so on.

The chief hazard during this period, in fact, lay in the Interim Government itself. There, the sharp, almost daily disputes between Congress and League members, according to Menon, 'caused Lord Mountbatten and his advisers more worry than any other problem'. In retrospect, many of these squabbles seem trivial; yet in a practical sense they mattered acutely at the time, for had they resulted in either party quitting the Government, as was threatened, the plan would have collapsed, and the Viceroy and the British Government been left on thin air. Only 48 hours after its public disclosure on June 3rd, Campbell-Johnson observed that, though it had 'led to a *détente* throughout the country as a whole, among the leaders in Delhi it has induced no brotherly love'. And three days later came a crisis, when 'the Cabinet meeting was only just saved, by a desperate diversion on Mountbatten's part, from breaking up in complete disorder'. This arose over a Congress proposal for appointing an Ambassador in Moscow, which the League objected to; and unfortunately the nominee turned out to be 'none other than Nehru's sister, Mrs. Pandit. Nehru asserted that, rather than tolerate League interference, he would immediately resign'. Somehow, the quarrel was patched up, to be succeeded by others, though of gradually diminishing significance as the date for transfer of power drew nigh.

Outside, even among those having scant knowledge of Punjab affairs, increasing anxiety was felt about the Sikhs. Clearly, the June 3rd announcement had not disposed of this problem; and among

[1] The Assam referendum applied only to Sylhet district.

the audience at Lord Mountbatten's Press conference in Delhi on
June 4th were some who left convinced that, if the plan foundered,
this would be the rock it did so on. He said he had been much surprised, soon after he reached India, to discover what the facts were
about the Sikhs. 'I found that it was mainly at the request of the
Sikh community that the Congress had put forward the resolution
on the partition of the Punjab. I was not aware of all the details,
and when I sent for the map, and studied the distribution of the Sikh
population, I was astounded to find that the plan which they had
produced divided this community into two almost equal parts. I
have spent a great deal of time seeing whether there was any
solution which would keep the Sikh community more together. I
am not a miracle worker and I have not found that solution.' This,
however, he stressed, was the actual present state of affairs regard-
ing the Sikhs; the resolution as passed had been primarily theirs;
the time remaining before Partition was very short; and whatever
steps were taken, would be based on the Congress resolution on the
subject, which – as he put it – 'the Sikhs themselves sponsored'.
And that, he seemed to think, was that.

But was it? Could the destiny of a martial and obstinate people,
conscious of their Imperial past, be disposed of in quite this slapdash
way, on the strength of paper resolutions agreed to by dubiously
representative politicians? Lord Mountbatten, unfortunately, was
not the only leading person in this drama unaware 'of all the details'.
As has been remarked there was little to suggest that either Mr.
Nehru or Mr. Jinnah knew much about the Sikh problem either.
Right up to the end of July, the prevailing assumption, fostered
doubtless by the not very impressive resistance of outnumbered
mainly mercantile Khatri Sikhs during the March riots in Northern
Punjab, was that Sikhs had become effete; that they were mere
modern materialists bent on money-making, with their former bodily
hardihood and religious zeal gone. Yet the persistence of the error
is odd; for besides Ismay, who certainly expressed misgivings, the
Viceregal staff included others with practical knowledge of the
Punjab such as Mr. Abell,[2] and the specially recruited Major Short.
And from outside came plenty of expert warnings that the Jat Sikhs
of Central Punjab were of different quality from the Khatris. They
were not predominantly traders, but peasants and retired soldiers,
landlords, scions of the princely families; men often of huge physique.
It could be guessed that, among such people, a chain-reaction against
the community's Rawalpindi humiliations might be developing,
rather as in the Calcutta-Noakhali-Bihar sequence of disorders

[2] Later Sir George.

during the previous autumn, but worse. The fact that the Jat Sikhs were individualists, and that the Sikh community was not well led, that as explained in Chapter 10 its best men had been sucked away from politics did not help; it made the problem more intractable.

By mid-June, signs of imminent trouble in the Central Punjab grew. Yet nothing whatever was done, whether by arrests or troop-movements, that in the event proved at all adequate. The ill-fated 60,000-strong Punjab Boundary Force was not brought into being until August 1st, four days before the outbreak started; and as we can see, the Sikhs' widely dispersed yet disciplined rural attacks, stretching over an area about half that of Ireland and much more populous, foredoomed its task to failure. But that is anticipating. Brecher states (without disclosing his source) that even before the June 3rd announcement, the Punjab Governor Sir Evan Jenkins had assured the Viceroy 'that large-scale violence was inevitable'. Moon is particularly interesting on the matter, offering a mass of well-authenticated detail, pungently expressed. Campbell-Johnson records that, prior to June 3rd, the two Sikh leaders Giani Kartar Singh and Master Tara Singh in effect told Lord Mountbatten they would do just what they actually did; and Ismay, at later dates not specified, quite failed to shift them from this formidable position. 'They arrived,' he writes – he and Sir Eric Miéville had two or three talks with them – 'carrying villainous-looking swords, and many volumes of Hansard from which they quoted interminably. They refused to budge from their preconceived ideas, and occasionally used threatening language. We told them that if they resorted to violence they would be very roughly handled; but we did not feel that our warnings had the slightest effect.'

On June 14th Campbell-Johnson, writing his diary in what he called 'the heart of the Sikh country', noted that 'the prevailing atmosphere is one of foreboding; Sikh unrest in the Punjab is growing hourly. The implications of the 3rd June are now all too clear to the Sikh people. They see that the partition of India means irrevocably the partition of the Sikhs, and they feel themselves sacrificed on the altars of Moslem ambition and Hindu opportunism. Their leaders, hopelessly outmanœuvred in the political struggle, begin to invoke more primitive remedies. Power is passing to the wilder men'. And by July, reports of Sikh intentions from Intelligence sources (gravely weakened though these were) had become precise. A plot was described, and a recommendation made for the imprisonment of certain leaders which, however, despite League protests, the Interim Government ignored. Ismay remarks that 'the giants of old, like the Lawrences and John Nicholson, would probably have clapped the Sikh leaders into jail at once'; but he goes on to say that the Governor of the Punjab, together with the two Governors-designate of what were to become the partitioned halves of the province, were unanimous in advising against this.

It would be wrong however to imply that Central Punjab was the only part of the map arousing concern, though we may be disposed now, knowing what we do, almost to think so. A mere ransacking of memory, however; talk with friends who shared the experiences of that extraordinary summer; a flipping of the yellowed pages of filed newspapers, or of books which reassemble the facts : such things suffice to remind one how far-reaching were the uncertainties; how impossible, at the time, to feel sure where the next big trouble would be.

Describing conditions across his far-stretched Eastern Command in June and July, Tuker says that, 'apart from the Meo revolt there was plenty of trouble elsewhere', instancing riots during the second half of June in the U.P. And everywhere the two major communities, Hindu and Muslim, 'were at work marshalling their resources. Both communities were now masters at setting a riot going. As preparations speeded up, so did the belligerents' zeal to acquire weapons and ammunition'. And he describes efforts to bribe or hoodwink members of the Armed Forces into giving up arms. Towards the end of June disorder in Calcutta again increased. 'On the 21st,' he recorded, 'incidents rose to 13; on the 22nd there were 21; on the 23rd, 12; on the 24th, 18. In Howrah were still other incidents, culminating on the 6th July in the killing of a Muslim police officer. (Next day) the officer's body was taken out in procession. Before it had gone far, hooligan elements slipped the bier away from its police escort. They then diverted the procession, gathering immense numbers of Muslims as they passed. As they went, they brickbatted Hindus'; and he tells how this episode alone resulted in 'at least 20 dead and 148 injured'. In another passage he refers to a 'new sport' then starting. 'Jeeps filled with Hindus were seen flashing through Muslim quarters, shooting up any who offered a target. Calcutta had passed beyond gangster methods, it was in the grip of anarchy.' These being still the conditions on the subcontinent's eastern flank, it is in retrospect astonishing that Partition only a few weeks later in Bengal should have passed off so smoothly. As the extract from Moon quoted at the end of the last chapter shows, there was, or at least seemed at the time to be, good reason why it should prove a horribly strife-torn process.

An ominous matter, during these weeks, was the evidence of

intensified recruitment of private political armies. Probably the most formidable was the Fascist-style Rashtriya Swayam Sevak Sangh (R.S.S.S.) of the Hindus. Although the authorities' channels of reliable police-information had been rapidly drying up, the expansion of this sinister body had caused the secrecy formerly cloaking it to lift somewhat, and even ordinary inquirers could now learn that it aimed at no less than complete Hindu domination over the subcontinent; that it had plenty of funds; and that it felt no Gandhian scruples about assassination or massacre. In the Punjab, recent enrolments were said to be particularly large, and it was running courses in weapon-training, bomb-manufacture, acid-throwing and so on. Less was specifically ascertainable about the two militant Sikh bodies, the Akal Fauj and the Shahidi Jathas, though it was noted that, during June, they amalgamated; and the views of extremist Sikh leaders were known. On the Muslim side the League National Guards had a large membership, and were in places fanatical; but in the Punjab, at any rate, did not seem well organised. A recent offshoot in the Frontier Province, the Ghazi Pakhtun, opposed the Red Shirt party's Zalmai Pakhtun, which though linked to the Congress seemed disinterested now in non-violence. There were also the volunteer groups of the Congress party proper; but these, still largely true to their pacifist traditions, confined themselves to squad drill, P.T., and control of crowds.

A big event of this time was Mr. Jinnah's decision to become Pakistan's first Governor-General. It had been supposed that, like Mr. Nehru, he would rather be Prime Minister. Further, the idea had been put about, probably by the Viceroy's staff, that at the start Lord Mountbatten would become Governor-General of both Dominions. Indeed, provision for this was made in the draft Indian Independence Bill, then being hustled through the British Parliament. So when Mr. Jinnah's decision was announced, early in July, it caused surprise.

There has been speculation about its reasons. Campbell-Johnson — who it must be remembered was Lord Mountbatten's Press Attaché — takes the view that Mr. Jinnah simply wanted 'power and glory'. But his diary is hostile to the League leader almost throughout. If that reflects Lord Mountbatten's own attitude at that stage, it is important. But Ismay's weightier evidence lends no support. Clearly, Lord Mountbatten and Mr. Jinnah differed much in temperament. And any visitor to Government House could learn that, whereas both Viceroy and Vicereine were on affable terms with leading Congressmen, they were not so yet with Mr. Jinnah or the Leaguers. But

Mr. Jinnah was not easy to become affable with. It seems doubtful whether Lord Mountbatten had yet really developed the hostility to him which he later showed.[3] And if he had, Mr. Jinnah was unaware of it. For it is a fact that, near the start of this episode, Mr. Jinnah pressed him to become 'a sort of super-Governor-General', with both Dominion Governors-General under him; and that when, after reference to London, this was turned down, he readily agreed to Lord Mountbatten's staying on as Governor-General of India only, and indeed got Mr. Liaquat Ali Khan to write saying he hoped this would happen. Possibly, as early as June, some Leaguers had come to suspect that Lord Mountbatten, in his proposed dual role, would subconsciously or otherwise load the dice against Pakistan, because of the friendships he and his wife had formed with leading Hindus. But Mr. Jinnah seems to have been above such suspicions.

Bolitho, Mr. Jinnah's biographer, offers another idea. He suggests that, in June 1947, Mr. Jinnah knew or guessed he had got the illness that he died of fourteen months later, and therefore decided that the Prime Ministership should go to a 'younger and stronger' man. For reasons which will be enlarged upon in Chapter 18, the present writer is sure there is nothing in this; Brecher, among the authorities, has reached the same conclusion by another route. The idea cannot be squared with the immense burden of work Mr. Jinnah at once undertook on becoming Governor-General, not only in that post, but as President of Pakistan's Constituent Assembly, and as Chairman of the Muslim League. Almost till death approached, he drove himself inhumanly hard. Nor does it tally with the tone of his remarks to the present writer during an interview in February 1948, as recorded in an earlier book.[4] But what clinches the matter is the medical evidence. Not until July 1948, did Mr. Jinnah's doctors discover anything seriously amiss.

According to Chaudhuri Mohammad Ali,[5] who though still a Government official was in the League leaders' confidence, Mr. Jinnah's decision was due to two practical points, the first of which – as an expert in legal niceties – he had at the outset pressed on Lord Mountbatten's attention. This was that he wanted it explained – because he could not see the answer – what would happen in the almost inevitable event, with relations between Congress and League so bitter, of the proposed Joint Governor-General being given

---

[3] See, for instance, the present writer's *Horned Moon*, pp. 113–115.

[4] *Horned Moon*, p. 50.

[5] Subsequently Secretary-General to the Pakistan Government; then Finance Minister; then Prime Minister.

conflicting advice by his two sets of Ministers, those in Karachi urging him one way, those in Delhi another. The second derived from a fact already touched on in Chapters 1 and 4: the shortage of trained Muslims at the higher administrative levels, both military and civilian, because of the community's backwardness in Western-style education. Owing to this, Pakistan at the start would need British officers to command her Forces, and British civil servants as Governors of some provinces. Might not Pakistanis themselves, as well as unfriendly foreigners, ask as a result whether she really was an independent country at all? But with a Muslim as Head of State, such doubts would go.

Whatever the decision's causes, it did not smooth the path towards Partition. Ismay describes it as 'a blow. We had all felt', he goes on, 'that the best hope of an orderly transfer of power, an equitable division of assets, and the establishment of friendly relations between the two new Dominions would be for them to start off with the same Governor-General'. And Lord Mountbatten himself seemed personally riled by it. Those brought in touch with him would doubtless agree that his weakness – perhaps the only one – was a curiously sensitive kind of vanity. Murphy's biography confirms this. That someone of his superb gifts should have had such a characteristic is odd; but evidently it was so. And it seemed noticeable at an editors' conference arranged the afternoon before Mr. Jinnah's decision was announced. Several of us inferred that the decision had not merely caused him political worry, but had hurt him. Perhaps he had set his heart on becoming dual Governor-General; the rebuff knocked against his most vulnerable point, his pride.

Whether Mr. Jinnah's choice proved right for Pakistan is a question uncommitted Westerners may prefer to leave open. With Pakistanis, his prestige stands so high that few would admit the possibility of his making any major error. In his lifetime, he became the acknowledged Father of the Nation; and his memory commands unquestioning reverence, rather like Ataturk's in Turkey or Mr. Gandhi's in India. And in further support of his decision it could be argued – and his advisers did argue – that as Joint Governor-General Lord Mountbatten would have spent less time in Karachi than in Delhi, the bigger Dominion's capital; and that while in the latter city, though functioning in part on Pakistan's behalf, he would have been so near Mr. Nehru, whom he liked, as to be influenced by him. And Mr. Nehru detested the very idea of Pakistan. The point undeniably has weight.

Nevertheless, the arguments to put on the other side are weighty too. For if, before July, Lord Mountbatten found Congressmen

more to his taste than Leaguers – as seemed unmistakable – this
does not mean he would have perpetrated major injustices. He had
a very quick mind. And he had his reputation in Britain to think of.
Vigilant Conservative eyes were bent on him from London; and un-
fairness to Muslims, while he remained responsible for them, might
have been just the sort of thing they were watching for. And as
Joint Governor-General he could have proved useful to Pakistan in
ways not then open to anyone else. There was the fact that, in the
division of assets, India started with the advantage of having most of
them in her physical possession. In his proposed dual role, he could
have prevented her dishonestly retaining, as she did, much of Pakistan's share of the military stores. Or again if, as most Pakistanis
believe – wrongly in this author's view – Lord Mountbatten or his
entourage somehow influenced Sir Cyril Radcliffe[6] towards finalising
his Punjab Boundary Award detrimentally to Pakistan, then it
follows that the Award might have been different had he at the time
been Governor-General-designate of both Dominions. We can even
imagine that if, in October 1947, troops had had to be sent to Kashmir to forestall the sack of Srinagar by Pathan tribesmen, he might
in his dual role have felt that considerations of quicker and easier
transport, of communal principle, and of probable reactions in the
British Parliament and Press, all pointed to their being Muslim
troops; men, in fact, of the Pakistan Army. And it is unlikely that, in
such circumstances, F.-M. Auchinleck as Supreme Commander
would have demurred.

On balance, most non-Pakistani historians, looking at the facts as
now known, may think Mr. Jinnah's choice about the Governor-
Generalship was a mistake. But that, of course, would be a judgement based on hindsight. A British official, who then held a post
near the heart of things, writes: 'I would add a point about Jinnah's
decision, which I suggest should be borne in mind. He had, after all,
almost alone created Pakistan – or rather, at that stage, had forced
through an acceptance by the British and the Congress of the idea of
Pakistan. The odds against it, only a year or two before, had been
terrific. What more natural, and perhaps more necessary, than for
him to carry the thing through personally until its success could be
seen, and crowned by his own headship of the State? On a cold-
blooded calculation, I would agree with an estimate, made now,
that it would probably have been better for Pakistan had Mountbatten, as proposed, been Joint G.-G. of both Dominions for a while;
I think that this might have averted some of the excesses in the Punjab. But in the political and psychological conditions of June and

---

[6] Later Lord Radcliffe.

M

July 1947 it was inevitable, I believe, that Jinnah should insist on being G.-G.'

As July moved on and August approached, the pace of events grew quicker. Everyone seemed borne forward on an immense wave of uncontrollable change, so swift and turbulent that the ordinary person could not grasp what was happening around him, or where he was being carried. Millions found it incomprehensible that the well-established British, after so many decades, and only a few months after winning a great war, were really about to abandon power and go, and that such of them as stayed on would be under Indian or Pakistani authority. Even among the educated, there were many unable fully to foresee that two distinct nation-States – very unlikely to be as friendly as (say) Sweden and Norway, or the U.S.A. and Canada – would next month exist where, for a century or more, had been overriding unity; that in consequence unfamiliar frontier-posts and customs-checks would spring up, along new boundaries wriggling for hundreds of miles down both flanks of the subcontinent; that overseas, separate Indian and Pakistani diplomatic missions would emerge, to reflect rival foreign policies evolved in Delhi and Karachi; and that the Armed Forces would soon be divided, new and perhaps hostile ones arising in their stead.

The June 3rd plan had in fact been brief in the extreme about the Forces' future. A firm decision that they must be split was however reached in the Partition Council on June 30th, at the insistence alike of Congress and League; and detailed instructions about this were now beginning to reach units and formations, to the bewilderment of unpolitical men. Although a single Supreme Commander was then intended to have authority over the Forces till the final sorting out along communal lines not later than April 1948, it was specifically stated that, from August 15th, each new Dominion must have some troops under its operational control within its own territory. According to Ismay, Mr. Jinnah had been vigorous in demanding this.

Behind all the rush and bustle, in knowledgeable minds, lurked uneasiness about two big omissions previously mentioned: effective disposal of the Sikh problem; and the future of the princely States. And apart from such large general matters there were the countless personal implications of the change to consider : small things, when set against the background; but vital for those concerned. Men whose homes or jobs lay near controversial parts of the map sometimes found it hard to decide which of the two new countries they would want to live in, or even, in the case of Government personnel, which of the prospective successor-régimes they would rather serve.

Members of the Forces, trained to ignore politics, were particularly at a disadvantage, the more so if they happened to be overseas or freshly back from there. It is a fact that in the Army quite a number of Sikhs, commissioned and otherwise, in the first instance opted unhesitatingly for Pakistan, for the simple reason that their families owned land in West Punjab. A Muslim flying officer whom this writer knew, who was then with the Allied Forces in Japan, unwittingly cut himself off from family and wealth on Indian soil, because he happened to like Risalpur, and wanted to get his next posting there. For folk such as these, whether cheerfully ignorant, or (as a few were) in agonies of doubt, choices which would affect the individual's and his dependants' whole future, his ancestral and personal property, his contacts with relatives and friends, might need to be made while his mind was quite unready.

Within the Delhi Secretariat, the slicing apart of an entire Governmental organism with its rights and obligations and material equipment, and the massive movement of its employees military and civilian, was being organised, so far – and if we make allowance for the task's complexity, and the lurid background of carnage against which it was occurring – in admirably quick, sensible fashion. But civilian officials such as Chaudhuri Mohammad Ali and Mr. H. M. Patel were not yet sundered by gulfs of antagonism as the politicians largely were. They had been trained as members of the All-India Services; they respected each other, understood each other's point of view. The pressure of tasks to be done within that hustling time-table must however at times have been almost unbearable. Writing from personal knowledge, Menon describes how, 'as the day for the transfer of power drew nearer, and as the sheets in Lord Mountbatten's specially devised tear-off calendar became fewer and fewer, the activity in the Government Departments reached fever pitch. There was no Department that was not in one way or another concerned with the Partition arrangements, and energies were concentrated almost exclusively on this'. He tells of the politicians' stunned reaction to a memorandum prepared by officials 'On the Administrative Consequences of Partition', of which Ismay gives fuller details; and goes on to describe subsequent procedures : the setting up of the Partition Council, under which functioned the Steering Committee, which in its turn co-ordinated the doings of ten expert sub-committees dealing with the entire field of administration including records and personnel; assets and liabilities; central revenues; contracts, currency and coinage; economic relations, domicile, and foreign relations. And then there were the Joint Defence Council, and the Armed Forces Reconstitution Committee, busy disintegrating what in those days – apart perhaps from Russia's Siberian Army – was the best fighting machine in Asia; and to the public eye perhaps most crucial of all, the Boundary Commissions for slicing in twain both the Punjab and Bengal, each consisting of two Muslim and two Hindu high court judges, with a single British chairman presiding.

About the end of July, the grim but not unexpected fact was disclosed that within these Commissions the Muslim judges on the one side, and the Hindu judges on the other, had totally failed to agree. Decision therefore by prior arrangement devolved solely on the British chairman, Sir Cyril Radcliffe. His awards, it was indicated, would probably not come out until just after Partition. There has since been much speculation, some of it ugly, about the reasons for this timing, and about its effects. Authorities on the subject differ. There was however what seemed to be one 'leak', possibly deliberate: the virtual disclosure that the huge turbulent city of Calcutta, the place where the civil war had started, would owing to its predominantly non-Muslim population be assigned to India; the frontier would have to run somewhere farther east. This information, almost certainly, though perhaps few at the time clearly foresaw it, had a major influence on the paradoxical way in which, after dire predictions and a full year of strife and turmoil, the processes of Partition, in the event, went through with the minimum imaginable amount of difficulty in Bengal.

But a week or so before, about August 4th or 5th, from the remoter rural parts of Central Punjab, 1,000 miles or so away at the other side of the country, came the first tricklings of the reports that portended disaster. Systematic attacks of a novel type were being made on Muslim villages by roving bands of Sikhs, usually on horseback, and operating under what looked like military discipline. The first such attack was made on the night of July 31st, at a place called Jhand. With increasing rapidity and on a large scale others followed, mainly in Amritsar district as yet; at Garwal, Talwandi Araiyan, and elsewhere. Menon and Campbell-Johnson both write as if knowledge of these developments did not reach Delhi until after the wildly enthusiastic Independence Day celebrations there on August 15th. That is not so, as study of newspaper reports of the preceding week or more will show. Lumby, back in London, who lacked personal contact with the events he describes and was writing afterwards simply on the basis of published data, records that 'Gangs led by ex-soldiers and armed with automatic guns, rifles and bombs were roaming the countryside, attacking and burning villages and massacring their inhabitants. It was estimated that, in the Amritsar

district alone, nearly 1,000 people were killed during the first fortnight of August'.

The truth is that, despite all the warnings, leading public figures
in Delhi quite failed, for ten days or so, to grasp the significance of
the news gruesomely pouring in from the Central Punjab. The
Sikhs' war of revenge, so long foretold, had begun, and in a way
which the hapless Punjab Boundary Force, belatedly formed, proved
incapable of dealing with, despite all its discipline and gallantry — a
fact necessitating its disbandment within a month. Like the great
Calcutta killing of nearly a year before, what was happening proved
once again to be 'a new order in disorder'; an affair the effects of
which flared out swiftly, in reprisal and counter-reprisal, to involve
the whole Punjab including its princely States; tracts also of Western
U.P., of Southern Kashmir, and of the Frontier Province; princely
States south of the Punjab such as Bahawalpur, Alwar, Bharatpur;
and which, when it reached Delhi, came within a hairsbreadth of
plunging the whole subcontinent irretrievably in confusion; an affair
which brought death to hundreds of thousands, and set in motion
millions of refugees. It was into conditions such as these — about nine
weeks after the decision on June 3rd, 1947, to create her — that
Pakistan was born.

Chapter 14

Birth of a Nation – II

CHAOS is not really a describable thing. The idea of it can be conveyed only by random choice of episodes, considered typical. Some such episodes, with supporting comments, will be offered in this chapter, to exemplify the sort of scene that Pakistan was born into; for the nature, temperament and policies of the Pakistani State cannot be understood unless the circumstances of her birth are kept in mind. Fuller details may be found in other books,[1] or in contemporary newspaper accounts. The broad fact about those appalling three or four months, starting early in August 1947, simply is that nauseating brutalities were done on an unprecedented scale, by Hindus, Muslims, and Sikhs. Some of the larger slaughters by Hindus and Sikhs had been carefully planned, whereas few if any instances of this sort of wickedness can be found on the Muslim side; but though important, that fact is secondary. And persons in Western countries, disposed at first to feel contempt that such foul things should have been done, may be reminded of things done in Europe, not in far-off times – such as the seventeenth-century religious wars, to which the Indian subcontinent's experience in the 1940's is sometimes likened – but recently; and not during temporary gusts of rage and excitement, but calculatingly, over years, as a matter of cold, set policy. Writings such as Lord Russell of Liverpool's, or the evidence at the Eichmann trial, serve as a means of comparing what happened under the Hitler régime in Germany – now Britain's ally – and the more hot-blooded atrocities in South Asia during the same decade.

Foreign newspaper correspondents at Partition-time were torn between determination to see conditions in and around the Punjab for themselves, and fear that, if they went far from their base at Delhi, disrupted communications would prevent their dispatches reaching their offices as soon as their rivals'. Several however managed long journeys. Perhaps the best of the resulting articles were those for *The Times* by Ian Morrison, who had previously been its war correspondent in North Africa, Burma and elsewhere.[2] The following

---

[1] e.g. Tuker's, Campbell-Johnson's, Menon's, Ismay's, Moon's.
[2] He was later killed while its war correspondent in Korea.

is from a cable he sent from Jullundur on August 24th, depicting occurrences of a sort that had been in progress for about three weeks.

'"More horrible than anything we saw during the war", is the universal comment of experienced officers, British and Indian, on the present slaughter in East Punjab. The Sikhs are clearing East Punjab of Muslims, butchering hundreds daily, forcing thousands to flee westward, burning Muslim villages and homesteads, even in their frenzy burning their own. This violence has been organised from the highest levels of Sikh leadership, and it is being done systematically, sector by sector. Some large towns, like Amritsar and Jullundur, are now quieter, because there are no Muslims left. In a two hours' air reconnaissance of the Jullundur district at the week-end I must have seen 50 villages aflame.

'The Sikh jathas, armed mobs from 50 to 100 strong, assemble usually in the gurdwaras, their places of worship, before making a series of raids. Many jathas cross over from the Sikh (princely) States. The Muslims are usually armed only with staves. When threatened, they assemble on their roofs and beat gongs and drums to summon help from neighbouring Muslim communities, and prepare to throw stones at the attackers. The Sikhs attack scientifically. A first wave armed with firearms fires to bring the Muslims off their roofs. A second wave lobs grenades over the walls. In the ensuing confusion a third wave goes in with kirpans − the Sikh sabres, which are also religious emblems − and spears, and the serious killing begins. A last wave consists of older men, often Army pensioners with long white beards, who carry torches and specialise in arson. Mounted outriders with kirpans cut down those trying to flee.

'British officers have seen jathas that have included women and even children with spears. Appalling atrocities have been committed; bodies have been mutilated; none has been spared − men, women, or children. In one village, out of 50 corpses, 30 were those of women. One officer found four babies roasted to death over a fire.'

The intensification of the Sikhs' systematic rural attacks during the first half of August; their obvious links with similar attacks in or from the Sikh princely States, notably Patiala and Kapurthala; the fierce retaliation some days later of parts of West Punjab, especially around Lahore; and (most disastrous of all perhaps) the disarming by the East Punjab authorities of the large Muslim element in the police,[3] brought about by Independence Day on August 15th a collapse of administration on both sides of the new frontier; with the

---

[3] In Amritsar district this was done on August 10th, five days before British rule nominally ended, on the orders of the new Hindu deputy-commissioner-designate.

result that, by the third week of the month, gigantic panic-stricken two-way displacements of population were in progress, moving under appalling physical conditions, on a scale probably never before experienced in human history.

Many of these people went in foot-convoys, often to be set upon, looted, and slain. Muslim convoys walking from East Punjab were more straggly than Sikh ones moving in the reverse direction, and therefore suffered more. But road-trudging emigrants were in less dire peril than those trying to get away by train; for planned attacks on refugee-trains, after they had been derailed or otherwise halted, became a horrible speciality of the whole affair, and continued far into the autumn. At least the people trudging along afoot had some scope for active self-defence; they could move about, try to hide in the crops, band together with others of their kind. But if huddled in a train's separate compartments after a contrived stoppage, when (as often happened) the escort (if any) had been overpowered or turned treacherous, they were trapped, helpless, at any slaughterer's mercy.

A previously unpublished account of one such train-outrage follows,[4] written by Col. Sher Khan.[5] 'On September 22nd I left Lahore, after a meeting, for Amritsar, and arrived in the area of the Khalsa (Sikh) College at 1620 hours. There were very big crowds with spears and swords, and more to the south of the road. There was firing going on. I stopped near a Garhwal Regt. post in the Khalsa College; here I was told a train was being attacked. I inquired if they had done anything about it and they replied in the negative. I proceeded to Bde. H.Q. to tell about the attack. The Bde. Comd. had already gone out, and had ordered one coy. to the station. At 2000 hrs. I went down to the train one mile outside the station. It appeared that practically everyone on it, except thirteen Hindu soldiers of the guard, had been killed, wounded or abducted. I saw a British officer, a Lieutenant, lying dead along with one Muslim Havildar. There were still thousands of people, mainly Sikhs, shouting slogans. I was warned by the O.C. troops that it was dangerous for me to be there, and returned to my bungalow. The troops were in position, and the crowd (about 5,000 strong) 400–500 yards away.

'The following morning I went to the station, where the train had been pulled in during the night. I found Miss Sarabhai,[6] with one stretcher squad and about a dozen volunteers, rendering first-aid

---

[4] The fullest source for descriptions of these outrages is Tuker. Ismay's book contains a vivid example.

[5] Subsequently Major-General; C.G.S.-designate, Pakistan Army; killed in an aircrash near Karachi, 1949.

[6] A well-known Hindu welfare-worker.

to the wounded and evacuating some to hospital. They had done
this all night. I talked to some survivors. They said they were refugees
from Alwar State, and were put on the train at Delhi. Most of
their belongings were taken away at Delhi station. They were asked
to surrender any sharp weapons at Ambala. Some who had knives
did so. They were fired at near Beas. An attack by about 100 Sikhs
two or three stations the other side of Amritsar was beaten off by the
guard. After passing Amritsar, the train slowed down, then stopped.
Soon after, heavy firing started from both sides. Then hundreds of
Sikhs rushed the train. They first started collecting valuables off the
women, and throwing out boxes. Anyone resisting was killed by
sword, kirpan or spear. Then they started pulling out women, saying
come with us, those resisting being killed. Having done all the looting etc. they started killing. There was some firing from the train,
presumably from the escort, but it died down. Several bombs were
thrown into the carriages.

'I then talked to the hinder members of the guard. They said they
did open fire, but the Lieutenant Sahib was killed, and when the train
was rushed they were hard put to it to save themselves. These soldiers,
thirteen in number, said they had eight Muslims as well, and the
Lieutenant Sahib in command. They thought all had been killed.
They belonged to R.I. Artillery.

'It is impossible to estimate the number of dead, as they were
piled on top of each other in the compartments; between 1,200–1,500.
Altogether, forty lorries were sent to Lahore loaded with wounded,
including about 200 persons who had escaped serious injuries. The
train was pulled out of Amritsar towards Jullundur. The police said
they were going to dump the bodies in the Beas river.'

Some dramatic accounts exist of journeys across the Punjab unwittingly done at the height of the calamity by uninvolved British
folk: among them Henniker's, and Moon's. Here is one, hitherto not
put into print, from Miss Janet M. Lane, who during August 1947
was on holiday in Kashmir from her post at a school in Dehra Dun
(U.P.). It gives grim glimpses of conditions on the Pakistani side.
'At the time of Partition,' she records, 'I was in camp with friends
at Sonamarg. As my term began in September, I had to leave earlier
than they did; I set off alone about August 26th. We had heard
little news, but many rumours. The bus from Srinagar to 'Pindi[7] was
very empty, and until we passed Kohala (where Kashmir State
meets the Frontier Province) the journey was normal – although we
were told that, the day before, the bus had been stopped and twelve

[7] Abbreviation for Rawalpindi.

Hindus taken out and killed. After Kohala, we were held up several times by lads armed with sticks, axes and occasionally a gun; all passengers were made to get out, and the boys searched under the seats and among the luggage for hidden Hindus. As we had few passengers, and none of them seemed to raise suspicions, we were allowed to go on.

'The bus reached 'Pindi station just as a train came in from Kohat. It had been shot up. Ambulances had come to fetch the wounded, who were being carried out; many passengers had been killed. The night train, which I had planned to catch, was cancelled; and I spent a rather grim night alone in the station rest-rooms, and was most grateful, next morning, when two British officers and an American professor came and insisted on my travelling with them. The journey as far as Lahore was uneventful, although we saw many burning villages, and processions of fugitives with their cattle and goods walking along the fields.

'Lahore station was in chaos; and as we got out of the train a man close to me was stabbed and fell. I was taken into the station-master's office, while my kind fellow-travellers went to arrange for an Army truck to take me to a missionary house in Lahore. I was told there would be no train on to Saharanpur (in U.P.) next day, but was advised to ring up frequently, in case one was arranged after all. In Lahore I got in touch with another missionary lady, Miss Rumbold, who had been camping at Sonamarg and had left there the day before me. On her way from 'Pindi she had had a trying experience. Having caught the night train it stopped in the middle of the night, and (her) door was opened and railway officials brought in a little girl aged about ten, who had had both hands cut off, and asked Miss Rumbold to look after her. The child's father, a Hindu station-master, together with his wife, had been killed before the girl's eyes.

'At last Miss Rumbold and I were told that a train would probably leave on the Sunday morning. We were put into a first-class carriage and locked in. The station was even more crowded than before; whole families of refugees with their goods and cattle were camping on the platforms. I saw one poor old man pushed off the platform in front of an incoming train. At about 9 a.m. we set off very slowly. We often passed groups of dead bodies which seemed just to have been left lying. At one place the train stopped, and the door of the next carriage opened, and an elderly, decent-looking Sikh was thrown out, (having been) stabbed, and was kicked down the embankment. It was a dreadful helpless feeling to be locked in unable to do anything. We reached Saharanpur about midnight.

The train that took us out of Lahore was, I think, the last that ran from Lahore to Amritsar until the service was eventually restored' (about 1955).

By the second week of September, the carnage in the now divided Punjab had spilt over heavily, as mentioned, into adjacent territories to north, south, east and west; and for a while seemed likely to pour uncontrollably on. And a curious point is that, of the four outflowings of disorder, it was the northward one – the one which then attracted least attention and indeed whose very existence, amidst the confusion, was largely unknown – that had the most intractable long-term effects.

This was the rising against the Hindu Maharajah of Kashmir and his officials, away up in that ramshackle great State's obscure Sudhnuti tract near West Punjab, by the sturdy Muslim peasantry, who included many ex-soldiers. They and their forbears had suffered long misrule under the princely régime; and the reports now reaching them of organised butcheries of their fellow-Muslims by Sikhs and Hindus on the plains, and their consequent fears for their own future under Hindu Raj, goaded them into action. Their country however is a wild tangle of bulky, forest-draped mountains, hard of access; roads through it, owing to intentional neglect by the Maharajah's Administration of a notoriously troublesome section of his subjects (very different from the pliant people around Srinagar), were few and bad; and communications across the Punjab to the main news-gathering centres in Delhi and Karachi had collapsed. So such knowledge of the rising as reached the outside world was fragmentary, and largely discounted. The best authority on it is Symonds; but his important material was not gathered till several weeks after it started. The next chapter goes into the affair further.

Not much was heard at the time, either, about the happenings in the south and south-east, in and near such princely States as Bahawalpur in Pakistan, and Alwar and Bharatpur in India. The bad but not disastrous Bahawalpur disorders have since been brilliantly depicted, from special contemporary knowledge, by Moon. More sinister were the events in Alwar and Bharatpur, which brought to an atrocious finale the struggle already mentioned, which had been intermittently going on since May in the adjoining Gurgaon district of the Punjab, between the local Muslim Meo tribe and their Hindu neighbours the Ahirs and Jats. This hitherto had seemed ordinary communal strife such as the locality had experienced before, though aggravated somewhat by visiting R.S.S.S. agents from Delhi. Then suddenly, early in August, the nearby tracts of Alwar and Bharatpur, which had been but little affected, became violently involved, and the conflict shuttled back and forth between the princely territories and what was still British India. Anyone reading the accounts of this development painstakingly assembled in Tuker's book could hardly avoid concluding that it was organised by Hindu officials of the two States, bent upon the Muslims' extermination. Particularly sickening are the reports of armed detachments of the State Forces repeatedly participating with Hindu mobs in determined onslaughts against Meo villages.

Tuker's concern in the matter was military. Meos had made good recruits, and many soldiers on leave or ex-soldiers on pension were scattered about the disturbed area. It is from these unpolitical men, or those who escaped, that evidence was obtained of organised massacres such as at Mandawar and Silgaon. Some of these hapless Meo survivors, while in flight, later became victims of the appalling attack by Sikhs outside Amritsar railway station already described. It is noteworthy that, early in the next year, the Indian Government itself stamped heavily on the Hindu fanaticism that developed in Bharatpur and Alwar at Partition-time, because of evidence that it had contributed to Mr. Gandhi's murder.

So much for the north and the south. The westwards – or north-westwards – overflow was to the Frontier Province. Rioting occurred in Peshawar and Nowshera between September 7th and 10th. This, too, got less attention than it deserved, because it synchronised with the eastwards overflow – the worse rioting in Delhi to which we shall turn in a moment. But the Frontier rioting, though soon finished, was important not only in itself, but because of its bearings later on the Kashmir affair. It had been preceded by premonitory 'incidents': a nasty one at Haripur on August 26th; casualties and arson soon after at Takhti-Bhai in Mardan district; and a bold attack on a train thought to contain Sikh and Hindu troops between Kohat and Khushalgarh.[8] On September 4th the Governor Sir George Cunning-ham[9] noted that it became 'obvious, about ten days ago, that unless the Punjab slaughters ceased it would be impossible to hold back our people; there have been so many revolting stories of massacres of Muslims in East Punjab, that even if they are 25 per cent true, they are enough to make our Muslims see red'. On September 7th, re-turning to Peshawar from a short visit to Nathiagali, 'we could see,' he wrote that evening, 'as we approached the Fort, that some-

---

[8] Probably the 'train from Kohat' mentioned in Miss Lane's account.
[9] He had retired from the Governorship in 1946, after seven years, but at Mr. Jinnah's request had come back for a further tenure in August 1947.

thing unusual was on, from the way people were standing about and looking; and we found all the gates shut against us. The trouble had started by a Sikh sentry of the 19th Lancers, shooting (possibly accidentally) a Muslim sepoy of the 3rd/8th Punjabis. The news had spread, and Hindus and Sikhs were being attacked. In the evening the murdering increased, and probably 100 Hindus and Sikhs have been killed, including many of our clerks and their families.' Next day, 'things (were) quieter in the cantonments, though with stray murders going on; but looting started in the city, and fire. This morning I sent for three platoons of Kurram Militia[10] to come and help, as our police are thin on the ground and troops few just at this moment. The trouble is that police and constabulary, and to a lesser extent Muslim troops, have really connived both at murdering and looting, in fact obviously having a good deal of sympathy with them. The animosity is primarily against Sikhs'. Affairs got worse as the day proceeded, and an official report says that large crowds of armed villagers, accompanied by Afridis from tribal territory, penetrated into the Dabgari and Gunj areas, where determined attacks were made on Hindu localities, and two serious fires started which continued throughout the night, despite attempts to prevent their spread by demolishing houses.

The situation had improved by September 9th, and Sir George recorded that 'the troops did excellently in the city last night. I have been sending some respected Muslims round in cars to talk to the people, mainly on the theme that this sort of thing is ruinous both to Pakistan, and to the Muslims who remain in India. In the evening I went down and had a round of golf; we were the only living things visible except for two caddies who turned up from somewhere'.

However, that same afternoon trouble broke out in Nowshera, eastward along the grand trunk road, and lasted two days. 'Local Khattak villagers,' observes the report, 'had been incensed by attacks on Khattak labourers by Sikhs in the Punjab; and a violent mob launched an attack on the Nowshera Sadar area.' This sort of thing went on throughout September 10th, the 'total approximate casualties being 122 non-Muslims killed and six women kidnapped'. During the period of these Frontier disturbances, traffic on the main line between Peshawar and the Punjab was stopped for four days, by derailment of a train between Jehangira and Khairabad. Before dawn on September 10th, however, all Sikh troops in the Peshawar area were successfully got away eastwards to India by road. 'This, I think,' wrote Sir George, 'will relieve things a good deal when it

[10] A unit of the Frontier Corps; see Chapter 12, p. 154.

becomes known'; and in fact the trouble in the Pathan country died out soon after.

The grave Delhi riots of September 7th–10th have been described by many pens: those of newspaper men writing at the time; or authors such as Campbell-Johnson, Menon, and Ismay – Ismay is particularly good – recording their impressions afterwards; and of private persons whose notes are available to inquirers. So details need not be offered here. Reliable estimates place the deathroll at about 2,000, and much higher figures have been given. But apart from this, the outbreak had a significance of its own, which justified widespread attention. First, it happened almost on the doorstep of the new independent Indian Government, where influential people of all sorts lived, and who could see and report what was going on. For the savageries against an outnumbered and terrified Muslim minority, the killing and burning and looting, were not confined to the crowded poverty-stricken areas of the old walled city, nor to the nearby villages; they swept at times unchecked along New Delhi's wide tree-lined avenues, past the huge Lutyens-Baker Government buildings of the recently extinct British régime, the arcaded modern shopping quarter, the comfortable bungalows of the officials.

Further, it was clear that, if the trouble was not decisively stopped at this particular point on the map, it would pour eastwards into the adjacent U.P.; already, the districts between the rivers Jumna and Ganges were dangerously disturbed, with communal 'incidents' becoming frequent. Delhi in fact, as before in her history, was serving as a strategic barrier against invasion from the west: this time, invasion by an acutely virulent type of communal disorder overflowing from the Punjab. If the capital of the new India failed to resist, if Delhi fell to the evil, anarchy seemed certain to rush on, east and south. No one could guess where it might halt.

It is worth remark that, in this crisis, India's leaders Mr. Nehru and Sardar Patel turned for aid to the British Governor-General they themselves had chosen, Lord Mountbatten, drawing on his experience in dealing with dangerous emergencies, and temporarily transferring much authority to him. And before the third week of September, thanks largely to his chairmanship of the riots committee that had been specially set up, and to Mr. Nehru's energy, the outbreak may be said to have been curbed, though as Tuker observed, 'for weeks afterwards, no Muslim servant from the residential quarter of New Delhi could venture out of his master's compound to visit the bazaar'.

Meanwhile, in fear and squalor, many thousands of Delhi's

Muslim citizens who had fled their homes lived herded in improvised refugee-camps, one of which, by an irony of fate, was the bastioned Purana Qila or Old Fort, built in the sixteenth century by the emperors Humayun and Sher Shah just when Muslim Raj in India was reaching its greatest phase. It 'was an appalling sight', says Ismay; 'there was no shelter, no doctor, no sanitary arrangements, no means of communication. I was surrounded, this time by a circle of men ten or twelve deep; and once more the cry went up, "Sahib, help us!".' Many of these Muslims were Pakistani-to-be; people who had opted for the smaller Dominion but been unable to get there, because of the slaughter and derailments in the Punjab: the poor, mainly; but members of the Delhi aristocracy also; Government officials high and low; mercantile people of all sorts. They may have seemed demoralised in the camps; but the spirit of fortitude bred amidst these adversities, when eventually they were taken to Karachi by air, helped Pakistan to get through the daunting stresses and confusions of her first few months of life.

There was indeed, at the start, little but human will for her to live on. At Delhi, the new Indian régime inherited all the splendid buildings and equipment of the Imperial Secretariat; but at Karachi the Pakistan Government scarcely possessed typewriters, telephones, desks, ink or stationery; and its personnel struggled with urgent tasks of creative nation-building not in palatial rooms of carved red sandstone, but temporarily in corners of shabby tin hutments and other structures left over from World War II. They focused their glowing hopes, in this shared new venture, on their Quaid-i-Azam, their own Governor-General and fellow-Muslim Mr. Jinnah. It was inspiring to visit Pakistan, and to feel the enthusiasms that did away with difficulties, in those early days.

Chapter 15

Mainly about Kashmir

MANY would agree that the root of all evil, in the post-Partition relations between India and Pakistan, has lain in the Kashmir dispute; in the bitter quarrel about the ill-constructed princely State in the subcontinent's northernmost tip whose ruler, as indicated in the last chapter, was Hindu, but whose inhabitants were mainly Muslim. Many Pakistanis, twenty years after Partition, have perhaps now rather forgotten what happened to Junagadh, and even to Hyderabad; to the never-delivered military stores, and to the financial balances which India withheld for several months in 1947–48. And other quarrels have proved soluble or partly so, for a while at least.

Most of the protracted bitter wrangles about refugees' property have now been disposed of, or petered out of their own accord. In 1951, India reluctantly brought herself to recognise that Pakistan had had the right, during the international currency crisis of 1949, to resist devaluation of her rupee,[1] and a sixteen-months' mutual economic blockade was called off. In 1955, as mentioned already, regular passenger railway services between India and West Pakistan, after eight years' cessation, were at last resumed and continued to run till September 1965. In 1959–60, better frontier demarcation on both flanks of the subcontinent resulted in a marked decrease, during the next four years or so, in the recurrent alarming affrays between the two countries' border-patrols. And in 1961 the very dangerous dispute about the irrigation waters of the Indus basin was settled after patient mediation by the World Bank. All these matters, over the years, proved in one form or another capable of some adjustment. But the Kashmir dispute, ever since it dramatically broke out in October 1947, has remained utterly deadlocked and a cause of passionate ill-feeling. It involved the two countries in fourteen months' localised fighting on Kashmir soil in 1947–48; it brought them to within a hairsbreadth of general hostilities in March 1950 and again in August 1951; and in September 1965, because of it, war between them did occur.

Its origins can plainly be traced – like those of the Sikhs' 'war of

---

[1] India then devalued hers, alongside sterling. Pakistan decided to stay as she was. India thereupon refused to recognise the Pakistani decision. See Chapter 17.

revenge', and of the Boundary Force's failure to cope with it – to the impetuous and (some might reckon) unprincipled haste with which the British, under Lord Mountbatten's lead, extricated themselves in August 1947 from their governing responsibilities. As was indicated earlier, the future of the princely States, a huge problem, territorially and historically, was never squarely faced by the British Government or the Viceroy until almost the last moment, a mere three weeks before the date fixed for the transfer of power, when a vigorous though morally questionable attempt was made to dispose of it in tidy and conclusive fashion. At an urgently summoned conference with States' Rulers in Delhi on July 25th – the first and last he had with them – the great-nephew of Edward VII in effect repudiated assurances of protection given by that monarch to the Princes in 1908,[2] and threw them to the nationalist wolves. They had the right, he acknowledged, after British paramountcy ended – as it was on the verge of doing – to try to stay independent if they wished, or to link up with either new Dominion; but there was no possibility of their getting help or encouragement from Britain after then. Their interests, in his view, simply lay in deciding, now, to accede on the best terms they could get – these might never recur – to the particular Dominion which their place on the map, and the communal leanings of the majority of their subjects, most pointed to; and he was ready to assist them in this.

However, the time left for these old-fashioned and often dilatory personages to make up their minds proved insufficient, and Independence Day arrived with the rulers of three States, one small, but two very large and important, still dangerously undecided. It is astonishing that there were not many more. No proper attempt had been made over the years by the British régime to prepare these hapless autocrats for the gigantic changes now so rapidly in progress, and their entire dynastic and personal futures were at stake. We may be sure that, had the Viceroy been someone less 'dynamic' than Lord Mountbatten, less persuasive and charming – and less Royal – had he, for instance, been as ponderous in action as Lord Linlithgow, the great majority of States' Rulers – and large and small they numbered over 560 – would have reached August 15th undecided too.

It could of course be said that Britain's assurances of 1908 to the Indian Princes were even more unwise – because bigger in geographical implications – than, for example, those of 1899 to her ally Portugal for protection of her overseas territories, which Mr. Nehru

[2] These assurances repeated those given by Victoria in her Proclamation on becoming Empress in 1858.

N

made such unpleasant nonsense of in 1961 by his seizure of Goa. Circumstances undeniably do alter cases; and realism is not a word to despise. Nevertheless, it remains true that, in neither instance – the abandonment of the Princes to Indian nationalism in 1947, or of Portugal to it in 1961 – did the British enhance their reputation for honouring their word.

The small State referred to, among the three dangerously undecided ones, was Junagadh, on the Kathiawar coast about half-way between Bombay and Karachi. Most of its inhabitants were Hindu; its ruler the Nawab – not an impressive person, by all accounts – was Muslim. Within the terms of Lord Mountbatten's advice, the Nawab's best course was to seek accession to India, because of his subjects' communal leanings; and a mild amazement was the general public reaction – for Junagadh in itself was of negligible importance, indeed most people had scarcely heard of it – when the fact came to popular notice in mid-September, amidst a welter of vastly bigger, bloodcurdling events, that he had in fact, a few days after Partition, asked to accede to Pakistan.

What the Government of Pakistan's motives were for agreeing to this, and presumably for having encouraged it, is not known. Campbell-Johnson, unkind as usual, hints at a complex 'trap', carefully set by the Pakistani Cabinet for India's detriment. But it seems likelier that the decision was rapidly made, on ill-considered though doubtless hostile impulse, amidst tremendous pressure of other business. In any case, it proved very unwise. It could indeed be upheld legally (and Mr. Jinnah perhaps attached too much weight to legal things); for as explained, the Princes strictly speaking were free to accede to either Dominion – or to none. And had the times been more normal, it might have been just sustainable geographically too, because of Junagadh's maritime position. But that seems about the most that can be said. It did Pakistan no sort of practical good; it ruined the foolish Nawab and his family; its subsequent uses in argument about Kashmir were not to Pakistan's advantage, for they could cut both ways; and relations at the time between India and Pakistan being what they were – acrimonious in the extreme – it caused India disproportionate anger. When it became clear that the Pakistani Government was serious in accepting the accession, the Indians moved troops towards the Junagadh area; soon, threatening displays of armed strength were being made; and a 'provisional government of free Junagadh' was permitted to function on Indian soil, headed by a distant relative of Mr. Gandhi. Then minor disorders within the State were fostered, or at any rate occurred; on

October 26th the Nawab fled to Pakistan; and a few days later the Indian forces marched in, and occupied the State 'to assist in maintenance of order'. A technique of aggrandisement had been learnt, to be reapplied later elsewhere : not only in 1961 successfully against Goa, and in modified form in 1950–51 and in 1961–2 against Nepal, but in 1948, as we shall now briefly describe, against another of the three princely States which on Independence Day had remained undecided, and a very much bigger and more important one – Hyderabad.

The Hyderabad affair needs examining here out of proper chronological sequence. It broke out several months later than the more intricate Kashmir affair, but it ended decisively and very abruptly; and though its geographical scale was quite different from that of Junagadh, its communal context was identical; namely, that history had so arranged things that a Muslim ruler, the Nizam – incidentally, not a very impressive person either – reigned over a population mainly Hindu.

Under the British Raj, Hyderabad had been acknowledged as the premier princely State of India. The Nizam stood in a class distinct from any other ruler, and was officially designated the British Government's 'faithful ally'. Since 1857, moreover, he and his forbears had been widely looked upon throughout the subcontinent as the main surviving inheritors of the Moghul tradition. Even excluding Berar – a large tract leased under duress to the British – the State covered about 82,000 square miles, an area roughly comparable, say, to that of Britain (including Scotland), or West Germany, or Rumania. Its total population at the 1941 Census stood at about 16 millions. As a potentially independent entity however, it had one great physical disadvantage. It was landlocked; August 1947 found it embedded in the Indian Union. Unlike Junagadh, it lacked access to the sea. And it contrasted with Kashmir in having no direct landward contact with Pakistan.

But despite that adverse fact the Nizam, relying on his State's size, and wealth, and historical prestige, indicated during the autumn a strong preference for avoiding accession to either Dominion and making it independent, as he had the legal right to do. Persuasion and pressure then began to be applied, by Lord Mountbatten and the Indian Government; indeed, there were some who said that a factor which had weighed with the Congress leaders, in asking him to stay on as Governor-General of free India, was that he and his Royal British associations might be used against recalcitrant Princes in exactly this way. Details of the protracted and sometimes ludicrous discussions which ensued need not be gone into, nor of the rash activities of an extremist Muslim organisation, the Razakars, within the State itself; for the fate of Hyderabad, after September 1948, lies outside this book's scope.

But what did at the time acutely concern Pakistan, because attempts, she guessed, would soon be made at applying it against herself – as indeed were plainly threatened, during the war-like crises of 1950 and 1951 – was the manner of Hyderabad's extinction: virtually the same as Junagadh's. Border incidents, fomented internal disturbances, and menacing military moves culminated suddenly – at the very moment, it so happened, of Mr. Jinnah's death in Pakistan, a frightful disaster for that country – in what the Gandhian pacifists ruling at Delhi euphemistically termed 'police action', headed by tanks and Spitfires. Large though Hyderabad was, and impressive in her Islamic traditions, the new Indian régime, helped by British military advisers, in an elegant little operation almost perfectly planned and executed, effectively subjugated it in less than five days.

In Kashmir, the third princely State which remained undecided on Independence Day, the communal roles, as mentioned, were reversed. It is that which has made the quarrel over it so disastrous, the 'root of all evil' in Indo-Pakistani affairs. The bulk of its people, about 77 per cent, were Muslim; but its ruler or Maharajah – in many ways a regrettable character – was Hindu. Yet India, by resort this time to a totally opposite set of arguments, not democratic but dynastic – and once again to armed force – contrived, in the latter part of 1947, to overrun the richer and more populous half of it, and has since remained there unbudged, professing moreover a legal right to the remainder. How so paradoxical and indeed shocking a position was reached must now be examined.

Kashmir – or more correctly the princely State of Jammu and Kashmir – was just a trifle larger than Hyderabad when deprived of Berar. And besides size, it had something which Hyderabad had not: great strategic importance, owing to its position in high Central Asia close to Russia, China, Afghanistan and Tibet. On the other hand its population amounted to only about 4 millions,[3] a quarter of Hyderabad's, owing to its mountainousness. Near its centre, around Srinagar, lay the renowned and fertile and fairly populous Vale – the real Kashmir as generally understood, and the main region which India laid hold of in 1947; a region of extraordinary scenic beauty, but perhaps unique also in its long record of human woe – exploited

[3] 1941 Census.

for centuries by conqueror after conqueror; by such appalling pre-Muslim monarchs as Mihirakula the White Hun, or the tyrannical Shankaravarman; then, in the fourteenth and fifteenth centuries, by a line of Muslim adventurers, who maintained themselves in independence of the Delhi sultans and included the fanatical iconoclast Sikander 'Bhut-Shikan'; then by the mighty Moghuls – who however gave it some splendid memorials in their ornamental gardens; and after them, by Afghans proper, mostly barbaric; by the brutal Sikhs of Ranjit Singh's day; and then by a Dogra Hindu dynasty of rather shady origins from the hills to the south. As a result of all this, the unfortunate inhabitants of the Vale, though talented in many ways, tended to be a spiritless, evasive lot, easily overawed; very different from the Dogras of the south of the State, the Sudhans of the south-west,[4] or the Gilgiti peoples of the north. Perhaps the most shameful part of the story was the abject condition to which they were reduced, by the rapacity of the Maharajah and his officials, between the Dogras' British-supported access to power in 1846 and the revenue-settlement which Lansdowne's Administration insisted upon in 1889. Vivid glimpses of this are to be found in Walter Lawrence's and E. F. Knight's writings.

So much, briefly, as introduction. Now for the events of the latter part of 1947. Kashmir had from the outset been looked on by Muslim Leaguers as geographically an integral part of the Pakistan-concept, and indeed, as mentioned in Chapter 4, the 'k' in Pakistan specifically stands for Kashmir. Soon after the June 3rd announcement however signs developed that influential Hindus were disinclined to let affairs rest on this basis. The ruler was Hindu; might not this be used to swing Kashmir into the Indian orbit? That such thoughts were astir seemed unmistakable from the Press, and from conversations. Mr. Nehru's emotional involvement in the State's affairs – he was a Kashmiri pandit by ancestry – had already shown itself, both in his writings, and in his odd conduct during the previous summer's negotiations with the British Cabinet Mission, when he dashed off to Kashmir on a relatively trifling political pretext. And during the few weeks remaining between the June 3rd announcement and Independence Day, the State had several other noteworthy visits: from Acharya Kirpalani, now President of the Congress party; from rulers of certain princely States in East Punjab, notably Patiala and Kapurthala, States where appalling slaughter of Muslims was soon to begin; and most suggestive of all, from Mr. Gandhi, who had never

[4] Occupants of the Sudhnuti tract already mentioned, part of the Poonch province of the State; see Chapter 14, p. 187.

shown marked interest in Kashmiri affairs during his political career as yet.

And before long much curious rumour got afloat – people experienced in the subcontinent's ways are wary both of believing rumour and of ignoring it – to the effect that Mr. Gandhi had succeeded where Acharya Kirpalani had failed; that his influence, coinciding with that wielded over the superstitious Maharani by a Brahmin priest in the princely entourage, had persuaded the Maharajah that accession to India was his destined and proper course; that he would announce this when opportunity arose; and that assurances of it had been privily passed to Delhi. On the other hand, there were those who said that the Maharajah remained in a mood of obstinate, feeble indecision – which seemed rather in character. That, evidently, was the impression formed by Lord Mountbatten, and later by Ismay, who successively visited the State in June and August to press on him the urgent need for declaring what he meant to do. At the crucial moment he evaded the former's attentions by sudden inability to be seen, owing to 'colic'. And Ismay has amusingly recounted the impossibility of engaging him in any political discussion at all.

But besides all this, some concrete facts did emerge. During July, he enlarged his army – it was overwhelmingly Hindu-Sikh, few Muslims were ever recruited to it, despite their being 77 per cent of the population – and moved units to the Poonch and Jammu areas, not far from the Punjab boundary. Those were doubtless reasonable precautions in themselves, at so critical a time; but they were made noteworthy by the simultaneous issue of orders that Muslim civilians in those areas having weapons must surrender them. And as Independence Day passed, and the State's future remained undisclosed, there were what seemed other pointers : the abrupt dismissal from the Prime Ministership of Mr. Kak, a Westernised Kashmiri pandit who was understood to have recommended accession to Pakistan on practical grounds; the appointment by Mr. Nehru as Minister without portfolio in the Indian Cabinet at Delhi of Mr. Gopalaswami Ayyengar, an able, reputedly anti-Muslim Brahmin who had been Prime Minister of Kashmir from 1937 to 1943; and then the very significant release from jail in Srinagar of Sheikh Abdullah, leader of one of the State's two political parties, the pro-Indian National Conference, although the leader of the rival pro-Pakistani Muslim Conference, Chaudhuri Ghulam Abbas, remained incarcerated. There had also, amid the fog of rumour during these weeks, been interesting reports of road-building projects or activities in the State's extreme south-eastern edge, near the Indian border. The atmosphere in the Vale at this time, heavy with whisper and suspense, intrigue and obscure surmise, is well depicted in Wilfrid Russell's book.

Meanwhile, in the Sudhnuti tract of Poonch province, an event had as we know occurred of which, at the time, the outside world learnt almost nothing, and which Indian propaganda has since persistently brushed aside; an event which, linked with its horrible and speedy sequel in Jammu province, bulks far larger, in human terms, than the much-publicised inrush of Pathan tribesmen via Baramula towards the end of October – which was the actual precipitating cause of the Indo-Pakistani crisis. Alarmed by the strengthening of the Maharajah's army, by his order that local civilians must give up weapons, and by the continuing lurid reports of rioting in the nearby Punjab, the Sudhan foresters and herdsmen and petty cultivators, from their dwellings amidst little terraced fields on the Himalayan slopes, rose in revolt against the princely régime, whose exactions they had long bitterly resented, and against which they had managed to stage a minor rising in the early 1930's. The revolt started with scattered incidents in the last week of July, and by the end of August was well under way. But confusion in the Punjab, then, was such that authentic contemporary news of it never reached the Press. The best authority on it, as mentioned, is Symonds,[5] who also gives particulars of the atrocious tax-system under which the Sudhans groaned. Essentially, theirs was a straightforward peasant revolt, the religious beliefs of the participants being irrelevant; an uprising of the oppressed against ancient feudal tyrannies; the sort of thing that ought to have got sympathetic acknowledgement from someone of Mr. Nehru's ideals. His then helper and confidant, Sheikh Abdullah, frankly stated the facts as early as October 21st.[6]

Besides being a sturdy lot, the Sudhans had some military experience to draw on. The recruiting authorities in British India had long ago recognised their qualities, and during World War II 40,000 or more of them had served in the undivided Indian Army. In consequence, despite woeful shortage of arms – which they strove to correct by sending inquirers to the village arms-factories away in the

[5] Then a welfare worker of the Friends' Relief Unit. Sarwar Hasan and Ferguson are also worth referring to. The present writer travelled in the Sudhnuti country in 1952, gaining some direct knowledge (see *Horned Moon*); his job in India had precluded his making the journey before.

[6] In a speech at Delhi. 'The people of Poonch had started a people's movement for the redress of their grievances. It was not communal.' In 1953, when the Sheikh's views deviated from the Indian Government's, he was imprisoned, and has remained so except for two brief intervals since.

Pathan tribal country – their revolt achieved quick successes against the Maharajah's forces, who worsened things for themselves by indiscriminate burning of Sudhan villages. The smoke could be seen from as far as the Murree hills in West Punjab, and is remembered to this day. By the end of September, large tracts of Poonch province had been freed of princely rule – permanently, as affairs turned out.

But in the Jammu province, things went very differently. There, unlike every other part of the State, Hindus and Sikhs slightly outnumbered Muslims; and within a period of about eleven weeks starting in August, systematic savageries, similar to those already launched in East Punjab and in Patiala and Kapurthala, practically eliminated the entire Muslim element in the population, amounting to 500,000 people. About 200,000 just disappeared, remaining untraceable, having presumably been butchered, or died from epidemics or exposure. The rest fled destitute to West Punjab. And although, owing to conditions in the now divided Punjab generally, the full truth about this appalling pogrom, as also about the extent of the State officials' and indeed of the Maharajah's personal complicity in it took some time to reach Delhi, leading Congressmen were well aware of it by November. This writer talked about it early in the following month with Mr. Gandhi, deducing that, even more than the carnage in and around Delhi itself, it explained the despairing mood of that great teacher of ahimsa[7] during his last few weeks of life.

It is against this background that the dramatic but over-notorious happenings set in train by the Pathans' irruption into the Vale up the Baramula road need to be set. Compared with events in Poonch and particularly in Jammu – which in the main preceded it – the sufferings which it caused were small.

As has been mentioned, the leaders of the Sudhnuti revolt – which later evolved into the 'Azad Kashmir' movement[8] – had sent men across the Indus plain into Pathan tribal territory to seek arms. At this time, and on into November, the future political relations (if any) of the quasi-autonomous Pathan tribes with Pakistan were entirely uncertain. Discussions had begun, and it was hoped that these formidable, restless people would decide to accede to the new-formed State, if only – by the cynical – because their scope for mischief would be greater otherwise; but the necessary jirgas[9] had not been held. It would be fair to say that the Pakistani authorities felt

---

[7] Non-violence.
[8] Azad means free.
[9] Tribal assemblies.

frightened of the tribes, and conscious that, at least for the nonce, they lacked the physical means for coping with them. The Pakistan Army as yet scarcely existed, it was in process of formation out of the previous Army of undivided India; bits of the latter were still being shuttled about the map, Hindu and Sikh ones remaining untransferred on Pakistani soil, and Muslim ones on Indian. And for decades, the tribes had proved an intractable, dangerous thorn in the flesh of the much stronger British régime. As recently as 1937-8, those of Waziristan alone, for months, had pinned down no fewer than 50,000 troops of the Imperial forces in sanguinary guerrilla warfare.

Two other factors need stressing. As was explained in Chapter 12, since the spring of 1947 the tribes had taken interest in the civil strife raging across the subcontinent's northern part. Increasingly, their Islamic fervour had been aroused; political officers found difficulty in curbing it. By September, the horrible incoming reports of their co-religionists' fate at Sikh hands in East Punjab had whipped this up almost to frenzy – which the outbreak of riots in Peshawar and Nowshera did nothing to allay.[10] And unfortunately, in one sense – here comes the second factor – several of the men holding high posts in the Pakistani Administration during those early days were British : men who, where zealotries of the Muslim Faith such as jihad[11] were concerned, Muslims had to assume were neutral if not hostile, and therefore needing to be hoodwinked. These points should be borne in mind, when the Baramula affair is approached.

It is not one in which the men involved, whether tribal or Pakistani proper, can retrospectively take much pride. Pluck and daring were shown; but also greed, and misapplied brutality. There had to be subterfuge about it, for the reasons explained; but as well, there was bad discipline and bad judgement. Worst, there was the grave practical stigma of eventual unsuccess. The affair opened suddenly on October 19th, when about 900 Mahsuds – the wildest tribe of all – set off in motor-trucks from Waziristan. Others from nearby soon followed: Wazirs, Daurs, Bhittanis, Khattaks, Turis; and some Afridis from farther north. And before the leading British personages on the Frontier – governor, chief secretary, divisional commander – knew what was happening, the spearhead of the force, about 2,000 strong, had slipped across the strategic bridges on the Indus at Khushalgarh and Attock, and was away towards the Kashmir border

---

[10] A publication entitled *Intelligence Reports concerning Tribal Repercussions to the Events in the Punjab, Kashmir, and India* (Lahore, Superintendent of Government Printing, 1948), provides detailed evidence.
[11] Religious war.

at Domel. Mohmands soon joined, also Swatis and men of Dir, some of these ferrying themselves over by rafts.

It seems clear that Pakistani politicians and civilian officials must have connived at this, helping the tribesmen to get vehicles and petrol and supplies, and ensuring that preparations were kept secret.[12] But it may be questioned whether, if the senior British officials had known what was astir, they could have stopped it – or would have been wise to try. For the tribesmen believed themselves on jihad; they were off to attack infidels, Hindus and Sikhs who had been butchering and outraging Muslims in the Sudhnuti country, the Punjab, and farther east. What would the effects on Pakistan have been, scared as she then was of the tribes, if Christian officials in her employ had sought to intervene? In her then new-born, unorganised state, she certainly could not afford a tribal war. And would Pakistani soldiers and police in such a case have obeyed orders to shoot, if given, originating from sources known to be non-Muslim? And if they had, might not enraged civilians then have rioted against the 50,000 or so Hindus and Sikhs still in the Province? Perhaps it was as well that the leading British personnel, kept in the dark by Pakistani subordinates, were spared the dilemma of having suddenly to decide on issues so delicate.

The tale of what physically ensued has been so often told that summary should here suffice. Helped by desertions among such few Muslims as the Maharajah's local forces contained, the tribesmen on October 22nd overran the awkward river-crossings at the entry to the State; and within a few hours had mostly moved off east along the good road through the Jhelum gorges towards the Vale. It was here that things began to go wrong. Unfamiliar with Kashmiris' dress and language, they failed to distinguish between Muslims and Hindus, attacking many of the former; and these insensate barbarities increased on October 26th when – after putting the Mahura power-station out of action, which caused consternation in Srinagar – they reached Baramula, a largish town where the Vale opens out. This place they violently assailed, killing and looting and burning, the survivors among the predominantly Muslim inhabitants fleeing panic-stricken to the hills. They incidentally also set upon a nearby Christian mission, killing five people including a nun; a bad but secondary episode, soon inflated out of all proportion by Indian propaganda aimed at countries of the Christian West. And the time lost over these misdeeds, we can now see, also lost them the campaign – it was of no avail that later waves of invading tribesmen

[12] Birdwood and other writers specifically assert that the Chief Minister of the Frontier Province was involved.

behaved much better, sometimes fighting superbly – for in Delhi, meanwhile, things had been happening very fast.

The present writer, then a newspaper editor, was there. He had moved specially from Calcutta a few days before, guessing that something important about Kashmir was going to happen. Mr. Ayyengar's appointment during September, in particular, had inclined him to believe that India was trying to organise the State's accession; and the tricklings of grim news from Poonch and Jammu, plus Sheikh Abdullah's release, suggested that a climax approached. The account that follows recapitulates or quotes from what he wrote about his experiences in a previous book, published in 1953,[13] and adds some knowledge gathered since.

First reports that Pathan tribesmen had broken into Kashmir reached the Indian Government confidentially on October 24th, fuller details coming next day. Early on October 26th, a Sunday, knowing nothing of this, but with the possibility of developments about Kashmir much in mind, the writer went to G.H.Q. on another matter, and happened to meet General Bucher[14] in a corridor, who gave him the facts as then known, saying that 'everyone was in a flap' – which indeed seemed to be so.

That evening he was invited to dinner by Lord and Lady Mountbatten, and noted afterwards:[15] 'I was startled by their one-sided verdicts on affairs. They seemed to have become wholly pro-Hindu. The atmosphere at Government House that night was almost one of war. Pakistan, the Muslim League, and Mr. Jinnah were the enemy. This tribal movement into Kashmir was criminal folly. And it must have been well organised. Mr. Jinnah, Lord Mountbatten assured me, was waiting at Abbottabad, ready to drive in triumph to Srinagar if it succeeded.[16] It was a thoroughly evil affair. By contrast, India's policy towards Kashmir, and the princely States generally, had throughout been impeccable. After the meal Lord Mountbatten took me aside. As editor of an important paper I should know the facts fully. Because of the Pathan attack, the Maharajah's formal accession to India was at that moment being finalised. Subject to a plebiscite, this great State, its inhabitants mainly Muslim, would now be legally lost to Jinnah. The Pakistanis had been crazy to accept

---

[13] *Horned Moon*, pp. 109–115.

[14] Then Chief of Staff of the new Indian Army.

[15] In a private memorandum. Its contents would never have been put into print – in *Horned Moon* more fully than here – had not Campbell-Johnson's book (p. 225) described these incidents misleadingly.

[16] Subsequent inquiries showed that Lord Mountbatten was wrong, and that Mr. Jinnah spent all the latter part of October in Karachi or Lahore.

the accession of Junagadh. Indian troops were to be flown into Kashmir at once; arrangements had been made. This was the only way to save Srinagar from sack by ruffianly tribesmen. It contained many Europeans, he pointed out. Outrages against helpless Europeans in the invaded regions were reported already. My memorandum records him as "persuasive, confident, charming, a successful commander on the eve of an important operation, who manifestly banked on hustling *The Statesman* into complete support". I was flabbergasted. The Junagadh affair I had perhaps wrongly looked upon almost as a triviality. But Kashmir was very different, a State recognised to be of first-class importance. The whole concept of dividing the subcontinent into Hindu-majority and Muslim-majority areas, the basis of the June 3rd plan, seemed outraged. At a Hindu Maharajah's choice, but with a British Governor-General's backing, three million Muslims,[17] in a region always considered to be vital to Pakistan if she were created, were legally to be made Indian citizens. I said little, except for expressing doubts whether a plebiscite would prove readily feasible; and went back much concerned, feeling that nothing but big trouble could come of this thing.'

Early next morning, October 27th, the airlift of Indian troops from Delhi to Srinagar started. This was quick work; no really firm news of what was happening along the Jhelum road had reached the Indian Government until late on October 25th. And the number of planes made available was large; they could be heard droning over steadily. When in Europe during 1944, this writer had as a war correspondent seen some of the difficulties of organising airborne operations; now, in his Delhi hotel, he listened and wondered.

Meanwhile, some of the more determined tribesmen, leaving their colleagues to finish looting and argument at Baramula, had pushed on, and that same morning had almost reached the edge of the airfield outside Srinagar, the only one in the entire Vale which troop-carrying planes could use. It was touch and go. But for the extreme speed of the Indian activities – Menon, as departmental secretary, had flown up to Kashmir twice within a few hours, to reconnoitre, and then to finalise political details – the airfield and probably Srinagar city too would have been in the tribesmen's grasp by afternoon. There was almost nothing to stop them, except Sheikh Abdullah's hastily-gathered local levies. The State army had disintegrated; and two nights previously, the Maharajah with all his entourage, and such valuables as he could collect, had fled by road to

[17] The figure of 4 million, given previously on p. 196, of course includes the State's Hindu and Sikh populations.

his dynasty's ancestral home beyond the mountains at Jammu. An Indian motorised force, sent overland – even had the eastern end of the Pathankot-Banihal route then been finished – could not have hoped to arrive nearly soon enough. Everything in this drama, the future not only of Kashmir, but of Indo-Pakistani relations into the 1960's, hinged therefore on decisions reached and translated into action at Delhi within hours.

The aforegoing implies that there must have been careful military planning as well as political intrigue by India beforehand. That was this writer's view at the time; he could not believe that so effective an airborne operation had been improvised. Yet exhaustive later inquiries have disclosed that on this point he was wrong. No evidence in support has been got; and specific written assurances are on record from senior British officers of the Indian Forces – which some Pakistani officers, then still in Delhi awaiting transfer, tend to confirm – that the airlift actually was an impromptu affair, enough aircraft happening to be on the spot or quickly obtainable: an instance, perhaps, just of 'Mountbatten's luck'.

But that by no means says that scheming of a political kind, for Kashmir's accession to India, had not been started in Delhi by leading Hindus long before, indeed as far back as June. The pointers towards this seem altogether too solid and many to ignore. And Indian politicians and civilian officials, doubtless, would have been at least as good as Pakistanis at concealing from temporary British superiors things undesirable for them to know.

The Pakistani Government's first enraged reaction, on learning what the Indians had done, was to decide to send in troops themselves. Orders to this effect were issued by Mr. Jinnah on the evening of October 27th at Lahore; and there are some who, looking back on the dreary intervening years of deadlock, wish he had been obeyed. But on getting them at Rawalpindi, General Gracey felt obliged to stall. He was then acting C.-in-C. of the Pakistan Army in General Messervy's absence; and a grave difficulty was involved, as we shall see. He decided he must consult F.-M. Auchinleck, Supreme Commander still, exercising diminishing authority at Delhi over both Dominions' Forces. The result was a visit by both officers to Mr. Jinnah at Lahore next day; the cancellation of Mr. Jinnah's orders; and an arrangement with Lord Mountbatten for a conference of the political heads of both Governments at Lahore on October 29th.

This however proved a fiasco : Mr. Nehru took to his bed from indisposition; Mr. Liaquat Ali Khan was also ill; Sardar Patel expressed inability to leave Delhi; and when, after a three days' postponement, Lord Mountbatten alone attended, he could do no more than undertake to refer to his absent colleagues the proposals Mr. Jinnah put forward. These were that a cease-fire within 48 hours should be proclaimed; that the tribesmen and Indian troops should alike withdraw; that if the former did not obey, joint Indo-Pakistani military action should be taken against them; and that the two Governors-General should be empowered to administer the State and arrange a plebiscite.

The Indian Government soon afterwards flatly rejected this (we may think) reasonable offer; and the stage was thus set for what, as 1947 passed into 1948, became for many months a sanguinary localised conflict between two fellow-members of the Commonwealth, and resulted in their profound political estrangement to this day.

Before considering the fighting, we must glance at what had separately been going on up in the sparsely-populated north, in Gilgit; a fascinating story, and as little known, owing to bad communications, as those of the Sudhans' rising, or of the frightful Jammu genocide.

Nominally, Gilgit formed part of the Maharajah's domains because of the Treaty of Amritsar in 1846; the much-criticised transaction whereby, at the end of the first Anglo-Sikh war, the previously obscure Dogra Hindu princely house of Jammu gained British consent to rule over enormous further territories including the Vale. But in practice, Dogra authority in Gilgit never became fully effective. The area could be reached only by mule-track over two passes of between 12,000 and 14,000 feet, which got snowblocked in winter; its inhabitants were 99 per cent Muslim; and until 1877 it continued, in reality, to be managed mainly by various local princelings. The British then stepped vigorously in, alarmed by Russian moves beyond the Pamirs; and Gilgit was made a political agency, modelled on those in the Pathan tribal country. In theory, however, it remained part of Kashmir State.

On Independence Day in 1947 the British political agent withdrew, and the Maharajah sent in a governor to replace him : a Dogra Hindu officer of his State forces. This was not locally liked; but it was tolerated in the belief that, as the State was a Muslim-majority one, the Maharajah, despite present hesitations, would soon act along the lines of Lord Mountbatten's advice to the Princes generally in July, and accede to Pakistan.

As in the Pathan tribal country, internal order in the agency was maintained mainly by the militia or scouts; a lightly-armed mobile force, recruited from the local tribes.[18] There was also – as in the Pathan country – an army garrison, though not in this instance of the Imperial forces but of the Maharajah's army. It was located mainly at Bunji, astride the Srinagar mule-track far from Gilgit town, and did not amount to much.

Ironically, the relatively smooth, swift course taken by events in the agency, after the startling news came on October 26th of the Maharajah's accession to India, depended largely on two young British officers still there : the scouts' commandant Major Brown, at his headquarters in Gilgit itself, and his colleague Captain Mathieson, some days' march down the curve of the Indus at Chilas. Circumstances could hardly have been more perplexing for them; and within hundreds of miles they had no compatriot or dependable official superior to consult. Local Muslims at once showed themselves outraged by the news; and so, which was graver, did their own fellow scouts' officers and the troops under them. Mullahs in the villages started preaching jihad against the Dogra régime; reports came that the neighbouring princely States of Swat and Chitral, which had joined Pakistan, were about to invade; Muslim soldiers in the predominantly Sikh garrison at Bunji, on the far side of the Indus, caused a disturbance; on the other hand, local Sikh and Hindu traders in Gilgit bazaar were known to have arms. By the evening of October 31st, tension locally became such that, in the commandant's view, mutiny and slaughter, resulting in general chaos, could only be forestalled by prompt acceptance of what unquestionably was the prevailing popular will. He therefore sent a platoon to request the Hindu governor to come to the scouts' lines for protection, and simultaneously ordered detachments from Chilas, as well as from Gilgit, to hold the Indus river-crossings and prevent Sikh or Hindu troops from Bunji getting over.

Some casualties ensued at the crossings, and indeed on the Gilgit residency's moonlit lawns too, because the governor resisted custody and fired on the scouts and their sympathisers from his windows, killing two. But within a few hours the affair was effectively over; and on November 2nd the Pakistan flag was run up amidst public acclaim. By November 6th, stragglers from the disintegrating Bunji garrison were on their way back to Srinagar over the passes; and not long after, the Hindu governor was spending afternoons amicably watching polo in his captors' company. A representative of the Karachi Government flew in on November 14th, to take formal

---

[18] See Chapter 12, p. 154. The Gilgit scouts were not yet formally part of the Frontier Corps however.

charge; and it is an interesting sidelight on Pakistan's complex geography that, until a jeep-track, usable only for a few weeks in summer, was built some years later from the Khagan valley over the 12,000 feet Babusar pass, her sole means of administering this vast, thinly-populated region was by aircraft and wireless.

Now for some comments on the fourteen months' fighting around the Vale and in Poonch province.[19] The big fact, for Pakistan, is that the fight was fought with her hands tied behind her back. She felt she could not send her Army in; at first not at all, and later only in bits and pieces, unobtrusively, and for defence rather than attack. Nor could she give air-support to the men fighting on the ground – the Azad Kashmir guerrillas, the tribesmen, and Pakistani volunteers. The only use she allowed her Air Force was for transport to and from Gilgit along the Indus gorges, far behind the lines.

Reasons for these handicaps were two. F.-M. Auchinleck, when in Lahore on October 28th, had made plain to Mr. Jinnah that, as General Gracey had guessed, entry of the Pakistan Army into Kashmir would mean forfeiture of its British officers. Certainly, he was not motivated in this by anti-Pakistani bias. As Connell's biography shows, he was by now totally disgusted by India's attitude towards her neighbour. 'I have no hesitation whatever in affirming,' he had written to London nearly a month before, 'that the present India Cabinet are implacably determined to do all in their power to prevent the establishment of the Dominion of Pakistan on a firm basis.'[20] But the point at issue was simple. Kashmir State, through the Maharajah's action – however wrong or absurd – had legally become Indian soil; if, therefore, the Pakistan Army went in, war with India – in a formal, comprehensive sense – might well ensue; and standing orders from Whitehall precluded involvement of serving British military personnel in any such situation. As Mr. Jinnah knew, Pakistan was at that stage even less able than India – owing to the Muslim community's relative educational backwardness, mentioned earlier – to dispense with the trained help of senior British officers in her employ. No doubt, too, he vividly realised that war with India must if possible be avoided anyway, owing to India's huge preponderance, not only in men but – by recent breach of the Partition-agreements – in munitions.

Besides this however – the second reason – Pakistan pinned high hopes, in those early days, on so flagrant a wrong as Kashmir's accession to India being righted, fairly, by diplomatic means. Britain

[19] Details may be found in such books as Birdwood's or Korbel's.
[20] The whole report deserves to be read: Connell, pp. 920–921.

might be induced to mediate; or the Commonwealth as a whole; and the U.N. could be appealed to – as was in fact done on January 1st.[21] And if the promised plebiscite was honestly conducted, Pakistanis had no doubt whatever of the outcome. Thus, though being militarily hamstrung was very unpleasant, it might in the end prove the best way to political success.

The trained Indian troops, soon after landing near Srinagar, had no great difficulty in pushing the tribesmen out of the Vale, out of Baramula, and down the Jhelum gorges to a point beyond Uri. But there they stuck. Their communication-lines were very stretched; and critics thought they were rashly risking sudden guerrilla onslaughts from the flanks, of the kind that, in the past, had often trapped small British forces on the North-West Frontier. But the analogy did not really hold; for the tribesmen, too, were fighting here far from their homes, on unfamiliar terrain. And in fact the positions on the Uri front changed little throughout the campaign, and interest shifts to the town of Poonch, where part of the Maharajah's army, some Indian troops, and a crowd of Hindu civilians had been besieged by Azad Kashmir irregulars.

This place, for about ten months, became a strategic 'running sore' for the Indians. Provisioning it by air was difficult, and their repeated efforts to get a relief column through on the ground came to nothing. However, during the winter, they had been steadily improving their main supply-route over the Banihal pass, augmenting their strength generally; and in a vigorous spring offensive, besides nearly reaching Poonch – which precipitated a fresh flow of Muslim civilian refugees into West Pakistan – they created, for a short while, a very dangerous situation militarily along the Kishenganga river near Tithwal, northwest of Uri, where a break-through was achieved against almost no resistance.

These formidable developments convinced the Pakistan Government that, whatever the consequences, something more positive must be done. Clearly, Azad Kashmir irregulars and the Pathan tribesmen could prove no match for the Indian Army, as now reinforced. Any further influx of refugees might overwhelm an already almost hopelessly burdened civilian Administration; and for reasons of future strategic security, Pakistan could on no account allow the remaining strip of Kashmir State territory adjoining her borders to be conquered. Accordingly, units of the Pakistan Army and of the Frontier Corps were sent in, with orders to hold specific defensive positions.

---

[21] By India actually. Pakistan however had previously proposed it, on November 16th. A suggestion that it might be done had originally been made by Lord Mountbatten on November 1st.

O

This happened mainly in May, as a result of an appreciation of the military facts put in on April 20th by General Gracey;[22] but it was not publicly acknowledged till August. It is not denied also that, earlier, individuals or small groups from the Pakistan Army, including a few fairly senior officers, had managed to find themselves in Kashmir while on leave, enthusiastically helping the irregulars. In theory this was wrong; in practice, not easy to prevent.

A remarkable diversion was then contrived. Some of the scouts from Gilgit, by a march over high ground and melting snows which at this season no one had supposed physically possible, suddenly appeared – to the Indians' concern – at the top of the Zoji-la, the main entrance to the Vale from the east. The Indians' response however was remarkable too. They got tanks up to this altitude, about 10,000 feet; thrust the scouts back; and proceeded to open up the route via Kargil to Leh, thus gaining firmer grip over the State's outlying Buddhist province, Ladakh.[23] During the summer, the not limitless resources in men, munitions, and energy of the rival Indian and Pakistan Armies – so recently one – got increasingly sucked into the Kashmir vortex, to the alarm of friendly foreign observers. In October, the Indians at last achieved the relief of Poonch town; and their accompanying strong offensive throughout that province gained them much ground, besides causing yet more Muslim civilians to flee panic-stricken into Pakistan.

The Pakistanis' reply was a bold move about which controversy persists. They pulled forces out from the Punjab plains around Lahore, leaving that city very thinly defended, and shifted them and other troops to a point west of Jammu town, near the Indians' recently much-improved main route to Poonch; and these, in December, were poised for an attack which, if made, might have put the whole of the Indian Forces farther forward in Poonch province, about two divisions, well 'in the bag'. For obscure reasons, partly doubtless uncertainty lest it might precipitate an Indian riposte against Lahore, resulting in unrestricted inter-Dominion warfare, the attack as such never occurred; but a well-maintained artillery-bombardment of a tract near the Indians' vitally-important bridge at Beri Pattan disclosed how dramatic its effects could have been. In some ways, the strategic conditions on this occasion interestingly foreshadowed those which developed during the three weeks' war of August-September 1965.

Events then happened fast. A few days after the Beri Pattan bom-

---

[22] Now C.-in-C., Gen. Messervy having left.
[23] A grip since prised loose, in places, by the Chinese, who by 1957 had built a motor-road across the barren Aksi Chin plateau in the extreme north-east.

bardment, both sides suddenly announced a cease-fire. The initiative had been General Bucher's.[24] Exactly why all concerned should at this moment have found themselves simultaneously of one mind, and what the respective calculations in particular were of Mr. Nehru and Mr. Liaquat Ali Khan[25] may never be known, for the arrangement seems to have been fixed up conversationally, direct or on the telephone. But it would probably be true to say that most Pakistanis, reflecting on the frustrations which have persisted ever since, think the cease-fire agreed to in December 1948 was a mistake.

[24] Now C.-in-C. of the Indian Army, Gen. Lockhart having left.
[25] Mr. Jinnah had died in September.

Chapter 16

Defence and Foreign Affairs

A FEW MOMENTS' thought, in front of a map, will begin to reveal how big and peculiar Pakistan's defence-problems are. Biggest, of course, is that she consists of two 'wings', 1,000 miles apart; in population-strength not very unlike one another, but utterly dissimilar in size, and in terrain and climate; dissimilar too – though the point can be exaggerated – in their peoples' physique and temperament, and in traditions towards war. No other unitary State in the world has a problem quite like this. Troops in large numbers, or heavy military stores, can only be got from one wing of Pakistan to the other by sea, via the coasts of Ceylon, a 3,000 miles' journey. It takes about ten days.

But other big problems, on consideration, soon become apparent. Pakistan is made up of the outer, north-western and south-eastern parts of the former Indian Empire that Britain administered. She therefore took over the bulk of the British régime's defence-problems. For in the north, along the Himalayan frontier up against Tibet and China that Mr. Nehru's new India took over, practically no defence-problem existed in British times; historically, India's present worries there are a novelty. But the problems of the North-West Frontier, which became Pakistan's responsibility, were notorious and grave; and though they have since changed in nature, and perhaps decreased somewhat, grave they potentially remain.

The existence along the North-West Frontier of the quasi-autonomous tribal belt indeed matters much less. There are now no Christian officers, no Hindu or Sikh troops in it for the tribesmen to fire at, no infidels, only fellow-Muslims – which is not so good. And since 1947 the tribesmen have accepted much closer educational and economic ties with Pakistan than they did with the British. Her initial misgivings about them, though prudent, seem to have been uncalled for; Islam – and considerations of self-interest – seem to be making them loyal Pakistanis. And farther south, Pakistan enjoys excellent relations with Iran; in fact the two countries felt so in accord, early in 1958, as to consider federating.

But the unfriendliness for many years of Afghanistan, beyond the tribal belt, created problems more perplexing for Pakistan – as we shall explain – than the British ever faced from that country; and

212

behind Afghanistan looms Soviet Russia, for several years unfriendly too, and much stronger than in British times. Since 1962 or there-abouts, relations with both of them have improved, but they are not yet perfect, and here is the region through which, in the past, all the main land-invasions of the subcontinent have come, from Alexander's in 326 B.C., to Ahmad Shah Abdali's in 1761 A.D. Though history does not always repeat itself, it can, especially if geography stands ready to help.

Nor can the subcontinent's other frontier, the south-eastern one adjoining Burma, be disregarded – which the British unwisely did, nearly till the end of their time. Pakistan inherited about a fifth of it, in the Arakan; and the Japanese, in the early 1940's, startlingly showed how penetrable by trained jungle fighters terrain such as the Burmese frontier can be.

And on top of all this are the problems of what may be termed Pakistan's inward frontiers, the products of the 1947 Partition; 3,000 miles of them, to east and west, hastily devised by a British lawyer unacquainted with the country, and lacking geophysical barriers of any kind in support; the frontiers with her fellow-member of the Commonwealth, the new India. In theory, these ought to be about as undefended and friendly as those between Canada and the U.S.A. In practice, they have caused her worse misgivings than all the rest.

And projecting north from the western one is something rather different again : the Kashmir cease-fire line, supervised by the U.N.; not an agreed permanent frontier at all, merely the ribbon of soil along which, on a particular day – January 1st, 1949 – fighting happened to be halted; as uneasy and problematical a boundary, and as vexatious for the ordinary person to get across, as Israel's boundary with her Arab neighbours.

Any foreign visitor can find out, by direct experience, without entering Kashmir at all, a reason for Pakistanis' strong feelings about this northward projection. Do a motor-trip from Lahore to Rawalpindi, choosing one of those brilliantly clear days of a Punjab winter, and making just ordinary use of eyes and imagination. You are on the grand trunk road here, the historic highway that traverses the Indo-Gangetic plain; and beside it runs the main railway linking Karachi and Peshawar. This parallel road-and-rail strip is veritably the aorta of West Pakistan's communications-system. And in full view from it, over your right shoulder all the way after you pass Gujranwala – 150 miles or so – stands forth in a splendour of blue and silver the Pir Panjal range, Indian-occupied, from whose clefts one day might again debouch, as in September 1965 near Sialkot, a numerically-strong foe to threaten the living transport-artery on which your wheels rotate.

It is not difficult, with these various problems' complexity in mind, to understand why Pakistan – like Israel – is a country of military flavour; why her Armed Forces have been made the very best that her limited resources can bear, and why – a big event we shall soon come to – American aid for them was accepted in 1954 so eagerly; why her moneyed classes endure the inevitable tax burdens with fair stoicism; and why, even to many of her intellectuals, it seemed right that, in a crisis of inefficiency such as developed in 1958, the generals should step in, sack the Ministers, overthrow the Constitution, and take firm grasp of affairs.

Creating two good new armies in 1947 out of the former undivided Indian Imperial one proved, actually, much less difficult than most people had foreseen, during the weeks before Partition. Sheer luck, the absence of any major trouble-stirring incidents, must have been a factor; but the main reason doubtless was the old Army's unimpaired discipline, stressed in Chapter 6, and maintained to the end – an achievement the more impressive when the effects of the I.N.A. and R.I.N. affairs in 1946 are recalled.

But headaches for the creators of the Pakistan Army were sharper than for the Indian. Apart from the fact, as mentioned, that Mr. Nehru's Government withheld from Pakistan quantities of military stores which, under the Partition-agreements, had been hers by right, and compelled abolition of F.-M. Auchinleck's H.Q. in Delhi which was to have supervised their distribution, geography had so arranged things that almost every ordnance factory on the subcontinent lay on what, for Pakistan, was the wrong side of the new frontiers. And so did most of the instructional schools, other than the famous staff college at Quetta; for instance, an entirely new junior military academy had immediately to be created at Kakul, in substitution for the one at Dehra Dun; a new engineer centre at Risalpur, and so on. At the start, too, the Pakistan Army was very short of technical experts, such as engineer and artillery officers. And recruitment had in the old days been extremely lopsided; decades would elapse before there could be a hope of the East wing's numerical representation in the Forces being brought up to something like parity with the West wing's. India, it is true, also had her problem of reputedly 'non-martial' races, but not to the same degree. There was also the fact that no homogeneous Muslim units had ever existed in the old undivided Indian Army; the so-called 'class' units were composed entirely of Hindus – Mahrattas, Dogras and so on; these went over to India intact. Pakistan got nothing comparable to this. At Partition, she obtained only fragments from units, and the Pakistan Army consequently took longer to put together. Birdwood observed that 'in October 1947, there was hardly a single formed unit in Pakistan. Several units still had Hindu and Sikh commanding officers, and Hindus held appointments at Pakistan G.H.Q.'. And a distracting preoccupation, during the opening months – proportionately heavier because Pakistan's Army was the smaller – had been the need for convoying and protecting masses of refugees. And then, in the spring of 1948, came the Kashmir fighting, in which, as Symonds remarks, the Pakistani troops were set 'a very delicate task. They were instructed to guard certain key points, but not to take any initiative. They were bombed, but had no air support. For several months their presence was a secret, so that they had no moral backing from the Press, radio, or from home letters.'

Nevertheless, within a few years Pakistan had built her Forces up to a high degree of efficiency, putting them professionally among the best in Asia. And they are popular; their compatriots look on them – which they do not always on the police – with respectful pride. Disgruntled politicians thrust from office by the military coup of 1958, or civilian officials soon afterwards dismissed for incompetence or worse, may at times make disparaging remarks about generals. But it is difficult to imagine anyone in Pakistan doing so about the Forces as a whole.

In the last analysis, one may say that a country's foreign policy is what enables her to exist; to keep independently in being. It may be shaped and defined with clarity; but it need not. Details can be kept vague. What matters is maintenance of the will, among her leaders and people, that she should survive. During her early months Pakistan's foreign policy amounted to little more than this. It had no precision. Mr. Jinnah's statements about it were studiously platitudinous. Goodwill was professed for all countries; belief in international honesty and fair play; readiness to contribute towards peace; and so on.

Nevertheless, certain leanings or attitudes, as contrasted with solid formulations of policy, soon became discernible – apart from fear of India, the big factor which swayed everything. One was a warmth of friendliness for Britain, coupled with faith in the practical value of being in the Commonwealth; sentiments which it was assumed would be reciprocated. A second was a naïve, undifferentiating Pan-Islamic enthusiasm for other Muslim countries. And both these instinctively-adopted early attitudes, most Pakistanis would now say, have in the main proved unrewarding and misplaced. Much disillusion has resulted.

In August 1947, Pakistanis were as happy as Indians to find themselves citizens of an independent sovereign State, free of foreign control; and popular jubilation, in Karachi as in Delhi, was immense. Theirs however was a double pleasure. They felt as glad to have escaped subjection to the new Hindu-majority régime across the new frontier, as to have emerged from British tutelage. The Muslim liberation-movement on the subcontinent had had virtually no direct quarrel with Britain, except briefly during the Khilafatist agitation of 1920–2.[1] The quarrelling had nearly all been between Britain and the political organisations of the Hindus : the professedly non-communal but Hindu-run Congress party, and the Mahasabha. During it, many hard things had been said and done; and some blood been spilt. Muslims perhaps have simple minds. They did not suppose that all this could be expunged from British memory. The decades of vilification from the Hindus since 1905 would they imagined be seen, by most British people, reflected against the background of neutrality, or something better, maintained by the Muslims. In particular, the Congress's 'open rebellion' as recently as August 1942, at the worst phase of the war, when the Japanese were thrusting against the fringes of Bengal, could surely not be forgotten. They therefore counted confidently, during the first few weeks after Independence, on their struggling new State being treated by the British Government at least fairly, and perhaps with some favour. Besides, it was a British tradition to champion small countries against grasping bigger ones.

They do not consider that fairness has ever been got. Always, at critical moments – in their view – the balance has been tilted to India's advantage, and by Tories as well as by Labour. Space precludes recital of the instances adduced;[2] for in this chapter we have Pakistan's relations with other countries to consider, and Britain's importance in her eyes has shrunk. But the trouble began soon. When, in her extremity amidst the Punjab carnage in October 1947, she appealed to Britain and the Commonwealth for help or mediation, the reply got from London, as Symonds remarks, was 'so coldly phrased that she took it as a snub'. By December, Mr. Jinnah felt bitter. Britain 'is treating Pakistan with indifference', he said; she should 'use moral persuasion to help settle differences between members of the Commonwealth; His Majesty's Government are, so far, shirking their responsibility'.

[1] See Chapter 4.
[2] Books such as Sarwar Hasan's and Siddiqi's present the earlier ones well.

The climax came in April 1949, when India was allowed to stay in the Commonwealth after repudiating the Crown and becoming a Republic. This, to Pakistanis, was incomprehensible; it changed the organisation's nature. Interest in it flagged. Their Government continued membership mainly now to prevent India exploiting hers, and for such secondary practical benefits as could be got out of it; in exclusive information for instance, or economic aid. Ishtiaq Qureshi's summing-up is not far wrong. 'Pakistan started with enthusiastic feelings of friendship for Britain,' he writes; 'since then, relations between the two Governments have been correct, but seldom warm.'

That however is not the whole story. Though her hopes of less fence-sitting and more positive friendship from the British Government have been dashed, as also her zeal for the Commonwealth, nevertheless her attitude in foreign affairs, until 1962, was firmly pro-Western. And other levels of relationship exist than the inter-Governmental. For the British people, British culture and institutions, British sports, English literature and language, a fund of goodwill remains. Pakistanis when in Britain – especially of course the Western-educated ones – find themselves in many subtle unexpected ways at home; as do British visitors in Pakistan. Countless personal friendships survive. These good things the political by-products of the 1947 Partition have not impaired.

Disheartened about the Commonwealth, Pakistan in the latter part of 1949 turned with vigour to cultivating relations with supposedly brotherly Muslim countries. In quick succession treaties of friendship were signed with about ten of them; cultural exchanges were arranged, mutual visits by Heads of State; and efforts made to hold Islamic conferences of various kinds at Karachi, only one of which – on economics – in fact functioned. By 1953 however it had become clear, to any but the most romantic Pakistani eye, that little of solid worth was emerging. New anti-colonialist, neutralist, and pan-Arab or otherwise racialist doctrines obviously in practice interested these countries more than ideals of an ancient Islamic brotherhood; and these doctrines happened, as well, to interest India very much, a bigger and more noticeable State than Pakistan. The leaders of Indonesia and Egypt – Muslim countries on which Pakistan had first focused special interest, because of the former's population-strength, and the latter's strategic place on the map – showed no disposition whatever, on Pakistan's account, to forego their contacts with Mr. Nehru. Exchanges with Turkey and Iran were indeed progressing well; but then the former, on her reckoning at least, ought not to be considered a Muslim State at all.

And Afghanistan, not only a Muslim one but adjacent, remained as mentioned for many years unfriendly, even hostile. This might at first seem less awkward than it actually was, Afghanistan being then (and to a large extent still) a weak, precarious State: landlocked, lacking railways and with few good roads, socially medieval and under a royal despotism, educationally and economically very backward, and with a population composite in race and language, and totalling only about 12 million as against Pakistan's 73 million.[3] But as explained in Chapter 3, part of the Afghan population, ethnically, is the same as part of Pakistan's, consisting of Pakhtoons or Pathans. Here lay the difficulty, worsened by the fact that the Afghan monarchy is not only of Pathan stock, but descended from the 'Peshawar Sardars', who 150 years or so ago ruled the richest tract of the whole Pathan country, the Peshawar Vale – in Pakistan.

This last fact was plainly what launched the Afghans on a foreign policy which by 1954 or thereabouts began to seem almost suicidally stupid. Misjudging, early in 1947, how events on the Indo-Pakistani subcontinent would shape, and foreseeing anarchy, they laid claim to all areas of the then expiring British Raj inhabited by Pathans. No one at the time paid this much heed; it seemed absurd; and Mr. Nehru, then head of the Interim Government at Delhi, brushed it aside. But it was the start of the long-drawn 'Pakhtoonistan' agitation; and in September 1947 soon after creation, Pakistan was amazed to find her fellow-Muslim neighbour the only country in the world to oppose her membership of the U.N. In December the Afghan Government went on to repudiate the Durand treaty of 1893, which had delimited the frontier bequeathed to Pakistan by the British.

Sporadic raids into Pakistani territory then began, which went on for years, supplemented by attempts to tamper with the tribes' loyalty, and at times that of minor princely rulers such as Kalat and Dir. India's complicity in this was of course surmised, and the Indians several times allowed 'Pakhtoonistan' jirgas[4] to be held in Delhi. Twice, diplomatic relations between Pakistan and Afghanistan were in effect broken off: in 1955, and again in 1961. Militarily, Pakistan in those earlier years could have coped with Afghanistan easily: the tribes on her side of the frontier were never seriously disaffected; and the Afghan forces were then so ill-equipped, poorly led, and underpaid that Kabul might have been captured by units

[3] 1947 estimates.
[4] Meetings.

of the 'militia' or Frontier Corps alone, without the Pakistan Army being used. But ideologically, things were less simple. That she should be in such disaccord with a fellow-Muslim State lying up against her frontier was obviously awkward. To mount a major punitive 'raid' into Afghan territory, though feasible, could stir up a diversity of foreign and domestic troubles, with incalculable results. And in 1955 the affair underwent an alarming new twist: the Afghan cause was espoused by hitherto uncommitted Russia, Mr. Krushchev supporting this with lavish offers of aid.

Russian influence in Afghanistan soon became paramount. The Afghan armed forces, so inefficient before, got Russian instructors and weapons. Modern motorways were planned, both through the Hindu Kush range by tunnelling, and around its western edge. And these, when joined to the roads already a-building with American aid near Kabul, would ensure quick access from the Turkmenistan tract of Russian territory towards the Afghan-Pakistani frontier at two strategic points: near Peshawar, and near Quetta. It was formidable.

However, after seven years or so the Afghan royal family apparently itself took fright. Might not dependence on Russia have gone too far? Other considerations were also at work, among them Pakistan's obviously greater stability under her military régime since 1958. At any rate in March 1963 Sardar Daud, one of the king's cousins – most leading men in Afghan administration were – who for nearly ten years had controlled Afghan policy as Prime Minister, abruptly and without explaining resigned. And from then on, Afghan-Pakistani relations have sweetened. Within a few weeks, through the Shah of Iran's help, the two countries' second diplomatic breach was formally repaired during a conference in Tehran (May 28th); and this has been followed by agreements and exchanges on numerous practical items: transit trade, air-services, 'tele-communications', short extensions of Pakistan's railway-system into Afghan territory, mutual visits by educationists, business men, cultural leaders, artists and so on. President Ayub has twice gone to Afghanistan: in July 1964 and in January 1966; and in February 1967 the Afghan king paid a return State visit to Pakistan. During the three-weeks' Indo-Pakistani war in September 1965 Pakistanis noted with pleasure and some surprise that, on balance, the Afghan Government seemed to favour their side; and though the Afghans have not yet officially withdrawn their 'Pakhtoonistan' claims much less is now heard about them.

Some while before Mr. Bulganin and Mr. Khrushchev plunged

into the 'Pakhtoonistan' affair in 1955 – and indeed doubtless largely what caused this – had occurred the most positive move yet in Pakistan's foreign policy : her decision as aforementioned in May 1954 to sign a mutual assistance pact with the U.S.A., which gave her military aid. This had been preceded, six weeks before, by a mutual assistance pact with Turkey; and soon afterwards she signed the SEATO and the Baghdad (later CENTO) pacts.

Till the spring of 1954 her foreign policy – so far as she had one – had nominally been unaligned as between the world's two contesting power-blocs, Communist and non-Communist. True, a perceptible leaning towards the latter in Mr. Jinnah's time, natural enough for ideological and other reasons, had seemed emphasised in 1950 when Mr. Liaquat Ali Khan evaded an invitation to Moscow and then went to Washington; but no commitment was made. This remained her position during Khwaja Nazimuddin's Premiership. Nevertheless, throughout all those years, fears of India's intentions persisted, and her efforts to find some reassurances, first from the Commonwealth and then from fellow-Muslim countries, had yielded nothing. So the decisions of 1954 seemed based on practical necessity. And as we look back, what stands out as remarkable is that they were made in Mr. Mohammad Ali of Bogra's time, just when she was entering her period of worst domestic instability, yet remained unchanged amidst the many twists and turns of four subsequent politically harassed Prime Ministerships.

The Americans had been careful beforehand, in 1953, to tell Mr. Nehru's Government just what they intended and why. They stressed that the aid would be defensive; Pakistan they believed needed buttressing against Communist penetration from the north; safeguards would be put into any agreement to prevent the equipment being used aggressively. And if any Pakistani – or foreign watcher of the South Asian scene – had doubted that a cardinal underlying Indian purpose was to keep her smaller neighbour weak and isolated for eventual re-absorption, his doubts should now have gone. This writer was revisiting the subcontinent at the time, and he watched, fascinated, the unfolding of the Indian propaganda. Every conceivable argument against the U.S.A.'s offer and Pakistan's acceptance of it was raised, every device of expert publicity applied. Much of the popular Indian clamour was no doubt honest, its subconscious motivation being unsuspected. But what it amounted to – and at the higher levels of India's Foreign Affairs Ministry this cannot have been subconscious – was that, in the average Hindu heart even now, years after a mutually-agreed Partition, Pakistan as an independent

State had no right to exist. She must not have a separate foreign policy; circumstances destined her to be India's satellite.

Observers friendly to India pointed out that she herself had been taking much American aid; admittedly not in a formal sense military, but economic; yet this had much strengthened her finances, enabling her to enlarge and re-equip her forces by purchases in Britain and elsewhere. So were not her protests rather illogical? The practical result seemed much the same. Besides, she had been helping Nepal militarily since 1952 on lines similar to those offered by the U.S.A. to Pakistan now. And might it not, at least in the abstract, be suggested that since Pakistan was a fellow-member of the Commonwealth, and had inherited from the British the task of defending the subcontinent's North-West Frontier, her increased strength, resulting from aid by a friendly outside Power, would redound ultimately to India's strategic benefit? None of these considerations carried the slightest weight. Early in 1954, the Indian publicity-campaign verged on hysteria; Mr. Nehru made speeches against the U.S.A.'s offer almost daily. 'It is a step not only towards war, even world-war,' he declared, but 'one which brings war right to our doors.' Perhaps the foremost of his arguments was that Pakistan's acceptance would disrupt the 'area of peace' which India had been building around herself. And if one looks at European colonialist literature of the early twentieth century another three-word term catches the eye which seems a synonym. Shift the two about from text to text, and the fit is perfect, they become beautifully interchangeable. The equivalent for 'area of peace' is the old-fashioned 'sphere of influence'.

Baffled in her efforts to stop the mutual assistance pact between Pakistan and the U.S.A., India began exploiting it over the Kashmir dispute. It put an entirely new complexion on that affair, she said; and she demanded recall of the American officers serving with the U.N. on the cease-fire line, saying they could not be impartial. She then, in a series of steps, pulled away from her promise, made when she first flew her forces in to Srinagar in October 1947, to ascertain the Kashmiris' wishes by a plebiscite. Already, she had discarded the two men without whose help she could never have got there. For the Maharajah, having been made use of to give legal basis to Indian actions, was exiled from his principality to Bombay in 1949, where he died in 1961. And as mentioned Sheikh Abdullah, Mr. Nehru's friend, when his views about India's policy in Kashmir began changing in 1953, was imprisoned; and except for spells of liberty in 1958 and 1964–5, he has remained so up to now, in the spring of 1967.

.   .   .   .   .

Like other ex-'colonial' countries, Pakistan has many diplomatic missions overseas. Some of these perhaps achieve little except remind busy people that she exists. And were it not for considerations of prestige – an imponderable thing – their staffs might be better used at home. Shortages of trained officials there remain serious. Actually, her foreign relations are important only with her neighbours or near-neighbours and especially the big ones – India, Russia, China; with the U.S.A.; and diminishingly with Britain and a few other Commonwealth countries.

Relations with India have been amply discussed. Now for more about those with Russia. A mere twenty miles – the fact is often overlooked – prevent Russia from being Pakistan's full neighbour. These twenty span the narrow easternmost strip of Afghanistan termed the Wakhan, which Britain and Russia in 1895 created as a buffer between their two Empires. Because of the ideological or religious factor, most Pakistanis look on the Soviet régime with some misgiving; as good Muslims they dislike avowed atheism. So Russo-Pakistan relations, never warm, and very chilly after Mr. Khrushchev's conduct in 1955, may not become intimate. However, since 1960–61 they have undergone a big change. A loosening-up in Pakistan's whole attitude towards the world's two contesting power-blocs then set in, because of what seemed to her a damaging shift in American policy. Whereas, during the Eisenhower-Dulles régime, the U.S.A.'s stand in the 'cold war' had been clear and indeed rigid, and her disapproval of neutralism such as India's absolute, President Kennedy seemed almost to think it praiseworthy. But in that case what was the point of Pakistan being non-neutral? Why should she risk it? Might not a more flexible, uncommitted course suit her better? If the Western bloc's strongest Power thought that good for India, why not for Pakistan? These were the startled questions bestirred in Pakistani minds, and F.-M. Ayub at that time was much more strongly placed to change course internationally than preceding Pakistani leaders had been. Glancing round, he and his advisers could see that alignment with the U.S.A., though in many ways useful, had been disastrous in others. Besides estranging Pakistan from most ex-'colonial' countries, which looked on her contemptuously as a mere American dependency, it had antagonised Russia – this being very much worse, for it had stopped the U.N. doing anything about the Kashmir dispute, possibly for ever.

So when, in 1961, Russia came cautiously forward with offers to help Pakistan in her domestic hunt for oil – the American and British oil companies having so far proved ineffective – she was not rebuffed. Russian geophysicists were soon at work on the Potwar

plateau near Rawalpindi, nine other areas being allotted to them, some in the East wing. It was unprecedented; the start of a vast slow thaw. And on this melting diplomatic soil a crop of technological and commercial deals has since arisen, not only with Russia but with some of the smaller European Communist States. Mr. Khrushchev's downfall in October 1964 helped. In April 1965 President Ayub visited Moscow; a trade agreement was signed, and arrangement made for Russian credits. Cultural and other exchanges followed, more credits being arranged in September 1966. As most Pakistanis see the matter, proof of the wisdom of their country's new policy lay in the evidence, since about 1963, that Russia's policy was changing in return. Her championship of India over Kashmir and of Afghanistan over 'Pakhtoonistan' began to abate; and by the time of the dramatic Tashkent meeting in January 1966 Mr. Kosygin's position, as between warring Pakistan and India, was scrupulously neutral. It was a big gain.

Even more fascinating has been the evolution of Pakistan's relations with Communist China. In so far as that country, ideologically, is nowadays more militant and propagandist than Russia, the religious obstacle to friendship is even stronger. Nearly all Pakistanis believe in God; Red Chinese cannot. But apart from that, relations with China, unlike those with Russia, have never been under specific strain. And in the Gilgit region, which Pakistan administers – it is nominally part of disputed Kashmir – she stands in full neighbourship with China, which the Wakhan strip of Afghanistan prevents her being with Russia. The Sino-Pakistani frontier, astride the Karakoram range, though it traverses very wild, almost uninhabited terrain, is quite long, about 200 miles; and in March 1962 the two countries agreed to define its exact alignment so as to avoid future quarrels. This was at a time when acute differences were already developing between India and China about their much longer common frontier astride the Himalayas farther east.

The rapidly increasing Sino-Indian estrangement, because of this, came to Pakistanis as a pleasant surprise; and when, in November 1962, it flared into open warfare, and an Indian army was routed, and Chinese forces broke into Assam, they showed undisguised glee. This amazed many people in Britain and the U.S.A., oblivious as always of the Pakistani point of view. But to such few Westerners as had bothered to understand the bitter frustration Pakistan has felt, almost since birth, owing to her supposed friends' failure to give her any practical help about Kashmir, her reaction at that moment was wholly understandable. On the long view, most informed Pakistanis probably feel some puzzlement or mistrust about their relationship

with the Peking régime, perhaps more so now early in 1967 than
before, owing to the unforeseeable effects of Mr. Mao's 'cultural
revolution'; but on the short, China happens to be their very welcome, unexpected helper.

For the rest, only Ceylon, Burma and Nepal need mention.
Though not contiguous with Pakistan, Ceylon must in a maritime
sense be accounted a neighbour, for without midway access to her
ports, Pakistan would find heavy sea-transport between her East and
West wings much more troublesome. Relations both with her and
with Burma, predominantly Buddhist countries, have so far always
been good; Islam of course stands nearer to Buddhism than to
Hinduism, owing to Buddhism's rejection of caste. Moreover, Ceylon
and Burma have both had domestic worry – Ceylon has it still –
from Hindu minorities on their soil. On top of this, by comparison
with India, they – and Nepal too – are small, and evidently sometimes eye their huge intervening neighbour with some alarm,
wondering what future form her idea of 'area of peace' might take,
and how far this might threaten their independence. Under the
Ayub régime, Pakistan has been energetic in fostering friendly under-
standings with all three.

Chapter 17

Some Economic Problems

PAKISTAN resembles most Asian, African and Central and South American countries in being what contemporary jargon prefers to term 'developing' rather than 'under-developed', both words however meaning simply that she is poor, and looks to the richer North American and European countries for financial and technical help. In this book we need not specify the many short-comings she shares with other tropical or sub-tropical lands; we merely mention here a few which seem distinctly her own.

Outstanding among her problems at birth was almost total lack of large-scale modern industries. The subcontinent was not devoid of these; but they nearly all happened to lie on the Indian side of the new frontiers. This was through sheer geological mischance. The main known mineral deposits – coal, iron, bauxite, mica and so forth – were beneath the areas predominantly inhabited by Hindus. Understandably enough, before the 1947 Partition, leading Hindu economists and business men therefore foretold that, apart from anything else, her mineral and industrial weakness would necessarily bring about her speedy collapse. And perhaps nothing so impressed the foreigner during her early years, as the vigour with which her leaders, full of the enthusiasms of that period, set about proving these hostile prophets wrong.

So anyone like the present writer, revisiting her at intervals, kept getting surprises. Each time, he found new factories built or building. By Western standards, these might not be large; and in the West wing especially, they were strewn over a vast area. But they were very noticeable. Probably most important was the change in the East wing, where at Partition an absurd state of affairs had existed. Though 70 per cent of the world's jute was produced there, it had not a single jute-mill; all of them had been put up in British times around Calcutta. But by 1952, this defect had been remedied, mainly by the huge new mill at Narayanganj, the biggest in the world; Pakistan no longer depended on India for processing her most lucra-tive product. By 1963 she had fourteen jute-mills altogether, dealing with over a quarter of her million-ton annual crop; the rest went for processing to Dundee, or other European and American cities.

Almost equally striking were the West wing's achievements in cotton textiles. What raw jute is to the East wing, the cotton crop is to the West : the farmer's main money-earner. In 1947, of the 1,500,000 cotton-bales produced, only 160,000 went to mills on Pakistani territory. By 1956 however, new mills had not only made Pakistan self-sufficient in the coarser types of cloth; she had begun to export. Remarkable progress has also been made in manufactures of wool, tobacco, sugar, cement, rubber-goods, fertilisers, and insecticides. Probably the most interesting area industrially nowadays in Pakistan is in the far north-west, near the triangle Rawalpindi-Peshawar-Daud Khel.

Pakistan's quick collapse was also prophesied from India because of lack of financial skills. Before Partition, most of the junior officials and clerks in banks and insurance companies, the big mercantile concerns, and the Government offices that dealt with economics had been Hindus or Sikhs; and their flight or withdrawal in 1947-8 did for a while cause something like chaos. But it was surprising what Muslims proved able to do in their stead. Hitherto unsuspected skills emerged; and where that was not so, enthusiasm and a friendly eagerness to help made good some of the shortcomings. Within nine months or so it seemed unlikely that collapse from this cause would occur, and the Hindu prophets were made to look silly, rather like certain people in London in 1956, who had predicted disasters in navigating the Suez Canal after withdrawal of the British pilots.

Then came the international currency crisis of September 1949, when Pakistan startled India and indeed the world by feeling able to disregard the rest of the sterling area and avoid devaluing – her stated reason being that she needed industrialisation, and that to lower her rupee would have made purchases of capital goods in the hard-currency area much more difficult. India's extraordinary response, in not recognising the Pakistani decision, and in effect imposing an economic blockade, besides doing her no good – she had to accept the Pakistani decision sixteen months later – was of psychological interest, as an early disclosure of the mental attitude that caused the acute controversy of 1954, described in the last chapter, when Pakistan signed her defence-agreement with the U.S.A. Apparently she could not bring herself to regard her small neighbour as entitled to evolve its own financial or other policies.[1]

And then, nine months later, came an unforeseeable stroke of luck: the Korean war, and the resulting boom in the world's commodity

[1] Pakistan devalued her currency to the general sterling level in 1955, after completing much of her dollar-area purchasing-programme of capital goods.

markets. Prices of Pakistan's raw materials soared. And unlike India, she was not then bothered by food-shortages, wheat in the West wing being in exportable surplus, and rice in the East in deficit only slightly. Thus the strain on her national budgeting – a recurrent worry ever since India temporarily withheld the agreed Partition-time cash-balances in 1947–8 – was relieved, and for a short thrilling period she became almost rich, and herself, in effect, a hard-currency area.

That this phase of unwonted prosperity was far from wisely used, rash expenditure during it contributing much to the instability of the 'bad years' 1952–8, is a sorry fact in her history. But at any rate the dramatic international events of September 1949 and June 1950 put her on the map as a State (to express it cynically) no likelier to collapse than most of the world's other 'developing' or under-developed ones.

Though her heritage in known mineral wealth at Partition was less wretchedly poor than in industrial installations, it gave no cause for joy. Compared with India's, it was very ill-balanced – which indeed largely explains why, in British times, industrial development in the areas that became Pakistan did not go ahead faster. They had practically no coal – producing only about 500,000 tons a year, of poor quality; no accessible iron-ore; very little oil, limited it then seemed to a small region west of Rawalpindi; no lucrative speciality such as India's manganese or thorium – unless the chromite in Baluchistan could be regarded as such. Good rock-salt lay in the Punjab hills, some of it being mined at Khewra; but its money-earning power was meagre. And that seemed about all.

Much activity since, by geologists and engineers, has not had proportionate results. As implied in the last chapter, there has been vigorous search for oil by British and American undertakings, but fresh discoveries outside the already known Attock oilfield have been negligible. However, a side-effect of great importance was the exciting find in 1952 of vast reserves of good-quality natural gas at Sui, in Baluchistan. This was quickly exploited; pipes soon took the gas to places as far off as Karachi, Multan, and Lyallpur, reducing Pakistan's fuel-shortage very pleasantly at small cost. The only other major item has been confirmation that immense amounts of high-grade iron-ore lie tucked away in mountainous Chitral; but getting it out, except at prohibitive cost, may always prove a physical im-possibility, unless perhaps the route via the Kunhar valley in Afghanistan could be developed.

One very important thing indeed, describable as mineral, has however not been mentioned – water; a means both of raising crops, and of generating electricity. Pakistan is excellently provided with it, in more manageable form of course in the drier West wing than in the much-flooded East; and her leaders, at the start, wisely concentrated on putting it to the utmost advantage. Many new hydro-electric undertakings are built or building, partly original, partly from old British blue-prints, and largely by foreign financial aid: in the East wing, on the Karnafuli river above Chittagong; and in the West, at a series of places on the Indus and its tributaries : at Warsak, Jaban-Dargai, Kurram-Gahri, Chickoki Malian, and Mangla. In addition, there are the great new irrigation-barrages in the West wing at Mianwali, Taunsa and Kotri, supplementing previous such works finished before Partition, the biggest of which, the so-called Lloyd barrage, is at Sukkur.

But even after completion of unfinished hydro-electric under-takings like the Mangla one, or the projected one at Gujranwala, the capabilities of the higher reaches of the Indus and its sister-streams for generating electricity will remain enormous. For instance, there is a place in the sudden bend of the upper Indus itself, above Bunji, which, if the necessary equipment could be got to so mountainous a tract at tolerable cost, could alone (it is reckoned) produce enough current to satisfy the needs of the entire West wing within any fore-seeable future.

On the long view, therefore, Pakistan's shortages in coal and (it seems) in oil may not greatly matter.

As is well known, a bitter dispute raged for years between India and Pakistan about apportionment of some of the Indus-basin waters for irrigation, this being only disposed of in 1961, not through direct agreement between the two contesting countries themselves, but through long, patient mediation by the World Bank. In British times, the canals that distributed water to the fields in the Indus basin formed an integrated whole : in those days the largest irrigation-system in the world. Partition in 1947 sliced right across the eastern part of it, leaving the upper reaches of three big tributaries – the Sutlej, Beas and Ravi – and also several of the canal headworks, in Indian hands. Pakistan was thus made dependent on her bigger neighbour's goodwill, and on such international law on these matters as existed, for regular flow of water to the plots cultivated by millions of her peasants – regularity being essential for farming in this dry climate. India's seizure of the Vale of Kashmir in the autumn of 1947 worsened things, potentially at least, by putting the upstream reaches of the Chenab and Jhelum also in her control; and in April

1948, she displayed her power for wreaking disaster on Pakistani agriculture by shutting off, for several weeks, all water-supplies to the rich lands around Lahore.

In some ways, this Indo-Pakistani dispute about the Indus-basin waters was even graver than that about Kashmir. It involved the possibility that splendidly fertile great tracts of West Pakistan would be reconverted to desert, and its industrious cultivators made beggars. And in passing we may note the curious resemblances, which have kept bobbing up through this book, between Pakistan and Israel – a State whose existence Pakistan, because of her Pan-Islamic foreign policy, refuses to recognise; for Israel, too, though the geographical scale is much smaller, has perhaps an equally dangerous water-dispute with her Arab neighbours about the Jordan.

The gist of the agreement pressed by the World Bank upon India and Pakistan, which eventually they accepted, is that the former should for irrigation-purposes use the three easterly streams in the basin – Sutlej, Beas and Ravi – and Pakistan the three westerly – Chenab, Jhelum and Indus; and that, to make good the needs of the Pakistani cultivators living downstream along the courses of the three former, and hitherto drawing water from them, a series of great link-canals should be built, cutting across the grain of the country – at huge cost, to come almost wholly from Western sources – so as to provide them, instead, with water from the three westerly rivers. Whether these canals, when finished, will prove tough enough to withstand the gigantic pressures of the floods which sometimes rush down the Himalayan gorges during the ten-weeks' rainy season in summer, apparently in ever-increasing volume because of deforestation on the upper slopes, is a headache more for engineers and cabinet ministers, than for the writers or readers of books. And besides floods, there could be earthquakes; the Indo-Gangetic basin is one of the world's great zones of seismic instability.

If you fly over the rich irrigated Punjab plains – whether Pakistani or Indian – you will see, dotted about the wide green productive expanse, irregular whitish, seemingly sterile or diseased patches; a sort of leprosy. These are the effects of 'waterlogging': uncultivable saline incrustations of the surface of the soil which, like the floods, are apparently increasing year by year; an unforeseen result of prolonged intensive irrigation, and now one of Pakistan's major economic worries. The process is that moisture seeps by stages downwards from the canal-floors, and the shallower earthy distributaries, and the fields themselves; that the general water-table is in consequence gradually raised; and that eventually, salts are thrust through to the good soil at the top, destroying its fertility. Pakistan has thereby been losing an estimated 100,000 acres of her best agricultural land annually. Remedies are expensive, and though progress since 1962 has seemed encouraging, experts on the subject – as on leprosy itself – are not wholly agreed about what is best. Some indirect benefit has however been got from the great increase under the second five-year plan (1960–65) in use of tube-wells, which have tended to lower the water-table.

The problem would be less awkward if Pakistan were still, as in 1947, a country feeling assured of an exportable food-surplus. But despite remarkable improvements since 1960 or thereabouts, her agricultural methods are still largely primitive; mechanisation has not developed as fast as was hoped; and since that first year she has created about 30 million extra mouths to feed. So here we are, back where we found ourselves at the end of Chapter 3, facing in bafflement what Feldman terms 'possibly the most productive aspect of Pakistan's economy, namely parenthood'.

Chapter 18

Politics and Constitution, 1947–58

ISTORICAL 'ifs' are fascinating things, and much has been written about them – with one curious exception. Few writers bother about the medical ones; about the occasions when human affairs might have taken a different course, but for the state of health of importantly-placed men. A striking example in the 1950's may jump to mind : would the British people have been involved in the humiliation of 1956 at Suez, if their Prime Minister had not had disease of the gall-bladder? Other instances will be thought of, ancient and modern; L'Étang, a doctor – probably the chief present-day writer on the subject – has collected a startling array of twentieth-century ones.[1] But all the thirty or so eminent men, whose physical condition at historically crucial junctures he discusses, were European or American. Asian leaders might offer an inquirer richer opportunities, for two reasons. Not only have they been less studied; in their part of the world, sheer personality certainly has a bigger impact on events than in the more educated, established democracies of the West.

Pakistan started her independent national life under a leader of extraordinary ability and prestige. Almost any constitutional, or political, or social innovation that Mr. Jinnah chose to ask for, during those early days, her people would have accepted readily. He wielded authority of an unquestioned, overriding, personal sort such as in India Mr. Nehru never quite accomplished, nor perhaps desired. And besides having this, he to a great extent controlled the actual levers of power. He was simultaneously Governor-General of Pakistan; President of her Constituent Assembly; and President of her main political party, the Muslim League. But within less than thirteen months of her coming into existence, he was dead.

What would have happened – here come two big 'ifs' together – if he had not died then, but lived for another ten years; and if, instead, the illness that killed him had removed Mr. Nehru? Though crude, when put in this form, these linked questions are not chimerical – as we shall explain. And it may be said at once that, had the two things postulated taken place, the entire South Asian scene, as now spread

[1] See Bibliography.

231

before an observer's eye, would have been transformed. Almost certainly Pakistan's 'bad years' – the period 1952–8 – would not have shaped themselves as they did.

It is very difficult for instance to imagine Mr. Jinnah tolerating eight years of dangerous wrangling about the form of the Constitution. One of two things might have happened. Either, on foreseeing bothers and delays, he would himself have laid down what form the Constitution should take. His personal prestige would have amply sufficed for this; besides, he was himself a legal and constitutional expert; and some authorities find signs that his mind was already sorting out the problem's most perplexing, federal aspect. Alternatively, accepting that the differences were deep, he would simply and decisively have shelved the whole thing – as Israel's Prime Minister did; and perhaps the cautiously pragmatic Israeli reasons, which Bentwich describes, would rather have appealed to him.[2] And we may be sure that he would never have let the Muslim League, his own political party, which had been the instrument for creating Pakistan, disintegrate as in 1955. Long before, he would have imposed his will on the quarrelling factions, pulled it together, and got himself re-elected its president if he had ceased to be so – as Mr. Nehru did with the Congress party in 1951.

When he died, Mr. Jinnah was not very old : only seventy. By mid-twentieth-century standards – those, say, of a Churchill, Adenauer or de Gaulle – that is not much. Thus to suppose him living and administering for another decade is reasonable. He had led a frugal, disciplined life. And he did not die of one of the diseases typical of the elderly; far from it. The facts here – as indicated already in Chapter 13 – are very strange. This writer has been at pains to inquire into them anew, seeking out his former doctors and personal staff; and it seems clear that he died of what Victorians would have called a galloping consumption. Not till July 29th, 1948, were his recent bouts of ill-health diagnosed as due to pulmonary tuberculosis; and he was dead on September 11th. In the previous December indeed, when he fell sick for three weeks in Lahore, his doctor there had suspected it. But such symptoms as were seen could have been caused by sheer fatigue from exceptional overwork; and he would not let himself be properly examined. Bolitho, in one passage, hints that he had been warned of possible tuberculosis at Bombay in 1944; but Bolitho's own text, at the relevant earlier

[2] Bentwich, op. cit., p. 107. 'The Prime Minister decided that, since Israel was no longer bound by the behest of the Assembly of the United Nations, it would be better to proceed circumspectly with the Constitution, and let it grow. They should follow the English principle of having no written Constitution. That course was adopted, and has prevailed to the present time.'

point, does not really support this;[3] and no other evidence can be traced.

During an interview with Mr. Jinnah at Karachi in February 1948, the present author touched on the subject of health; and the following summary of what ensued has been more fully recorded elsewhere,[4] and brings out the human quality of the problem. 'Yes, Mr. Stephens, I am better. They say I have been ill; I have not. I know. I get tired. It is natural that I should; I am not young; I have responsibilities. So when I get tired, I rest. It is simple. I tell my doctors to go away. I know what to do. I will not have them fussing; they might annoy me. No, I was not ill at all.' One of the consultants who were called in to examine him in August told this writer later that, when he listened through the stethoscope, at first he could not believe his ears; two-thirds of one lung seemed gone, and about a quarter of the other. It was scarcely credible that a Head of State, without anyone realising it, should have got into such a condition.

Had the disease been discovered before, modern treatment might have checked and perhaps cured it. Presumably the bacilli, halted years earlier by the body's resistances, had lain dormant, and then been suddenly activated by the continuous extreme strain that Mr. Jinnah subjected himself to, in the months while Pakistan was being created. On the known facts, Mr. Nehru was really the likelier tubercular victim. He worked as hard, and in a tenser, more emotional way; and he had been much exposed to infection, for his wife died of the disease after long suffering in the 1930's. To a medical eye, the two men were rather of a type : lean intellectuals, who lived 'on their nerves' and probably did not eat enough.

And if Mr. Nehru, rather than Mr. Jinnah, had died in 1948, his successor would have been Sardar Patel: a sturdy realist who had no use for doctrines and abstractions, a staunch Hindu rather than a believer in secularism, who had been the first among leading Congressmen, in the spring of 1947, to recognise the practical necessity for Partition. And by September, the logic of events had plainly brought him – though he would not have acknowledged it in these words – to accept Mr. Jinnah's 'two-nation' theory as a fact; he even pressed for much bigger population-exchanges than occurred. From undercurrents in talks with the two Indian leaders, this writer – who apologises for personally intruding yet again – formed the opinion (as did others) that on several subjects their views, or at least their angles of approach, differed much. Among these subjects was

---

[3] Bolitho, op. cit.; cf. pp. 211 and 148.
[4] *Horned Moon*, p. 50, shortened.

that 'root of all evil' in Indo-Pakistani affairs, the Kashmir problem. Officially, this was Mr. Nehru's job, so Sardar Patel left the handling of it to him; but it could be deduced that his inner mind doubted the wisdom of trying to embody in the new India a compact bloc of 3 million Muslims dwelling near a frontier. He reckoned that in a crisis they would prove disloyal; that mattered more, as he saw things, than any secularist experiments. And unlike Mr. Nehru, he had no sentimental family attachment to Kashmir. So it is not fanciful to guess that, had he been Indian Prime Minister, a trouble-saving deal might before long have been offered, India (say) to retain the Jammu and perhaps Ladakh provinces of the principality, and an internationally-supervised plebiscite to be quickly organised in the Vale. Pakistan, at first, would not have liked this; she claimed the whole principality. But she had claimed the whole of Bengal and the Punjab – and accepted about half. We may surmise that, if Mr. Jinnah had been alive, ready to exercise his immense authority, such an offer might not have been turned down. Whether Mr. Liaquat Ali Khan would have felt politically strong enough to accept it seems more questionable.

It is interesting to speculate along these lines when such great affairs, involving the fate of millions, may be said – depending on how we look at it – to have hinged on a thing so tiny as the tubercle bacillus: on its virulence, and choice of victim. Historical 'ifs' may well also be asked about other smallish things, bullets or bombs for instance. But these deserve less time; the incalculables are too many. The jerk of an assassin's wrist, the trembling of a trigger-finger, mere hairsbreadth deviations from accuracy in a split second, can indeed (like a disease) mean much more than the difference between death and life for a single man. But they happen instantaneously; the damage one way or another is done. Mr. Nehru escaped attempts at assassination; as did President Nkrumah; neither Mr. Gandhi, Mr. Liaquat Ali Khan, nor other Afro-Asian leaders such as U Aung San or Mr. Banderanaike did so. It seems a mere matter of chance.

And Mr. Liaquat Ali Khan's death, in October 1951, coming so soon after Mr. Jinnah's, in a State new-made, which had proportionately less experienced leadership to draw upon than India, led as we know straight to the much-publicised muddles, the shameful intrigues, the self-seeking and disillusion of 1952–8. Looking back, it may seem a wonder, to some, that after such catastrophic losses of her only two acknowledged statesmen so early, a country like Pakistan, very extraordinary anyhow in its geographical structure and ideological basis, managed to struggle through those years at all.

But then, to some, mere politics seem more important than they are. The speeches and Press statements, the devious manœuvres, the falls and reconstructions of Ministries in Pakistan during that period bulked very big and formidably, to newspaper-readers there and abroad. But other things exist in a country's life than these. The mass of the people, urban and rural, and much of junior officialdom, almost ignored them. And although to senior personnel in the armed forces or the civil services, and to leading business men, the politicians' goings-on might well appear unpleasant, at times worrying, and even – when they spared time to consider them – dangerous to the point of something needing to be done, they meant less in practice than the publicity implied. In this, Pakistan during the 'bad years' rather resembled France, at about the same time.

So low did the reputation of politicians in Pakistan sink, so without substance did their activities appear, that it is often overlooked that in effect three 'coups d'état' took place during those years, not one. Of these, the first two, in April 1953 and October 1954, whose results after a few months rather petered out – details will come later – were inspired by some leading civil servants, the chief of these being (by origin) the Governor-General himself, Mr. Ghulam Mohammad;[5] then followed the third more decisive coup by the Army in October 1958. And all three, though they ruthlessly thrust aside politicians widely supposed to be influential, were accomplished – this is the point – without the slightest bloodshed or disorder. As Binder puts it, writing of the 1954 coup, 'no public protest was raised, no procession taken out, no further agitation went on; the man-in-the-street was unconcerned, completely indifferent.'

Probably many people now will take the view that, at any rate after the double disaster of Mr. Jinnah's and Mr. Liaquat Ali Khan's deaths, the continued effort to give Pakistan a written Constitution was an error. Rivalry with India largely explains it; that country had agreed upon her new Constitution in 1950. But it absorbed too much of the now dangerously weakened Pakistani leadership's energy; and Pakistan's affairs could have been carried on almost indefinitely by the means already in use – the Government of India Act of 1935 and the Independence of India Act of 1947 – further readjusted occasionally to suit her needs. Indeed, large lumps of the 1935 Act were eventually transferred almost verbatim into the first of her two Constitutions, the 'Islamic' one, adopted at long last in 1956. However at the time, after Mr. Liaquat Ali Khan's death in

[5] Until a year or so before Partition, his entire career had been in Government employ.

1951, the decision was made to proceed with Constitution-making; it was assumed that public opinion wanted this; so we must try to explain why it got so stuck.

The chief reason was the Constituent Assembly's inadequacy. It had not been elected for the job. It was inherited; a broken-off part of the intended All-India Constituent Assembly, which had been created in 1946 as a result of the British Cabinet Mission's Plan from the then existing Legislatures, and which, themselves, were the result of the All-India general election in the previous winter.[6] And when, after Partition, it became the Constituent Assembly of Pakistan its membership amounted to less than eighty – in the circumstances not nearly enough; and its sessions were much too short, partly because it had to serve as well, distractingly, as Pakistan's Central Legislature; its personnel, too, was always in flux, the ablest members being sucked off for other duties; and towards the end, after the provincial elections of 1954 in the East wing, it became absurdly unrepresentative. Callard describes its shortcomings well and in detail.[7]

But there were two further reasons – subtler ones: the peculiar federal difficulties, due not merely to the existence of Pakistan's two wings, but to the fact that the West wing, unlike the East, consisted of several units; and the even more peculiar mental chasm, educational in nature and often unbridgeable, between her Westernised intelligentsia and her theologians. These interacted on one another, offering the politicians irresistible scope for intrigue. In consequence, it never seemed possible to tackle one without the other getting in the way.

As indicated, the East wing in 1947 happened to start off as a single administrative unit. But the West, by contrast, was a weird hotch-potch : three Governors' provinces (West Punjab, Sind, and the Frontier Province); two fairly large princely States (Bahawalpur and Khairpur); plus the national capital of Karachi – these all being down on the plains; and in the hills, the former British Baluchistan, plus the four Baluchistan princely States; together with the tribal agencies plus the four princely States of the North-West Frontier. The logical answer to this was to amalgamate the units; then the East and West wings would be brought into balance. But to attempt it was risky. Historical and linguistic factors were involved, of the sort mentioned in Chapter 3, which might prove explosive. Mr. Jinnah could have done it; Mr. Liaquat Ali Khan might have. But it was unattainable by the smaller politicians who came after; and it had to await the chance opened up by the civil servants' coup in

[6] See Chapters 7 and 8.
[7] Callard, op. cit., pp. 77–85.

1954, when it was hustled through as the 'one-unit' reform, prior to the passage of the 1956 Constitution. Meanwhile, intriguers had a happy time, playing off the various West wing units, and the two wings themselves, against one another.

The third reason – the chasm between the English-speaking intelligentsia and the theologians – is unique. Nothing comparable exists in Western countries, and many Western visitors to Pakistan scarcely realise its existence. While there, they meet the Westernised, fairly affluent upper classes – and the poor. But they probably meet no theologians. Those people, however, the so-called mullahs, are there; and plainly, in a State professing at any rate in part to have religion as its basis, they must be important. The trouble is that the Westernised Pakistanis themselves seldom meet them either, mentally at least – a state of affairs primarily ascribable to that pioneer of the subcontinent's Muslim renaissance, the creator of Aligarh, Syed Ahmad Khan. It was his one big failure. He proved too modernist for his time. He pushed the theologians too hard, tied as they were to a rigid tradition; with the result that religious and secular education within the Muslim community split apart. As Albiruni emphasises, this happened even at Aligarh itself; Syed Ahmad Khan had 'to hand over all religious affairs of the college to a committee of orthodox Muslims, and promised to have nothing to do with these matters'. Later, his distinguished pupil Shibli left, drawing off followers after him, to coalesce with the rival orthodox camp. The resultant educational cleavage persists to this day, causing sometimes a sort of schizophrenia in the Pakistani national mind.

We have on the one hand in Pakistan the typical product of the Aligarh movement,[8] culturally very much a Muslim but lax in religious observance, English-speaking, an eager participant in the world of the present. On the other, there is the mullah, the theologian, steeped in Arabic and the past, in traditions brought from seminaries such as Deoband near Saharanpur, or the Nadva-tul-Ulema at Lucknow.[9] And although the Aligarh product may look on the mullahs with fond romantic eye, feeling sincere respect for what he imagines they stand for, he would be outraged at the thought of their running his country's affairs, and would resist any efforts towards it. And he may in fact know less of their real thoughts and aims, indeed of Islam itself doctrinally, than does your scholarly Western visitor. Incomprehension between the two types can be

---

[8] Aligarh now lies in India; but the movement which started there spread to other universities, including those in Pakistan.

[9] Both now in India also. New seminaries have been founded, in Pakistan, at Quetta and Dacca.

almost complete, to an extent scarcely imaginable in Protestant
countries of the West where future clerics and laymen tend to be
educated together, often parting company only after graduating.
This being the case, it was inevitable that spokesmen of the two
types, nurtured almost in different worlds, should to their surprise
and distress at times find themselves in total, blank disagreement
about the form their country's Constitution should take.

When Prime Minister Liaquat Ali Khan was murdered in October
1951, no evident successor could be seen, and the arrangements made
to replace him caused surprise. They were ingenious. Khwaja Nazimuddin, an experienced East Pakistani politician, who had been
made Governor-General after Mr. Jinnah's death in 1948, stepped
down to take on the Prime Ministership; and the Finance Minister
Mr. Ghulam Mohammad, a former civil servant, who had been un-
well, became Governor-General instead.

The new Prime Minister was a respected figure. Of distinguished
family, he had integrity and was liked; moreover he was known to be
a devout practising Muslim. But it is plain, now, that he lacked an
essential quality for the job : force of character. Perhaps, also, history
has been unkind to him. He took office at an adverse moment. Signs
of coming storms, constitutional and economic, had appeared in Mr.
Liaquat Ali Khan's lifetime, but were not fully recognised. In
November 1950, the report of the Constituent Assembly's basic
principles committee had had to be withdrawn, under pressure from
the mullahs; and the boom caused by the Korean war, so helpful to
Pakistan's finances, was collapsing. Harvests had been bad, and
might cause a food-shortage.

At all events, within a few months of his assuming the Prime
Ministership, the impression grew that the nation's affairs had got
dangerously adrift. Decisions were not taken; files were said to pile
up. And though he strove, with admirable loyalty, to proceed with
his predecessor's policies, it seemed that in tackling the more difficult
ones he had not the necessary prestige. Early in 1952, for just this
reason, he ran into heavy trouble in his own home province. Mr.
Jinnah and Mr. Liaquat Ali Khan – perhaps unwisely – had
foreshadowed that Urdu would be made Pakistan's national
language, despite the strong claims of Bengali. Khwaja Nazimuddin repeated this, and moreover in Dacca, though himself a man
of Bengal. The result, in February 1952, was serious rioting in
that city – some students were among the casualties – and an
underswell of subsequent anger throughout the province. The

whole question of a national language had ignominiously to be shelved.[10]

But worse was to follow : the anti-Ahmadi agitation in the West wing, referred to earlier;[11] perhaps Pakistan's gravest domestic upheaval since her birth, because sectarian hostility between Muslims was involved. That remark however begs the main question; for whereas the Ahmadis, or Qadianis, say they are Muslims, many Sunnis deny it. Consequently, dislike of the Ahmadis' doctrines soon got tangled up with the seemingly pressing problem of Pakistan's future Constitution, because Sunnis said that Ahmadis must be declared a separate non-Muslim community, like the Christians or Parsis. A further ugly item was the extent to which the orthodox ulema[12] eventually let themselves be dragged into the affair; people who, throughout Muslim history, have as a rule avoided direct conflict with established secular authority. Details of the whole complex controversy, and of the course which it took under conflicting pressures from the politicians, are set out in the Munir report,[13] an official document which makes good reading.

Khwaja Nazimuddin's Government at Karachi, until almost the last moment, did very little to check the developing crisis. Its growth had been slow. It first seemed getting dangerous in May 1952, after a speech there by Sir Zafrullah Khan, the Foreign Minister, an Ahmadi. It was of course intrinsically perplexing; and the Prime Minister's religious cast of mind, and his respect for the ulema, must have made it the more so for him. On the other hand, its instigators undeniably were people perhaps still unpatriotic, who had been indifferent or hostile to the idea of Pakistan almost up to her birth: people such as the Ahrars, and Maulana Maudoodi's group the Jama'at-i-Islami. At any rate, the months of inaction proved disastrous, enabling the West Punjab provincial Government under Mr. Daultana, during the winter of 1952–3, to switch the mounting popular clamour against Karachi, and then, in February, virtually to forego responsibility, abandoning Lahore to the mob. Between March 3rd and 7th, conditions in that city verged on the anarchic.

In this final emergency Khwaja Nazimuddin acquitted himself with credit. He concurred in recommendations by officials that

[10] It was eventually disposed of in May 1954, by giving Urdu and Bengali equal status.

[11] See Chapter 3.

[12] The terms mullahs and ulema are often used interchangeably. The latter is more correct, and narrower; the former – the more popular term – would also include comparatively heterodox religious figures such as Maulana Maudoodi.

[13] Formally, the *Report of the Court of Inquiry into the Punjab Disturbances of 1953* (Lahore, 1954), presided over by Mr. Mohammad Munir, then Chief Justice of the Lahore High Court.

several religious leaders in Lahore must be arrested, and agreed to
immediate imposition of martial law. These measures broke the back
of the disorders within hours. He then went to the city; got Mr.
Daultana dismissed and replaced by Mr. Noon; and returned to
Karachi almost in triumph. But the civil servants had had enough.
On April 17th came their answer to the long shilly-shallying: an
abrupt announcement, ironically by the Prime Minister's successor
in the Governor-Generalship, Mr. Ghulam Mohammad, formerly
for about twenty years a member of the Audit and Accounts Service.
'I have been driven to the conclusion,' he declared, 'that the Cabinet
of Khwaja Nazimuddin has proved entirely inadequate to grapple
with the difficulties facing the country. I have felt it incumbent
upon me to ask the Cabinet to relinquish office, so that a new
Cabinet, better fitted to discharge its obligations, may be formed.'

This new Cabinet – and once again, surprise was caused – had as
its head a rather obscure, agreeable, youngish ex-politician, Mr.
Mohammad Ali of Bogra, who since 1948 had served abroad as
Pakistan's ambassador in Rangoon, Ottawa, and Washington, and
done well there; a Bengali, like his predecessor – indeed his connection by marriage – but unlike him, almost without popular following.
His pre-Partition political career had been limited to Bengal; the
nation as a whole had scarcely heard of him. So it seemed, at first,
that he would prove little more than the Governor-General's
nominee. Alongside the dismissed Prime Minister three other politicians of national standing were flung out: Sardar Abdur Rab
Nishtar, Mr. Falzlur Rahman, and Pirzada Abdus Sattar. The rest,
six in all – perhaps some had been sounded about the coup beforehand – trooped over without demur to join the new Prime Minister's
team; and with various provincial office-holders such as Mr. Noon,
they soon made nonsense of the hapless Khwaja Nazimuddin's efforts
to stay in politics – he still nominally had a majority in the Legislature, and was President of the Muslim League – by refusing membership of his new working committee. Thus it seemed obvious where
power now lay: with the bureaucracy; in particular with Mr.
Ghulam Mohammad, backed by another former civil servant,
Chaudhuri Mohammad Ali, who had been Finance Minister since
1951; an even abler man perhaps, though less iron-willed. As Callard
remarks, from this time on 'the office of Governor-General was to
cast a shadow over that of Prime Minister' – because 'what had
happened once, could be repeated'.

The theologians who had thwarted Mr. Liaquat Ali Khan over
the basic principles committee's report in November 1950 were now,

temporarily at least, as a result of the Punjab disorders, in total eclipse. Several lay in jail, and two under death-sentences,[14] martial law in Lahore having been harsh. And as the Central Ministers considered unsuitable had been got rid of – Sardar Nishtar for instance had favoured the theologians' views on the Constitution – the way seemed clear for secular-minded Westernised officials to press on strongly towards permanent stabilisation of the country's affairs.

Reports soon began to circulate that an 'Interim Constitution' was being prepared; and the Government during June confirmed them. Its text never emerged; but it was intended, apparently, to by-pass all the abstract points of difficulty which had blocked progress hitherto – whether Pakistan should be termed Islamic, and so on – and to consist simply of mechanism for co-ordinating the working parts of the 1935 Act, as so far used, with the modifications made since Partition. According however to contemporary Press reports, which Binder summarises interestingly, there was a supplementary aim. Dissolution of the existing Assembly would be involved; it had become unrepresentative. And the new one would not be sovereign, wide powers of veto being reserved to the Governor-General, since governing 'had become too complicated to be left to inexpert politicians; the old theory of parliamentary sovereignty had to change'.

If something of this sort had gone through – shorn, even, of that sting in its tail, the Governor-General's wide veto-powers – Pakistan might have been spared much trouble. But the new Prime Minister, back in politics, proved more agile and spirited than perhaps had been foreseen. And the Governor-General and his supporters never felt really sure of their ground, whether with the public (and of how far the mullahs might sway the public); or with the law; or with that final depository of strength the Army, which, so far – except for fulfilling efficiently but with distaste its tasks in Lahore – had held aloof.

And a fresh factor was intruding : the need for provincial elections, next year, in the country's most populous part, the East wing. The three West wing provinces, starting with West Punjab in 1951, had already had theirs; and the Muslim League – in places by questionable means – had successfully got back. But in the East, where a vague popular sense of grievance was known to exist, they had been postponed. And as the summer advanced, it became clear that League organisers there reckoned their electoral prospects to be poor, unless they could disengage from this 'Interim Constitution' project evolved in Karachi. They might have doughty foes; politicians such as Mr. Fazl-ul-Haq and Mr. Suhrawardy, who had fallen

[14] Maulanas Niazi and Maudoodi. The sentences were later remitted.

Q

out with Mr. Jinnah before Partition, but now seemed to be getting popular again. And on September 17th, 1953, shortly before the Constituent Assembly was due to meet in Karachi – it had been put into recess after the April coup – they announced their opposition formally.

And almost immediately after it met, proposals unexpectedly emerged, under the Prime Minister's lead, for solving the long-standing question of provincial representation in a future federal Legislature. Known as the 'Mohammad Ali formula', these were passed unanimously in October by the League parliamentary party in committee. The civil servants' whole 'Interim Constitution' project then had to be shelved. This was a heavy personal rebuff for the Governor-General – now in serious ill-health. The effects of the April coup seemed almost destroyed. Politicians and the old Constituent Assembly became pre-eminent again; and the Assembly resumed its Constitution-making, some of the compromises on matters such as the State's Islamic quality, embodied in the abortive 1956 Constitution, being due to work done at this stage.

However, the Assembly-members – more than half of whom were Bengalis, chosen we must recall as long ago as 1946, before Pakistan was born – had no idea what was coming at them out of the East wing. Nor had anyone. Detached British observers of the electoral scene, like indigenous experts, forecast that the League, as elsewhere, would struggle back, though perhaps with a much reduced majority. The result, in April 1954, dumbfounded all. It was a rout. The League got ten seats; its opponents, a motley combine calling itself the United Front which fell to pieces soon after, got 223. And henceforth an element of sheer unreality, almost of farce, invades the Pakistani political stage. Parties and principles alike fade, then vanish. Only a confused turmoil of rival struggling personalities remains. Through the dust of conflict, little is discernible beyond ineffective clutchings, on the one side, for private profit and place, and on the other, for the public weal and national survival, between men of varying moral statures whom fate thrust temporarily to the forefront.

Within two months of the newly elected East wing Cabinet taking office at Dacca, the Central Government at Karachi felt obliged to dismiss it. Mr. Fazl-ul-Haq, the Chief Minister, unwisely revisiting Calcutta, had made remarks there interpreted as treasonable to Pakistan; and at Narayanganj, in the huge new jute-mill of which the country was so proud, an appalling riot occurred – apparently through sheer administrative ineptitude – in which over 400 people were killed and about 1,000 injured. The provincial Cabinet was thereupon evicted on Karachi's orders, and General Iskander Mirza, then Defence Secretary,[15] sent over to rule as Governor under the 'breakdown' clause of the 1935 Act.

Meanwhile at Karachi the Bengali members of the nearly eight-years-old Assembly, forgetful it seemed that, after the East wing elections, they represented almost nobody, had proceeded on a legislative path unmistakably aimed at a systematic pruning away of the Governor-General's powers. They found support among the re-emboldened mullahs, and among Pathan and Sindhi members jealous of the Punjabis' numerical strength. These activities culminated, during October, in an attempted amendment of the Government of India Act of 1935 which some construed – Callard gives details, and they were certainly peculiar – as no less than a conspiracy to seize power, instigated by one of the former Central Ministers, Mr. Fazlur Rahman.

The ailing Governor-General, on October 24th, then hit back suddenly and hard. It was the civil servants' second coup, more thorough than the first. He dismissed the entire Assembly which, he said, 'as at present constituted, has lost the confidence of the people, and can no longer function'. And he drastically reconstructed the Central Cabinet, keeping the Prime Minister and three others, but dropping the rest, and appointing nine new ones, none of whom then had seats in the Assembly. They included the evidently reluctant Commander-in-Chief, General Ayub Khan, who for a while agreed to be Defence Minister; General Mirza, recalled from the East wing to be Minister of the Interior; and two able politicians from beyond the pale of the Muslim League, men who indeed in 1947-8 had been looked on almost as enemies of Pakistan, Mr. Suhrawardy of Bengal, and Dr. Khan Sahib of the Frontier. And within a few days General Mirza – obviously now a rising figure, because nothing but almost superhuman will-power still kept the physically-stricken Governor-General in office – was talking of the need for Pakistan being 'under controlled democracy for some time to come'.

Thus transformed, the Central Government during the next eighteen months pushed right ahead with constructive tasks hitherto stopped by the politicians' disagreements. A fantastic tangle which soon arose about the legal implications of what the Governor-General had just done – apparently, every act passed by the Assembly since Mr. Jinnah's death in 1948 had been technically invalidated –

---

[15] Subsequently Governor-General, then President. Sometimes spelt Sikander. A member of the Political Service since 1926, he had entered it from the Army, and so kept military rank. He had recently become major-general.

did not seem to put it much out of stride. First among the tasks was unification of the West wing; the critical 'one-unit' reform alluded to earlier. Clearly, the two wings' contrasted internal structures – one a single administrative entity, the other a hotch-potch as explained – had been a big factor in the country's troubles so far, opening up superb opportunities for intrigue; and the Cabinet almost overreached itself in its efforts to get the change made quickly, thrusting provincial Ministers in or out of office for the purpose with complete lack of scruple – conduct helped by the evident fact that, now, the only political party in Pakistan that mattered, the Muslim League, was breaking up.

Within less than a year, the required unification was achieved; perhaps the biggest internal change in Pakistan's history. It went through without serious public protest or legislative hitch on October 14th, 1955. Meanwhile, General Mirza had taken over the Governor-Generalship from the dying Mr. Ghulam Mohammad. And Mr. Mohammad Ali of Bogra had ceased to be Prime Minister – daily tightrope-walking between the bureaucracy and the politicians having proved too much for him – and been replaced by someone of similar name but very different origins already mentioned, Chaud-huri Mohammad Ali the Finance Minister, trained in the same branch of the civil service as Mr. Ghulam Mohammad himself. And a useful way of outflanking the aforementioned legal tangle had been found. On the federal Chief Justice's advice, a fresh Con-stituent Assembly had been elected, indirectly indeed like its prede-cessor, but from provincial Legislatures themselves elected since Independence in 1947. So the new body could thus not be charged, as the earlier one was, with being altogether unrepresentative. And it was this Assembly which, ably piloted by Chaudhuri Mohammad Ali, managed at last, on March 23rd, 1956, to pass Pakistan's first Constitution.

Historians are unfairly advantaged over men living amidst events. They can look back. It is not difficult, now, to see why the Constitu-tion of 1956 failed. But those who, at the time, did not expect inevitable breakdown, and who for months after its passage kept hoping that it would establish itself, and healthily renew the coun-try's political life, were not obtuse. In many ways, it was a well-built thing.[16] What scarcely anyone recognised, then, was its basic flaw: that it assumed, as axiomatic, the feasibility of making Parliamentary institutions copied from those of Westminster permanently func-

[16] Details are in Callard, pp. 330–341.

tional, in Pakistani conditions such as had actually come to exist in the later 1950's.

Had such a Constitution been enacted while Parliamentarians of the quality of Mr. Jinnah or Mr. Liaquat Ali Khan were alive, men who knew how to work such institutions, and who controlled a coherent, disciplined party, the prospects of success might have been bright. In West Pakistan, at any rate, no intractable minority-problem existed – the factor which has often nullified Westminster-style Parliamentary democracy elsewhere. But those good days were no more; vanished with the smoke of an assassin's bullet in October 1951. And after the chequered political experiences that Pakistan had since undergone at Mr. Ghulam Mohammad's hands, in the provinces as well as at the Centre, and with the Muslim League – the instrument by which she had been created – now almost self-destroyed, and with similar non-Parliamentary men, professional bureaucrats, members of the former British Imperial Services installed both as President and Prime Minister, the optimists' hopes lacked grip on reality. And there was the further consideration that, for the historical and educational reasons of nineteenth-century origin stressed earlier in this book, the chances of British forms of democracy proving transplantable to Pakistani soil were probably anyhow, from the start, intrinsically poorer than to Indian.

The rest of this chapter's sorry tale can soon be told. Between the spring of 1956 and the autumn of 1958 – and we are strongly reminded again of France, around that time – Pakistan had four Prime Ministers. Only about a fortnight after the Constitution's enactment, Chaudhuri Mohammad Ali's hold on office was shaken, and General Mirza's future tenure more subtly undermined, by completely unprincipled conduct on the politicians' part. President and Prime Minister had decided that the best person to be Chief Minister of the West wing was Dr. Khan Sahib; and they had got an assurance of Mr. Daultana's influential support in fixing this. But at the last moment he and other Muslim Leaguers defected, on the pretext of Dr. Khan Sahib's anti-Pakistani past. Not to be outdone, that politician – who could play tricks too – contrived by promises of ministerial posts to lure several Leaguers to his side, and went on to form a party of his own, the Republicans – with which President Mirza soon let himself get identified. Disruption among Leaguers, as soon as the President's leanings became apparent, then naturally spread to the Centre; for he would have future political plums to offer. By August, all but ten of the 36 Leaguers in the Assembly at Karachi were Republicans. East wing affairs then got involved. And when, in the course of a complex triangular wrangle in October, Chaudhuri Mohammad Ali lost his majority – though he could easily have arranged another one – he abandoned the Prime Ministership in disgust.

His successor was Mr. Suhrawardy, leader of the Awami League, a component of the East wing's so-called United Front after the 1954 elections. And although President Mirza, not long before, had been reported as saying that this controversial gentleman would only become Prime Minister of Pakistan over his dead body, the two of them, for a while, made an effective team. Temperamentally, indeed, they had resemblances. Clever, and aware of it; bold; personally ambitious, and rejoicers in power for its own sake; thoroughly Westernised and secular; and not noticeably shackled by ethical scruples, they were well qualified, in partnership, to give the country resolute leadership. Pakistan, but for them, would certainly have quit the Commonwealth during the Suez crisis of November 1956. For Sir Anthony Eden's policies put an unparalleled strain on Anglo-Pakistani relations; the public felt outraged by what seemed to them a wanton attack, by an infidel Christian-Jewish combine, on a weak fellow-Muslim country, and widespread anti-British disorders occurred. The Mirza-Suhrawardy partnership also coped well with an awkward domestic problem: that whereas the West wing wanted continuance of separate electorates[17] in the nation-wide general elections intended to be soon held under the new Constitution, the East wing favoured joint ones.

But the pair mistrusted one another, as was natural. And a sudden move by Mr. Suhrawardy in October 1957, aimed it seemed against the Republican party, stirred the President's immediate antagonism and cost him his job. For he still had not much popular support to draw on; his disloyal attempt – as many regarded it – to sabotage the Pakistan-project in July 1947, when he was Muslim League Premier of undivided Bengal, had not been forgotten. The titular leader of what remained of the Muslim League, Mr. Chundrigar, then found himself Prime Minister; but no juggling with figures could get him sure backing among the Assembly factions, where personal feuds between Republicans and Leaguers had become acute, and he had to resign before the end of the year, to be succeeded by Mr. Noon.

By now, mere stratagems to retain or capture office were practically the sole preoccupation of politicians, Central and provincial, because of the prospect of general elections early next year – the first in Pakistan's history. Everyone assumed that, whoever held

[17] See Chapter 4, p. 71

Ministerships at the time in Karachi, Dacca or Lahore would rig the results and so keep power. Manœuvrings of the most shameless sort therefore intensified – and meanwhile, the country's affairs slid towards chaos. The national finances were in frightening disarray; prestige abroad had slumped almost to nil; corruption or allegations of it flourished everywhere, and there could be little doubt that it had reached the higher ranks of the civil service. In the East wing, during September, a meaningless vendetta in the Legislature resulted in the Awami League faction getting the Speaker formally declared insane; whereupon, two days later, its rivals of Mr. Fazl-ul-Haq's Krishak Sramik party, in an organised demonstration, hurled pieces of furniture at his Deputy – causing his death.

The Army – and we may find it odd that apparently the struggling politicians scarcely gave such a possibility a thought – had now, however, like the civil servants earlier, had enough. During the night of October 7th-8th a group of generals led by the Commander-in-Chief seized power, and by means of a proclamation issued through the President, abrogated the Constitution of 1956, dismissed the Central and provisional Cabinets 'with immediate effect', dissolved the Central and provincial Legislatures, abolished all political parties throughout the country, and imposed martial law.

Chapter 19

Military Revolution, 1958–62

PAKISTAN'S military revolution of October 1958 seems likely to go down to history as the most efficient and benign thing of its sort that the twentieth century has seen. This writer was there at the time, and indeed had a post in G.H.Q. at Rawalpindi, so can write on it with confidence. It was entirely bloodless; was certainly popular; and in its treatment of the evicted politicians showed a magnanimity, and an acumen, which other countries that have since gone through similar changes – Pakistan's ally Turkey for instance – might well have copied.

First reactions from nations having special concern with Pakistani affairs, such as India or Britain, were adverse however. Mr. Nehru, whose disapproval of earlier military coups elsewhere – of Colonel Nasser's, Brigadier Kassem's, or (in nearby Burma) General Ne Win's – had not been very noticeable if felt at all, showed extreme annoyance at what had happened.[1] Rude remarks poured from him. 'Naked military dictatorship', despotism 'without a veil', shameless betrayal of the democratic cause were the sort of things he charged General Ayub with; and he wanted to get Pakistan expelled from the Commonwealth, because of her régime's obnoxious nature. The British, too, were shocked. Amiably convinced that their ways of doing things are always best, and proud of having, as they believe, invented the Mother of Parliaments (they forget the Icelanders), they regard all un-British forms of government, the American included, with puzzled disfavour; and with their experiences under Cromwell in mind, they keep specially cold looks for military dictatorships. Mr. Nehru, they would have agreed, was going rather too far; but that such an overthrow of established Westminster-style institutions should happen in the Commonwealth, of all places, was really quite improper. So with pursed lips they turned away, misconstruing the nature of the Pakistani innovation. And within three weeks, something happened which stiffened this disapproving mood: the new

---

[1] The sequence of Afro-Asian military coups, from 1952 to 1962, was thus: Egypt, July 1952; Iraq, Burma (the first coup), Pakistan, Sudan, respectively July, September, October, and November 1958; Turkey, May 1960; Burma (the second coup), March 1962. Except Turkey, all these countries had once been British dependencies. There have been many more coups since.

248

régime's treatment of President[2] Mirza, who had influential British friends. The episode needs a section to itself.

As President, he had concurred in the Army's take-over on October 7th–8th; indeed, the formal proclamation of it, and on October 24th of the revolutionary Cabinet's membership,[3] was made in his name, which gave it a cloak of legality. And past utterances of his, to which we have referred, had plainly denoted no repugnance to the idea of Pakistan being paternalistically ruled. Yet on October 26th he was suddenly got rid of, General Ayub becoming President instead; and six days later he found himself on an aircraft, London-bound, and in effect exiled. It was startling; it gave the coup an unstable, almost Levantine air, and cast the deposed President rather in the role of a Neguib. In Karachi, newspaper reports soon had it that a reason for his exit was that he had been found financially corrupt; but retrospective considerations show that this, in broad terms at least, must certainly have been unjust, and should be expunged from memory. Indeed the most horrifying thing about the Pakistan of 1952–8 was the readiness with which such charges were made – and believed. No one could judge where corruption began or ended; the evil fed upon itself; there was undoubtedly much of it, and Pakistanis are talkative folk. Years of flagrant self-seeking by the politicians had brought public affairs so low that the average person, hearing such a charge, at once gave it credence.

The substantial cause of President Mirza's going is however fairly clear : he had let himself get entangled, it seemed beyond scope for withdrawal, in political faction and intrigue. The 1956 Constitution, under Chaudhuri Mohammad Ali's guidance – and with Mr. Ghulam Mohammad's interventions in mind – had demarcated the limits of the Presidential powers exactly. But President Mirza soon managed to outflank these, by active personal support for individual party leaders or groups, to his own position's benefit – as also, he no doubt believed, to that of the State. He had virtually fathered the Republican party which, so far as most people could see, had no intelligible programme beyond mere capture or retention of office. General Ayub explained the episode thus : 'The feeling existed,' he said on October 31st, 'that Mirza was as responsible for the political deterioration as anyone; it had been his job to stop it.'

Woodruff's book, written six years or so before, contains a

---

[2] The Governor-Generalship lapsed on the launching of the 1956 Constitution, and Gen. Mirza thereupon became President instead.

[3] It consisted, besides Gen. Ayub, of three generals – one of them medical – and eight non-political civilians.

character-sketch of the man who became Pakistan's first President. Officials on the North-West Frontier in British days, he says – Mirza spent most of his time there – were of two sorts : the dedicated enthusiasts such as 'Bunch' Parsons, and the 'bon viveurs'. And he names Mirza (and one other, a British official) as typifying the latter; as someone who 'enjoyed the Frontier in rather the same way as the Pathan'; who liked 'getting the better of a man by a cunning trick, intercepting, for instance, a piece of intelligence that had been bought by the other side, buying it back before it was delivered, and substituting something else'; as one of those people who care little 'about what might happen in five years; opportunists hoping to get over the next hurdle, and perhaps obtain some amusement'. And he recounts the fascinating tale of how, on an early occasion, Mirza got an intended troublesome political procession put to rout, by contriving a wayside offer of hospitality, the hot tea supplied having been well laced, beforehand, with a quick-acting aperient. As President of Pakistan from 1956 to 1958 he unquestionably served her efficiently, according to his lights. But those lights were not of a clear, reformist tint; and had he remained Head of State, it seems improbable that, in the public's eye at least, the military revolution could have kept its lustre. Indeed, rumour had it that already, during those three weeks after the take-over, he had been up to his former game, trying to play off one important Army personage against another; and that recognition of this was what speeded his exit.

Another cause for criticism of the régime by outside commentators, during its first few months, was economic. Business men thought its methods too crude. Blackmarketing, profiteering, illegal trade in import-licences, smuggling and so on had been jumped on very heavily, under the martial law regulations; and prices crashed, some by 33 per cent or more – at first to the public's joy. But the more junior Army officers seemed to think the country's economy could be permanently managed by simple issue of orders, as on the parade-ground. What in fact happened, within a few weeks, was total stoppage of much normal trade; goods vanished from the market as soon as visible stocks had been cleared. Shortages and confusion became quite serious.

These troubles were in due course disposed of by the régime's deliberate rehabilitation of the civil services, the Army officers being steadily reverted to their normal jobs. Civilian officials meanwhile however had undergone a thorough 'screening' by special committees set up under martial law. Detailed statements of private wealth had been demanded from all senior personnel in Government

employ; possible past misdemeanours and political contacts were looked into; and some highly-placed civilians – though magnanimously not shorn of their pensions – found themselves sacked and in public disgrace. In the West wing, 84 officials of various sorts were eventually either 'compulsorily retired', dismissed, or downgraded; and in the East, 124 suffered a like fate. Others, however, though probably guilty too, after being well frightened were kept on; for at Partition-time Pakistan only got about 50 members of the former I.C.S., and as yet simply had not enough trained officials to go round. And from the moment of the take-over General Ayub was determined that the Armed Forces – except for the briefest possible initial period – should not get bogged down in civilian affairs. Their job was national defence, and they must be kept in efficient readiness for it. To purge the civil services therefore and restore their morale; to simplify their work by better procedures; and then to hand administration back to them under the safeguard of martial law was one of his firm aims of policy. And by the spring of 1959, it could be said that much towards this had been done. Many senior civil servants were delighted by the changed conditions. They could do their jobs without hindrance, now, from Ministers perpetually trying to buttress up precarious majorities in the Legislatures on the shifting sands of party faction; and members of the new Cabinet actually came with regularity to the office, and dealt with files fast. It was rather like what serving under a good Viceroy's Executive Council must have been, in the old days.

As indicated previously, the régime's handling of the dismissed politicians was extraordinarily intelligent. It achieved the practical results wanted with liberality, and the minimum of fuss. These fallen public figures got no scope at all – as Turkey's so tragically did – for becoming martyrs. The idea was that the worst of them should be made ridiculous – and then let drift into obscurity. Hangings or shootings were never suggested. Only one Central Minister, Mr. Khuhro of Sind, a notorious man, who ironically enough held the Defence portfolio at the time of the coup, was even arrested – in his case, on a specific blackmarketing charge. Five politicians who had formerly been Ministers in the East wing at periods prior to the coup were also jailed for a while on suspicion. All the others, Central and provincial, were told, in sum, that their doings would be vigorously investigated; that if something bad came to light, trials under martial law would ensue; that these would be fair, and that accused persons would get due facilities for their defence; that if the charges were proved, the likely penalty would be disqualification

from public life for a term of years; but that if, instead, they would rather volunteer beforehand not to stand for trial – which might save trouble all round – that would be all right, but the same penalty would apply. Many of them chose the second course. In the West wing alone, over 40 politicians including eleven former Chief Ministers of provinces were disqualified for six years; and at the Centre, two former Prime Ministers were among those similarly dealt with.

This remarkable arrangement, coupled with the facts that the coup had gone through entirely without bloodshed or disorder, and was obviously welcomed with heartfelt relief by the great mass of the people, should have shown critics, in Britain and elsewhere, that Pakistan's military revolution was something out of the ordinary, which needed friendly study. There was further the consideration that, at this early stage, what seemed honest effort was being made to find a way back to more democratic constitutional arrangements, perhaps of indigenous making – as had indeed been promised by General Ayub when he assumed the Presidentship. Something of the régime's distinctive flavour is conveyed by an experience of the author's. Staying with friends in one of the cities at the time when the politicians' past doings were under active inquiry, he learned that at lunch next day he would probably meet a leading ex-Minister, whom he knew. Being then temporarily in the Pakistan Government's employ, he rang up the local general, to ask what one did in such circumstances. 'Go right ahead, old chap, it'll be a good party I'm sure. Everyone knows what he's been playing at. The last thing we want is to drive these fellows underground. Glad you phoned me, though.'

For tax-evasion, which had been gross, and to which some politicians in office had turned an obstinately blind eye, lest they lost votes that powerful evaders such as the big landlords might control, the régime used the same medicine : its own special blend of liberality and shrewdness. Evaders were told, in effect, that officialdom knew much about what had been happening; that the ex-Ministers themselves however were partly to blame; that people who had not paid would therefore now be allowed a fixed time in which to make true statements of their affairs; if they did so, and actually paid up, they would be spared punishment; but that if not, they would very soon learn what being punished under martial law meant. The result was the disclosure, within about three months, of undeclared income amounting to £99,000,000 and the recovery of £18,000,000 in taxes.

Even more dramatic, though on a smaller scale, was the disruption

of the gold-smuggling gangs. Senior police officials had long been aware of their doings, and even of the whereabouts of much of the gold – mostly in underwater hideouts along the Karachi coast; but they had been curbed from doing anything effective – this was perhaps the old régime's worst scandal – by eminently-placed political persons. Within a few days of the military coup, the police got full freedom to proceed; and during October and November alone, illegal hidden gold was brought to the surface worth about £1,500,000.

General Ayub took early opportunity for trying to put relations with India on a happier footing. The feud between the two countries, he felt, was plainly absurd. Regardless of the larger strategic background and of Communist threats from the north, they were frittering away their limited energies and funds, which ought to be used for the peoples' uplift, on futile squabbling. Except perhaps for the complex dispute about Kashmir, there was little between them which commonsense could not settle. He approached the problem with a soldier's directness; and as someone who, unlike previous Pakistani leaders, need not worry about precariously-poised votes in a Legislature. Diplomatic soundings were taken; and then, seeing a chance of tackling it while on an air-journey from Karachi to Dacca – and ignoring Mr. Nehru's earlier aspersions – he proposed a halt at Delhi, for a talk with him.

This took place on September 1st, 1959. Nothing much resulted. During it, he apparently went so far as to suggest India and Pakistan working towards a joint defence policy. A pause ensued – of more than a year. Not until September 19th, 1960, did Mr. Nehru return the visit, various preoccupations being adduced; and vexation on the Pakistani side grew. Eventually, discussions were held over five days, mainly at Rawalpindi and Nathiagali. Reports afterwards indicated that the two men, as was scarcely surprising, had not found themselves temperamentally akin. And if we exclude routine contacts at Commonwealth conferences in London, they did not subsequently meet.

Looking back, it seems that the only solid outcome of F.-M. Ayub's initiative[4] was the arrangement of 1959–60, mentioned in Chapter 15, about better frontier-demarcation and prevention of border affrays. The treaty of 1960, on apportioning the Indus valley's waters for irrigation, though very important, was an international affair, brought about more by long patient mediation from the World Bank, and promises of vast foreign financial aid, than by anything the two disputants did. It would probably be no exaggeration to say that, by

[4] He became field-marshal in October 1959.

the spring of 1961, F.-M. Ayub and his advisers had concluded that to try to reach fundamental understanding with Mr. Nehru was mere waste of time; that his very gifted and in many ways wise and tolerant but now septuagenarian mind had become so fixed in its anti-Pakistani attitudes that nothing could move it.

An episode of a military sort during the new régime's first few months, which much annoyed it, resembled in a curious way the notorious international affair of the intruding U2 American aircraft in May 1960. Reconnaissances early in 1959 over the West wing by planes of the Indian Air Force were noticed, at heights above what the Delhi authorities presumably thought Pakistani interceptors could reach. The routes taken by the intruders were carefully plotted on graphs. Particularly deep penetrations occurred on the great Id-ul-Fitr festival, April 10th, at the morning hour when Muslims might be expected to be at prayer in the mosque. One Indian aircraft, a Canberra equipped for photography, got as far as Rawalpindi, about 150 miles inside Pakistan from the nearest point of the Indian frontier. The Pakistanis, however, had perhaps guessed that some such trick might be played; and one of their interceptors, a Sabre, flying actually rather above its ceiling, managed to shoot the intruder down – without killing the occupants. Instead of an apology for so crude a violation, the Pakistanis got nothing but prevarication and abuse from the Indian Defence Minister, Mr. Krishna Menon. But this was an incident, merely. Much graver and more significant, as fresh illustration, in most Pakistanis' eyes, of India's basically expansionist aims, of her wish in due time to reunite the entire holy soil of Bharat Mata, by force if needs be, and regardless of international law or Gandhian pacifist teachings, was her subsequent armed annexation, in December 1961, of Goa. They did not fail to notice the contrast, here, between her conduct and that of the Communist Chinese, who had not yet sought to conquer Hongkong, much smaller in area, though what happened in 1941 showed this to be tactically easy. And beyond such matters, of course, lay an uglier one still : her continued obduracy, in defiance of past pledges, about the promised plebiscite in Kashmir.

Domestically, the new régime's chief first achievement was resettlement of the urban refugees, especially at Karachi: an achievement visible and indeed spectacular, and the more striking for this reason. That during the first few years after Partition in 1947 Pakistan should have felt almost overwhelmed by the refugee problem could be well understood; in scale alone – as indicated in Chapter 3 – it was enough to daunt even any long-established Government. But,

equally, it was not understood why the country's capital should enter its second decade since Independence, with the pitiable condition of the scores of thousands of indigent fugitives there still, in broad terms, no whit better, and in some ways such as sanitation certainly worse than at the start. Swarms of destitutes lived homeless on the sidewalks, under improvised shelters of rusty tin and sacking; estimates showed that, in 1958, Karachi had no fewer than 120,000 families of such people. The multitudinous continuing filth, and stench, and wretchedness were indescribable. And one of the worst clusters of grossly overcrowded shacks and hovels, unfit for animals to live in, lay beside the main route from one of the airports to the rich centre of the city. Visiting foreigners were appalled – not merely by what they saw and smelt, but by the apparent helpless apathy of successive political Cabinets towards this mass of human misery unmitigated on their doorstep. Probably nothing so discredited Pakistan internationally, during the confused years before the military coup, as the persisting shameful squalor along the pavements of her capital.

The task of setting things right was given to General Azam, one of the five Army officers who had shared responsibility for the coup with General Ayub : a warmhearted extrovert Pathan of overflowing energies – who later endeared himself to the Bengali public when Governor of the East wing. He arranged a quick survey, getting the help of local people including university students; made a rough general plan; called in a foreign firm of architectural consultants backed by the Ford Foundation; and by June 1959 had got some good, clean, but not lavish housing built at the first of his new satellite townships – Korangi, a breezy, sandy wilderness about seven miles east of Karachi, near where the R.A.F. had had a seaplane base during the war – and some of the capital's unhoused refugees were already beginning to move in. Before the end of the year, 75,000 of them had been settled there – and back in the capital, bulldozers had destroyed the loathsome shanties that they left, and cleared up the mess. Similar settlements, now, were being built elsewhere : at Malir in the Karachi area, and in less afflicted regions scattered about the East wing as well as the West. But Korangi, and the transformed streets of Karachi itself, became for some while symbols in the public's mind of the military régime's humane spirit, right sense of priorities, and capacity to get things done.

More basic, though less visually noticeable, were its bold agrarian reforms in the West wing, first announced on January 24th, 1959, and supplemented by a detailed ordinance next month. Though big eventual economic benefits were looked for from them – improved farming techniques, larger crops, lessened foreign food-imports, a

more prosperous and contented peasantry – their main aim was
political: to smash the power of the West wing's feudal landlords.
This had been among the banes of recent Pakistani national life, and
a major cause of the country's instability.[5] Adult suffrage – as introduced in the last elections – had paradoxically worsened things.
Landlordly influence grew. For some of the estates in the Punjab and
Sind were huge, and the aristocrats owning them soon saw the value
of their tenants' votes, and learnt how to sway them. In the Punjab,
6 per cent of the landowners held more than 20 per cent of the entire
cultivable area; and conditions in Sind, because of local customs as
well as mathematically, were in some ways worse. In consequence, a
very corrupt landlords' 'lobby' had grown up in the Legislatures.
And its influence on national policy was worse than merely negative;
for besides being self-interested and reactionary, its behaviour on
detailed issues was unpredictable, owing to latent feuds between the
landed chiefs. No previous Pakistani Cabinets – because of vote-
gathering calculations, and their own membership-structure – had
dared to touch this dangerous social nettle. But the landlords' doings
had by this time antagonised even sections of society normally conservative : military and civilian officers of the moneyed families, and
the West wing's rising industrialist class, notably the textile magnates.
Many of these now recognised that agrarian reforms were inevitable.
And the interests of the Army as a whole were of course mainly rural,
and tallied with those of the politically-stultified tenants on the big
estates.

While harsh, the reforms were not brutally expropriatory. Observers of Leftist leanings indeed thought them not nearly drastic
enough. But that they achieved their main aim was clear. The big
landlords' power was broken; a political lobby such as had existed
could never revive. The whole scheme was based on a report by an
expert commission which had worked to a time-table. President
Ayub's method before launching big changes. Under the confirma-
tory ordinance of February 1959 no landlord could keep more
than 500 acres of irrigated or 1,000 of unirrigated land, together with
150 of orchard. The rest would be offered for sale among the tenants
already farming it, at a fixed sum payable by them in 50 half-yearly
instalments. Landlords would be compensated for the land surrendered – on a scale however that fell as the size of their holdings
increased – in heritable bonds bearing 4 per cent taxable interest,

[5] Land-tenure in the East wing had been on different and perhaps even more
outmoded principles, derived from the 'permanent settlement' of 1793. But since
Independence, reforms had already occurred there, helped by the fact that many
of the Hindu proprietors had eschewed Pakistani nationality and become Indian
citizens. The main enactments had been in 1950 and 1956.

and having a 25-years' redemption-date. These bonds' actual worth, at a rough market reckoning, would average about a quarter or a third of what the land might earlier have fetched. That might seem hard; but it was often less so than the facts really warranted; for alert landlords such as ex-Ministers, guessing that strong measures must come, had of late been quietly parcelling out their holdings among relatives. Some indeed had begun this before the coup; or else had gradually been selling land and buying up urban property or industrial shares instead. And even 500 acres of well-farmed irrigated land can yield a big income.

The reforms' scale can be grasped from the following figures. Nearly 6,000 landowners in the West wing were affected, the amount of land formally brought within the ordinance's scope being no less than 9·1 million acres. But many of them were only smallish holders, owning acreages not much beyond the prescribed maximum. Thus the land actually surrendered and transferred to tenants amounted to 2·3 million acres. The tenants who took it – on payment as described – and who thus themselves became proprietors, numbered about 150,000; and provision was made for helping them to farm efficiently by Government 'taccavi' loans of up to Rs. 1,200 per family, a total of Rs. 30 millions being set aside for this good purpose.

Also at about this time – the régime was a quick mover – news got about that President Ayub had some political innovation of a 'grass-roots' sort under study: a scheme whereby everyone could vote, but the ordinary person would vote only locally, for men or causes he knew or could grasp, and would thus be represented on the parish council as it were; and that a constitutional structure might be built up on this, through ascending tiers to the provincial and then the national one, in which the elective principle would operate, but only indirectly. It seemed interesting. But these, surely, were early days for thinking about votes or political changes at all. The plain man – if you could talk to him in something like his own language, to your orderly's uncle out in the village, to the police constable, or the taxi-driver or small shopkeeper in the towns – was obviously uninterested in elections or else disgusted by them, and wanted nothing more than clean, efficient rule such as he was now getting – and rough use of martial law against the rich. Cynicism could also at first be sensed among senior officials and foreign residents; such a scheme, they evidently felt, could amount to little more than renewal of old familiar local self-governing bodies like the panchayats and union boards.

The scheme was formally announced on October 26th, 1959, just

R

a year after F.-M. Ayub had become President. And to a historian, looking back on it some years afterwards, it stands out as the first step, or rather, as the first and third ones in effect taken together – a second, the most difficult, had yet to be worked out – in about the most remarkable feat of suicide, or shall we say planned abdication, by a military autocracy that the world has witnessed : statesmanly and far-sighted in high degree, perhaps; but perhaps premature and rash, perhaps an outcome of the martial mind's liking for mere speed – as arguably also in Lord Mountbatten's case twelve years before. We are too near it, yet, to judge which epithet best fits. But this can confidently be added. It was actuated by a spirit totally unlike what Mr. Nehru and many British people supposed, when the coup took place. It was liberal; was progressive in a spontaneous way, and was made from strength. At the time, no significant public pressure for any change existed. Even many of the intelligentsia then favoured continuance of the régime as it was for a while – and the attitude of the masses has been stated.

Choice of October 26th was deliberate. F.-M. Ayub remembered, though many did not, some words he had put in his broadcast on the occasion of President Mirza's dismissal. Other despotic régimes throughout history have made similar promises, have told the people that they would restore basic freedoms – but then have forgotten to do so. Most persons who heard or read the relevant passage paid it little heed; that it lacked any specified fulfilment-date doubtless lessened its impact. 'Let me declare in unequivocal terms,' he had said, 'that our ultimate aim is to restore democracy – but of a type the people can understand and work. When that will be, events alone can tell. Meanwhile, we have to put this mess right.' The scheme now announced was the result.

It must have come up for discussion in the revolutionary Cabinet very early, for on December 2nd, 1958, an official statement had disclosed that the régime had the possibility of a future Constitution in mind. But all sorts of other fascinating things were then going on, and distracted interest : the arraignments for corruption before the martial law courts, for instance. On January 15th however a pre-liminary commission was appointed to look into the matter. Formal conferences of Cabinet members and officials, to consider this body's ideas, were held at the end of April and again on June 12th–13th. And on September 2nd, general agreement was reached.

Though the anniversary announcement of October 26th was limited almost wholly to the 'grass-roots' aspect of the scheme, this and the opposite end of it – the future functions of the Head of State – had in fact been tackled simultaneously. Thoughts about the latter started from the axiom that, whatever Pakistan's future political set-up might be, it must differ radically from that of the past. British-style Parliamentary democracy had been tried for eleven years, and had failed disastrously; much time had run to waste; plainly, that particular kind of democracy must be unsuited to Pakistani conditions; something else must be found. The American kind seemed to offer possibilities : a system involving a clear separation of executive and legislative powers; and a President who was no seeming figure-head, but a working chief executive and fully empowered as such; who was chosen not by the Legislature, but in a separate election directly by the people, for a fixed term; and moreover who, with his Cabinet, was irremovable by the Legislature's vote. Some adaptation of this might suit the Pakistani environment well. Thought along these lines had already been current before the coup – General Mirza being among those attracted by it. The idea was now, plus the scheme's 'grass-roots' part, decided on in principle; and during the winter of 1959–60, as we shall see, the two parts – summit and base – were joined together.

Mental approach to the 'grass-roots' part had started from frank recognition that at least 80 per cent of the Pakistani population was still illiterate.[6] To suppose, therefore, that the average peasant or street-vendor could get his mind round complex national or inter-national questions as efficiently as the educated electorate of Western countries (which might not mean very much) was plain nonsense – whatever neighbouring India's experiences might so far suggest; and events during Pakistan's 'bad years' (1952–8) had proved con-clusively that such a supposition thrust far too many opportunities for gain into unscrupulous hands. Working from this postulate, the régime evolved what it termed the 'basic democracies'; a system which, when set forth in detail on October 26th, 1959 – and still more, when put into practice – could be seen to have greater originality than cynics had thought.

Under it the whole country, its East and West wings alike,[7] would be broken up into very small constituencies of between 800 and 1,000 people; and the system's essence lay in that phrase 'very small', meaning that the people would vote, not for some professional poli-tician who arrived at rare intervals from afar, gathered a (perhaps paid) crowd, harangued it, and dashed off, but for one of themselves, a candidate whose faults or merits they really knew. This novel type

[6] 85 per cent in the 1951 census. (The 1961 census showed a reduction to 81 per cent.)
[7] The East wing was politically the more sophisticated, and the union boards there, established in 1929, already had considerable powers.

of constituency would be the 'basic democracy'; and after election, the successful candidate would be grouped with those chosen by ten other such constituencies into a union council.[8] These bodies would administer local taxes, and be given a secretary to prepare their budgets and their minutes; they would be the new constitutional structure's first tier. The Government would nominate some additional members to them, and in larger numbers if local interests such as religious minorities, or women, seemed insufficiently reflected in the personnel chosen. Above this tier would be others – much as rumour had earlier suggested: the subdivisional council; the district one; the divisional (or regional) one; and then, for each of the country's wings, the provincial one. To these, too, nominated members would be added; but the elected element would remain, though diminishingly, so that when the final tier was reached, at the level of a National Assembly, the system would still keep some of its first 'grass-roots' contacts.

Neither the National Assembly nor the two provincial ones could be set up now. That was the difficult intermediate step yet to be taken, which would depend on the actual drafting of a new Constitution. But meanwhile, as mentioned, the other two steps would be tied together, by getting the basic democracies established, and by making the 80,000 elected members of the union councils an ad hoc electoral college for formal choice of the country's President. These things were done during the winter of 1959–60, F.-M. Ayub being confirmed in office by 95·6 per cent of the votes cast, and being sworn in on February 17th, 1960. A fresh Commission of distinguished membership was thereupon appointed, to work out the new Constitution's details, and especially the rights and duties of the National and provincial Assemblies.

A striking feature of the basic democracies system, as indicated, was the small size of the primary constituency, composed of 1,000 or fewer people. This ensured an intimacy and coherence usually lacking in the old self-governing bodies, whose dimensions could vary much; and it doubtless contributed towards the scheme's striking efficacy in practice, which won enthusiastic comment from foreign visitors such as the Indian Socialist leader Mr. Jai Prakash Narain, and later Mr. B. G. Verghese, and from Rushbrook Williams, and other British and American commentators. Perhaps the profoundest observations on it however have come from Spear, who points out that 'the system seems to have close resemblance to the successive tiers of Soviet people's councils', and goes on to remark that all it has

---

[8] In the towns, termed a union committee. These councils or committees, in statements on the subject, are themselves also often termed the 'basic democracies'.

apparently lacked is a party to animate it. This, he argues, would need to be 'something more drastic and closely knit than the Congress party in India'; and he has put forward practical suggestions on how such an organisation – not Communist or Fascist of course, but Muslim in flavour – might be evolved.

After about 14 months' work, which included considering more than 6,000 answers to a questionnaire, the Commission on the Constitution put in its report on May 6th, 1961. Its chairman had been Mr. Shahabuddin, a former Chief Justice. Committees of the revolutionary Cabinet under the President then started studying it, taking ten months or so over the job, and making several changes. The Foreign Minister, Mr. Manzur Qadir, himself a lawyer, played an important role in this. The resulting finalised Constitution was signed on March 1st, 1962, by F.-M. Ayub, who broadcast, explaining it, the same day.

Constitutions are complex things, and this is not the place for trying to dissect Pakistan's new one fully. The nature of its rather original 'grass-roots' base, and of its strong Presidential summit, have been indicated already. The middle connecting part – the National and the two provincial Assemblies – was to consist of single-chamber Houses of 150 members each, to be chosen in the same way as the President, that is, by an electoral college formed by the successful candidates returned from the basic democracy constituencies. These persons, incidentally, would now increase – from 80,000 to about 120,000 – because on the new Constitution's inauguration, Governmental nominations to the basic democracy councils would cease. Besides their ordinarily elected members, the three Assemblies would also have a few seats reserved for women – six in the National Assembly and five each in the provincial ones. The term of the Assemblies would be five years.

A few other features may be picked out for mention. The two provinces, or wings, got more autonomy than had been thought likely. The federal Centre was given its own list of subjects, national in character; all the rest were reckoned provincial – unless the Centre used its own overriding reserve powers in the interests of security or co-ordination. 'Such occasions should be rare,' said F.-M. Ayub; 'the theme is that what can be done on a provincial basis ought to be so done.' A remarkable provision, aimed at ensuring harmony between the two wings, in effect gave the country two federal capitals : a political one at Dacca, where the National Assembly would meet; and an administrative one at Rawalpindi (or nearby Islamabad). The same purpose was sought by providing that, if the President was absent or sick, the elected Speaker of the National Assembly should act for him; and that if the person who held the former post was a West Pakistani, the latter must be an East Pakistani, and vice versa. Defence was to be safeguarded by stipulating that, unless the President himself had high military rank, the Minister in charge must be a member of the Forces with at least lieutenant-general's status. To prevent the clashes about finance between the Executive and the Legislature, characteristic of the American governmental system, an ingenious provision was included, whereby the latter could not bring projects spreading over years to a halt. As F.-M. Ayub put it, 'to ensure continuance of on-going schemes, the previously-passed budget shall not be altered without the President's permission; but new taxation shall not be levied without the Assembly's consent'. The President's own position was strong. Only a three-fourths majority of the Assembly could override his veto; and, in that event, he could order a referendum, or else dissolve the Assembly and seek re-election himself. Further, he was buttressed against possibility of frivolous charges against him. Under the Constitution he could be impeached; but this required the votes of not less than three-fourths of the total Assembly members; and should such a motion not get the support of half the membership, the impeachment-notice's signatories – who must amount to at least a third of the House – would forfeit their membership forthwith. Finally, we should mention an item relevant to the perplexities about the nature of Pakistan, discussed in Chapter 1. In his broadcast, F.-M. Ayub flatly termed her 'an ideological State'. A Council of Islamic Ideology would therefore be set up, whose opinion the President and the Legislatures should seek when law-making. Its functions however would be advisory only.

Elections to the National Assembly were held on April 28th, and to the two provincial ones on May 6th. The outcome far from tallied with expectation. Despite the electorates' small size – 80,000 persons only – and the drastic restrictions on the amounts of money candidates might spend, surprisingly many old-style professional politicians, mainly of the former Muslim League, managed to get elected, instead of the new men, simple and plainly honest and of 'grass-roots' origins, whom the régime had reckoned on. F.-M. Ayub proceeded undeterred however. On June 8th, when the National Assembly met, martial law was lifted as had been promised, and the new Constitution came into force. Pakistan's military revolution of 1958, whether prematurely or not, had of its own accord dissolved itself.

Chapter 20

Epilogue, 1962–67

EVENTS since that unusual act of abnegation in 1962 fall into three phases. The first, which lasted several months, caused many Pakistanis and their friends abroad anxiety. The President, doubtless keen to make his experiment work, let the politicians push him out of several of his supposedly strong opening positions, to the bewilderment of the unsophisticated masses and some detriment to his prestige. The process went so far and fast that to critical eyes he seemed to have lost his grip and leadership. Within a few days of the Constitution becoming operative he agreed, under pressure from East wing members of his Cabinet, to abrogate its article 104 – the 'removal of difficulties' section of article 224 seemed to allow this – so as to let Ministers hold seats in the National Assembly, rather than merely having the right to address it as in the U.S.A., which was what he had wanted. This seemed a big surrender, perhaps damaging to the Constitution's whole spirit; and as we shall see, it was no more than luck plus some Opposition politicians' stupidity which afterwards set things back where they were. Also at an early stage the Assembly decided, which was known to be flatly against his wishes, but which constitutionally they now could do, that political parties, all of which were banned by the coup in 1958, should revive. And before long, instead of resisting this, he so far gave way as to announce his own enrolment in a branch of the Muslim League.

What seemed another big surrender – which, too, later righted itself though in a different way – was his reluctant consent in principle that members of the National and provincial Assemblies should be chosen by direct election instead of indirectly through the basic democracies. Further retreats were to permit the tabling of a Bill of Rights, which would make enactments under the martial law régime 'justiciable' and thereby expose them to annulment; and to allow cancellation of a clause which he had approved in the Education Commission's report about the length of university courses. It also, for a while, seemed that he might succumb to clamour instigated by the mullahs through some politicians for regressive changes in the régime's Muslim Family Laws Ordinance, described in Chapter 3. This however did not occur.

263

Counter-clamour from feminist groups and social reformers helped to prevent it.

Nevertheless in Asia as in Western countries, and perhaps more fundamentally so, politics are seldom quite what they seem. The inherent strength of the Presidential office under the 1962 Constitution was very great – much as it is in contemporary France – and the politicians must at times have felt very conscious that, if outvoted in the Assembly, F.-M. Ayub could appeal over their heads to the public by referendum. And the more perceptive, glancing around the globe to West or East, to Turkey and Iran, or to Burma, if no further, would have been reminded of what can happen when leaders who have Army backing are pressed too far.

To say precisely when the second phase opened, and circumstances started improving for him, is not easy, nor even whether the main causes were domestic or foreign. But so thorough was the change, that by February 1964 a British newspaper could describe him and his Government as 'firmly in the saddle'. The antagonism, it said, which had 'burst out last year' was now 'spent, divided, leaderless or suppressed'; and Pakistan was apparently 'for the first time in its short history entering a period of political stability'.[1] And certainly, one factor in the transformation was external: the dramatic episode of China's attack on India in November 1962, as described in Chapter 16, and the much-changed international scene that this created.

As will be recalled, India in that sudden crisis momentarily flung her much-publicized 'non-alignment' aside, and pleaded with the U.S.A. and Britain for supply of arms, which were promptly, freely sent. To most people in those countries, the former of which at any rate was obsessively anti-Communist, such a response seemed natural: China was Communist, India a Western-style democracy or striving to be one. But Pakistanis' reactions were very different. For them, India was their great antagonist; and though in the Commonwealth like themselves, she had held aloof from the 'cold war', and often proved peculiarly bothersome and unhelpful to the West. They, contrariwise, were the U.S.A.'s and Britain's declared allies; and on most matters, despite sneers from other Afro-Asian countries, they had steadfastly backed the Western cause. Yet they now found themselves treated by their supposed friends as expendable or virtually non-existent, and obliged to watch helplessly while military equipment of modern types was rushed to Indian soil; equipment which, without firm guarantees – and it was hard to see what these could be – might later, to judge from what had happened to Goa,

[1] *The Times*, despatch from its own correspondent, Karachi, Feb. 24.

Hyderabad, Junagadh and (abortively) Nepal, be turned against themselves or used for diplomatic coercion. According to their Intelligence reports, about 80 per cent of India's army, at the time of the Chinese thrust into Assam, was still strung along the frontiers facing Pakistan and not facing China at all. And President Ayub and his colleagues made very clear at the time that, for logistic and other reasons, they completely disbelieved the Anglo-American assumption, supported in Delhi, that China planned any serious or permanent invasion of India. They reckoned the attack was simply a raid, brought about largely by Indian diplomatic and military clumsiness – an opinion which, when looked back on in 1967, seems justified.

Pakistanis therefore naturally felt outraged. Popular clamour immediately arose for a total break with the West. What good were these alliances? Always, in emergencies, the Westerners' dice seemed loaded in India's favour, doubtless just because she was big, and regardless of right or wrong. There had been several other earlier instances, though smaller. During that November, President Ayub bluntly termed Hinduism a worse threat to Pakistan than Communism; and one of his Ministers, soon after, proclaimed Pakistan's unconditional friendship for China. And links with that country have in fact, since, been vigorously maintained and developed despite strong American objections. The decision of March 1962 to demarcate the Gilgit frontier was soon ratified; an agreement followed in January 1963 for trade by barter; and then, in August 1963, an airlines agreement – the first ever made by China with a non-Communist country – which so annoyed the Americans that they stopped their promised grants for improving Dacca airport. In February 1964 Mr. Chou En-lai visited Pakistan, and while there, helped doubtless by the growing ideological feud between China and Russia, he pronounced in Pakistan's favour over the Kashmir dispute – Pakistan responding by promising support for China's entry to the U.N.; all of which was much to the Pakistani public's taste. And since the Indo-Pakistani war in September 1965 – to be touched on later – Pakistan has been re-equipping her Armed Forces partly from Chinese factories.

Meanwhile the Kashmir dispute itself, that 'root of all evil' in Indo-Pakistan affairs, had been going through strange new twists and turns. During the November 1962 crisis the Kennedy and Macmillan administrations, forced eventually by rough remarks such as those of President Ayub and his Ministers to remember that Pakistan did exist, persuaded an obviously unwilling Mr. Nehru, in return for their gifts of arms, to promise more talks on the problem. Most Pakistanis, knowing his utter obduracy about it hitherto, felt sceptical of any result. And they proved right. After dragging on intermittently from December 1962 to May 1963 the talks foundered. And during that time Pakistanis, with amazed exasperation, had to watch free military aid for India being organised by the U.S.A. and Britain not merely for the 'emergency' as foretold, but on a long-term basis. It would be fair to say that, by the latter part of 1963, Pakistan's relations with the West had never since her birth been so estranged.

In December of that year Kashmir affairs were given yet another convolution by the theft, never explained, of a Muslim relic said to be a hair of the Prophet from the Hazratbal mosque near Srinagar. What followed soon showed that, despite outward calm during 16 years' occupation by up to 100,000 Indian troops and armed police, most of the predominantly Muslim populace of the Vale remained quite unreconciled to rule from Delhi. Demonstrations of grief and protest were held, and increased, till the local puppet administration installed by Mr. Nehru in 1953 when Sheikh Abdullah was jailed, and which still seemed controlled by Bakshighulam Mohammad though he had recently quit the Premiership, virtually collapsed, power passing to self-constituted local committees. For weeks, against a background of armed force, complex political manœuvres ensued, conducted on behalf of the now ailing Mr. Nehru mainly by Mr. Lal Bahadur Shastri (later his successor), which in April 1964 culminated in the second temporary release, mentioned in Chapter 16, of Sheikh Abdullah.

And this Kashmir upheaval was far from being local. It had formidable effects 1,200 miles or so away on the subcontinent's eastern flank. Tension there had been evident already, for during the autumn of 1963 the Pakistanis once more alleged that the Indians were pushing out their own Indian Muslims from Assam destitute into East Pakistan. Next, the Pakistan Government demanded closure of the Indian diplomatic mission at Rajshahi, which with a staff of no less than 150 was said to have been trying to subvert the Hindu minority in the province and doing espionage. Early in January 1964 a Muslim gathering, held at Khulna in East Pakistan to protest against the theft of the Kashmir relic, developed into an anti-Hindu riot. Reports of this, reaching West Bengal, gave rise to anti-Muslim riots there. Characteristic panicky two-way movements of minorities on both sides of the frontier then began, these themselves causing more riots, as at Partition-time in 1947: at Dacca in East Pakistan, at Calcutta and elsewhere in West Bengal, and then on into the industrial areas of Bihar and Orissa, and as far West in India as Madhya Pradesh. For much of the spring of 1964, conditions for the minorities in both countries became more frightening than at any time since the threats of Indo-Pakistani war in March 1950; and the fundamental unsolved problems of Mr. Jinnah's 'two-nation' theory and Mr. Nehru's secularist doctrines re-emerged in full vigour. Pakistanis felt they needed a leader, and in President Ayub they had one.

During this second phase there had been domestic factors in Pakistan as well which helped to strengthen his position, though mostly of the diffuse sort difficult to pin down to dates. Chief of these doubtless simply was the contending politicians' inability to combine – no new thing. We need not detail here the intricate rivalries among them which emerged after political parties became legal again. Suffice it to say that the departure of Mr. Suhrawardy – he spent the summer of 1963 abroad and died in November – removed the one man who might have cemented the shifting sands of Pakistani politics into something firm enough to subvert the new Constitution – his evident aim. But even his capabilities in this line may have been over-stressed, for though he had great skill, his questionable role in Muslim affairs during the summer of 1947, which many remembered, was a drawback, and his ambitions had made him enemies.

Another item was the grotesque reversal, already mentioned, of the President's surrender in July 1962 to East wing members of his Cabinet by abrogating article 104 of the new Constitution. For the sake of mere harassment perhaps, Opposition politicians soon afterwards rashly appealed to the Courts against it, claiming that the surrender itself was unconstitutional; and to the surprise of many the appeal was upheld, first by the High Court at Dacca, and then in May 1963 by the Supreme Court. In consequence the governmental system as in the U.S.A., which the President had always wanted, was restored; and such members of his Cabinet as now held seats in the National Assembly had to surrender them. The two ensuing by-elections[2] brought further success, Opposition candidates being defeated by nominees of the now seatless Ministers. His regained popularity was further shown, during the next few weeks, when routine by-elections to the National and provincial Assemblies resulted in his supporters winning 16 out of 17 contests.

As mentioned, the politicians during the first phase after the new Constitution's launching had urged that martial law enactments

---

[2] There would have been three, but for the death shortly before of Mr. Mohammad Ali of Bogra, the Foreign Minister.

should be made 'justiciable' under a Bill of Rights. Even the Opposition in the Assembly however now saw that, on practical grounds, not all such measures could be so treated; social chaos would for instance ensue if the West wing's land reforms became reversible. So a compromise was reached; and from the Bill agreed to in December 1963, 31 martial law measures were excluded, among them, besides the land reforms, being the at least equally important Muslim family law reforms.

Finally, the franchise. In response to clamour that indirect election through the basic democracies, as provided for by the Constitution, should be replaced by direct election as before the military coup, President Ayub passed the problem to a commission headed by a civil servant. In the summer of 1963 this body reported. It favoured a mixture: indirect election to the Presidentship; but direct to the National and provincial Assemblies. In a broadcast talk soon after, the President indicated that he disagreed. The problem then went in December to a committee of the Assembly – where by now, as explained, owing to the politicians' weaknesses and quarrels, his position was much better. A majority there favoured indirect elections throughout; and a Bill to that effect went through in April 1964. Thus ground conceded in 1962 had been regained; and not this time by mere luck, as in the affair of Assembly seats for Ministers, but by deliberate exercise of political strength. The moment was auspicious too, for general elections to the basic democracies, to the Presidentship, and to the National and provincial Assemblies were due under the new Constitution early in the following year.

This crucial coming event opens the third phase of Pakistan's affairs since martial law ended in June 1962. However, it got linked with two others: Mr. Nehru's death in May 1964 plus happenings shortly before and after that; and policies towards Kashmir evolved by the Indian Government about nine months later. These two latter items can be dealt with first and together.

Though the evidence is inconclusive, it seemed during Mr. Nehru's final weeks that his views about Kashmir were changing. If so, the reason almost certainly lay in the horrifying renewal of Hindu-Muslim strife all over the eastern parts of the subcontinent, Indian and Pakistani, triggered off during February and March by the faraway Hazratbal incident. Some of the atrocities against hopelessly outnumbered Muslims in Orissa and Madhya Pradesh were peculiarly horrible and shocked all well-meaning Hindus. The elaborate propagandist edifice of secular theory, built up before an admiring or sceptical world by independent India since 1947 seemed in peril. Would-be mediators began to be listened to with more respect, notably the temporarily-freed Sheikh Abdullah, and Mr. Nehru's former rival for headship of the Congress party Mr. Jai Prakash Narain, since turned holy-man. In many kindly hearts, on the subcontinent and abroad, faint but genuine hopes stirred that a new era in Indo-Pakistani relationships might be dawning; that that 'root of all evil', the Kashmir dispute, could somehow be compromised over, put aside and buried; and the two countries then go forward together in sensible collaboration for the common people's good.

But Mr. Nehru suddenly died. His successor Mr. Lal Bahadur Shastri had nothing like his authority. Reaction set in; time passed; extremist voices were again heard. The opportunity, if it was one, was let slip. And by December, not perhaps so much to provoke Pakistan as to placate or reconcile contesting political groups in Delhi, Srinagar, and Jammu, the Indian Government began something new: open moves towards indissoluble union with India of the parts of Kashmir which it held, by modifying or abrogating article 370 of the Indian Constituion – this being in defiance of promises given long before to the Commonwealth and the U.N. To President Ayub and his advisers it seemed the last straw. Thus by the end of 1964, instead of being on the way to settlement as had momentarily been hoped, the Kashmir dispute was worse than ever.

Meanwhile, campaigning had been in progress for Pakistan's general elections, the first ever held.[3] It soon took a form disquieting to F.-M. Ayub's supporters, because an entirely unexpected rival for the Presidentship appeared: Miss Jinnah, sister of the founder of the State. Septuagenarian now, an austere, aloof, talented, Western-educated lady, she had been wont, since her brother's death in 1948, to issue enigmatic pronouncements on national 'days' implying criticism of those now in authority, but had otherwise not been in politics. It seemed inconceivable that, if elected, she could manage to hold together the miscellaneous, mutually competing groups who ranged themselves behind her. Chaos might ensue. But her name carried immense influence. Possibly, in the end, her sex cost her some votes, for to the old-fashioned and the religiously-orthodox the notion of a woman as Head of State in a Muslim country was strange. This is guesswork however; and almost certainly she was the most dangerous rival to F.-M. Ayub who could have been found.

[3] There had been elections previously to the provincial Assemblies, viz.: West Punjab (March 1951), N.-W. Frontier Province (Nov.-Dec 1951), Sind (May 1953), and East Bengal (March 1954), but not to the Central Assembly.

Impartial commentators in the main thought the campaign fairly contested. At any rate, there was a great deal of free speech and print. Some in-built bias in favour of the 1962 Constitution doubtless existed in the entire electoral system, for the basic democrats naturally wanted their own self-continuance. But probably no electoral system devised by man can be wholly just; the present British system is unquestionably unjust to Parliamentary representation of the Liberals. Alarm was felt beforehand by F.-M. Ayub's supporters lest, as a West Pakistani, he might fail to get a majority of the votes cast in the East as well as in the West wing. If so, prospects for Pakistan's national cohesion might be dark. But he did not. On January 2nd, 1965 – the contest's most crucial date, it went through three stages – the elected basic democrats, formed into a Presidential electoral college, cast 49,647 votes for F.-M. Ayub and 28,343 for Miss Jinnah – the former achieving majorities in both wings though in the East one not big. And when the dates later came, respectively in March and May, for elections to the National and the provincial Assemblies, squabbles among Miss Jinnah's backers had become so acute that support for the President greatly improved; and in the National Assembly – the most important of course – no fewer than 118 out of the 150 chosen members belonged to the branch of the former Muslim League which he had joined.[4]

While this was going on domestically, there had been grave developments outside: Indo-Pakistani relations were fast worsening. In particular, 'incidents' along the U.N.-supervised cease-fire line in Kashmir – endemic since its creation in 1949 though seldom reported in any overseas newspaper – multiplied steadily, involving more men and heavier casualties. So did frontier skirmishes along the subcontinent's eastern flank. And then suddenly, in April, an unprecedented set-to started near the southern end of the subcontinent's other, western frontier: in the sterile, brackish, periodically flooded wilderness known as the Rann of Kutch which separates Sind from Kathiawar. Forces on a scale never before used in Indo-Pakistani affrays were engaged, including armour. Why this happened is obscure; we are now entering a period in South Asia's history about which many facts remain hidden. The Rann, worthless in itself, almost uninhabited, and due for submergence soon anyway by the summer inundations, seems to have been the scene chosen for a kind of military experiment, for a probe or test preliminary to something else; and we may feel reminded here of the Russo-Japanese border affrays in Manchuria in 1938–39, or of episodes in the Spanish civil

[4] Now entitled the Pakistan Muslim League; formerly, it had been the 'Conventionist' M.L., as contrasted with the 'Councillor' M.L.

war. Ostensibly, British mediation ended the affair on June 30th, but in fact the duly arrived floodwaters had done so.

And before they did, something like an anti-Indian insurrection was being attempted by the hitherto docile Kashmiris of the Vale. Its chances of success were slim indeed; about 100,000 Indian troops and armed police were there to prevent it, and the Vale is a flat compact easily traversable area only about 20–24 miles broad and 84 long. But the re-arrest of Sheikh Abdullah in Delhi on May 8th after return from foreign travel quite enraged them. Unprecedented turmoil broke out in and around Srinagar, which spread into the countryside and then up the side-valleys, particularly those just behind the Indian troops posted along the cease-fire line bordering on Azad Kashmir – the tract held by Pakistan. Within that tract, especially among the tough Sudhnuti hillmen, enthusiasm for the evident efforts of their co-religionists in the Vale to rid themselves of Hindu dominance became extreme; armed volunteers began infiltrating across the cease-fire line to help them, with Pakistani officials' connivance sometimes doubtless; the Indian authorities naturally became alarmed; 'incidents' along the line between the alerted Indian and Pakistani troops became bloodier and bigger, the Indians on May 19th claiming over 40 Pakistani soldiers dead; during June and July this went on, intensifying yet more; and then during the second half of August the Indians, so as to block infiltration from beyond the line, deliberately violated it in three sectors, those of Kargil, Tithwal, and Poonch, pushing their forces some distance into Azad Kashmir territory—a grave step which the Pakistanis could not ignore.

On September 1st came their retaliation: a strong thrust by an armoured task-force across the southerly end of the cease-fire line near Chambh. Strategically this was very dangerous to the Indians, because if successful it could cut the road whereon most of their supplies to Kashmir travelled, and reduce their army there almost to impotence. On September 6th followed the Indians' dramatic rejoinder. Without any declaration of war they attacked in two columns across the international frontier in the Punjab towards Lahore; simultaneously, their planes started bombing Pakistani airfields; soon after, they launched a second ground attack from Rajasthan aimed apparently at Hyderabad in Sind; and, before long, yet another from the Jammu area inside Kashmir towards Sialkot in Pakistani Punjab. Three weeks of unrestrained warfare by land, air and sea had broken out between fellow-members of the British Commonwealth.

It was a professional war. Except near airfields or perhaps by mistake the civilian populations were scarcely affected by the air-raids, though there was naturally great excitement. Damage to such industrial installations as the two countries possessed was negligible; their economic life – except as a result of reductions in foreign financial aid – was thus not seriously disrupted. Casualties among the fighting men on both sides were however heavy, considering the war's brief duration, and much gallantry was shown. Wastage of equipment and fuel became very rapid. This indeed, coupled with a resolution by the U.N. unique for its vigour and unanimity, was what, on September 23rd, brought the fighting to a halt. For it so happened that, at the moment, no great Power – China included – wanted the subcontinent to fall into confusion. Militarily, the war was a draw. The Pakistanis did well to prevent Lahore's capture, for the Indians' violation of the international frontier only 20 miles eastwards from the city seems (rather strangely) to have taken them by surprise. They then immediately had to call off their Chambh thrust just when it was very near success, and to switch forces back in haste. On the other hand, their counter-attack from Lahore, made about 35 miles or so south of the Indians' main entry-points, spear-headed by the American-built tanks in which they had such hopes, soon petered out, partly because the ground was boggy after the monsoon. The Indian tank-thrust launched soon after towards Sialkot, probably their most formidable move of all, was however sturdily resisted and also failed. In the air, the Pakistanis certainly did the better; their pilots achieved astonishing successes. The two navies' exploits though interesting were not important.

To try to analyse the aims and conduct of the Pakistani and Indian leaders during the crisis would be useless. Insufficient publicly available data exist. Perhaps each side largely misjudged the others' intentions, and so got jerked, by stages, into an escalating conflict which it neither fully foresaw nor wanted. But some of the consequences, at any rate, now stand out clearly. First, in present-day circumstances, war between India and Pakistan cannot be won; within days, this must have been evident to the generals on both sides. No neat conclusive military victory was attainable; only chaos lay ahead. Next, the Pakistanis could feel proud of their country, its resources and numbers being so much fewer than their enemies' and its geography so odd; proud both of their civilians' morale, and of their fighting men's gallantry and skill. But to offset this the simple faith which some Pakistanis had in Muslims' necessary invincibility against Hindus in war lay broken; the Hindus had fought well. But also broken lay the outside world's belief – if in 1965 it still existed – that India's international dealings stood on a loftier moral plane than other countries', raised there by Gandhian principles. The Hydera-

bad and Goa episodes should have shattered this but in some minds
it had not. But now the truth was undeniable: India could be as
ruthless and unscrupulous as any; could violate cease-fire agreements, could launch undeclared war across an agreed international
frontier against a comparatively small neighbour.

All these lessons were perhaps healthy. And other items emerged,
among them China's importance. Whether a link existed between
her policies and Pakistan's during the crisis is not known, but the
Indians thought it did; and after their army's experience at Chinese
hands in 1962 this much alarmed them. In March 1965, President
Ayub had visited China; and on September 4th – an interesting
date – China's Foreign Minister Marshal Chen-yi was briefly in
Karachi. India guessed that mutual assurances must have been
given. When two days later Indo-Pakistani war broke out, the
Chinese avoided direct involvement. However, they almost immediately seized on a petty, long-standing border dispute with India
in the far-away Darjeeling area and blew it up to a separate crisis
on its own, issuing an ultimatum to India about it. Though the exact
motivation and effects of this remain obscure, it seems to have done
two things, which most Western commentators failed to notice owing
to the absurdity of Chinese demands for return of stolen yaks and
sheep. First, it reinforced what must already have been the Indian
general staff's belief that military victory against Pakistan could not
be got; and it strengthened President Ayub's position both at home
and abroad. For he could now say, which was important because
many East Pakistanis had felt unprotected and forgotten during the
war, that the Indians would never anyway have overrun East
Pakistan for fear of China.

After the U.N.-imposed armistice on September 23rd, long uneasy
weeks of friction and gory incidents ensued during which – as in a
smaller way in Cyprus and elsewhere – the U.N. control-officers had
the utmost difficulty in preventing unrestrained hostilities flaring up
again. Ultimately in January 1966, an agreement between the two
ex-belligerents was patched up at Tashkent under Mr. Kosygin's
urgings, Russia being the only non-Asian Power which had contrived
to avoid exasperating them during the struggle. However, India's
Prime Minister Mr. Lal Bahadur Shastri died in Tashkent within a
few hours of the agreement's signature; and such personal under-
standings as he may have reached with President Ayub during their
talks died too. Since then, practically no progress towards disposal of
Indo-Pakistani differences has been made; and at the time of writing
(April 1967), the entire Indo-Pakistani frontier from Kashmir to the
Arabian Sea is still declared closed.

s

Politically and economically, the three-weeks' war of 1965 seems to have done Pakistan less internal damage than might have been expected. President Ayub's régime looks stable; more so, at any rate, than many others throughout the Afro-Asian world today, and he showed no hesitation in permitting return to public life on schedule, early in 1967, of the politicians disqualified for malpractices under EBDO[5] during the martial-law period. Cessation or lessening of foreign financial aid has inevitably caused a setback to Pakistan's admirable third five-year plan. It can scarcely now prove the un-qualified success which the second one did. And in the West wing, owing to drought, shortages or high prices of food have been a worry. But in general, when we look round at a swift-changing, often dis-orderly and afflicted world, prospects for Pakistanis seem fairly bright.

This book ends, as books must which venture forth from the fairly firm ground of history proper to the quicksands of current affairs, leaving large questions open. Was Pakistan's military régime wise to give up power when it did, less than four years after seizing it, or would delay have been better? Other much-needed reforms could then also have been pushed through with martial speed; for instance, in the cumbrous working of the law-courts and the rules of evidence. Or again, to carry this line of thought farther, need Pakistan – a question applicable as much in 1956 as in '62 – have a written Con-stitution at all? Not every country does so, even among the firmly democratic ones; neither elderly Britain nor new-born Israel, to mention the two examples adduced before. And are most Afro-Asian countries, anyway, suited to Western-style forms of government, whether of American, British, or other European origin? The con-tinuing instability throughout their areas, the countless recent coups especially of late in Africa scarcely suggest so. Perhaps Spear is right when he suggests that, in Pakistan's case, her political viability depends on 'a strong authority embodying in some measure the leadership principle. The temperament of the people demands it; their tradition and habit of thought confirms it. The authority must be visible and personal'.

And behind these questions stand the profounder military and diplomatic ones, especially Pakistan's relations with her huge un-friendly neighbour India, and with the countries of the West, the U.S.A. in particular, with whom she allied herself but from whom she nowadays feels estranged; questions of the kind uneasily looked

[5] i.e. the Elective Bodies' Disqualification Order (1959); implicit in Ch. 19, pp. 251–2).

into only a few pages back and in Chapter 16. And, as well, the even more profound ideological, cultural, social, economic and demographic ones, of the sort pondered over in Chapters 1 and 3. To speculate or attempt prophecy about these would however be profitless at this point. The most pressing among them are the economic and demographic problems conjoined: for how can the lot of Pakistan's endearing pitiable poor possibly be bettered and their living-standards raised amidst a 'population-explosion'? But that – luckily in a way – is not exclusively a Pakistani conundrum. It faces, frightens, and at present totally baffles those responsible for governing nearly all the world's so-called 'developing' countries.

Bibliography

Bibliography

Aga Khan, *The Memoirs of* (Cassell, 1954)

Ahmad, Mohammad, *My Chief* (Longmans Green, Lahore, 1960)

Ali, Ameer, *The Spirit of Islam* (Methuen – University Paperbacks – 1965)

Ambedkar, B. R., *Pakistan and the Partition of India* (Thacker & Co., Bombay, 1946 Edn.)

Andrus, J. R., & Mohammed, A. F., *Trade, Finance and Development in Pakistan* (O.U.P., Karachi, 1966)

Attlee, C. R., *As It Happened* (Heinemann, 1954)

Ayub Khan, Mahommad, *Pakistan Perspective* (printed for Pakistan Embassy, Washington D.C., 1966)

Azad, Abul Kalam, *India Wins Freedom* (Orient Longmans, 1959)

Barstow, A. E., *Sikhs* (Government of India Press, 1940)

Bazaz, Prem Nath, *The History of Struggle for Freedom in Kashmir* (Kashmir Publishing Co., New Delhi, 1954)

Bentwich, Norman, *Israel Resurgent* (Ernest Benn, 1960)

Binder, Leonard, *Religion and Politics in Pakistan* (University of California Press, 1961)

Birdwood, Lord, *A Continent Decides* (Robert Hale, 1953)

Birdwood, Lord, *Two Nations and Kashmir* (Robert Hale, 1956)

Blunt, Wilfred Scawen, *India under Ripon, A Private Diary* (T. Fisher Unwin, 1909)

Bolitho, Hector, *Jinnah: Creator of Pakistan* (Murray, 1954)

Brecher, M., *Nehru, A Political Biography* (O.U.P., 1959)

Burbidge, Wm. F., *The Military Viceroy* (John Crowther, 1943)

Callard, Keith, *Pakistan, A Political Study* (Allen & Unwin, 1957)

Callard, Keith, *Foreign Policy of Pakistan* (N.Y., Institute of Pacific Relations, 1959)

Campbell, Robert D., *Pakistan, Emerging Democracy* (D. Van Nostrand Company, Inc., 1963)

Campbell-Johnson, Alan, *Mission with Mountbatten* (Robert Hale, 1951)

Cantwell Smith, Wilfred, *Modern Islam in India* (Gollancz, 1946)

Cantwell Smith, Wilfred, *Islam in Modern History* (Princeton University Press, New Jersey, 1957; O.U.P.)

Caroe, Sir Olaf, *The Pathans* (Macmillan, 1958; re-issued 1965 as a paperback)

Choudhury, G. W., and Parvez Hasan, *Pakistan's External Relations* (P.I.I.A., Karachi, 1958)

Choudhury, G. W., *Democracy in Pakistan* (Green Book House, Dacca, 1963)

Collins, Maj.-Gen. R. J., *Lord Wavell (1883–1941), A Military Biography* (Hodder & Stoughton, 1948)

Connell, John, *Auchinleck* (Cassell, 1959)

¹Connell, John, *Wavell, Scholar and Soldier, to June 1941* (Collins, 1964)

Cragg, Kenneth, *The Call of the Minaret* (O.U.P., New York, 1964; a Galaxy Book, paperback)

Crocker, Walter, *Nehru* (Allen & Unwin, 1966)

Cumming, Sir John (Editor), *Political India, 1832–1932* (O.U.P., 1932, especially articles by Sir Theodore Morison and Sir Hugh McPherson)

Cunningham, J. D., *A History of the Sikhs* (1st Edn., 1849, John Murray)

Curran, J. A. Jr., *Militant Hinduism in Indian Politics: A Story of the R.S.S.* (Institute of Pacific Relations, New York, 1951)

Darling, Sir Malcolm, *The Punjab Peasant in Prosperity and Debt* (4th Edn., O.U.P., 1947)

Darling, Sir Malcolm, *At Freedom's Door* (O.U.P., 1949)

Edwardes, Michael, *The Last Years of British India* (Cassell, 1963)

Feldman, H., *A Constitution for Pakistan* (O.U.P., 1956)

Feldman, H., *The Land and People of Pakistan* (Black, 'Land & Peoples Series', 1958)

Feldman, H., *Pakistan, An Introduction* (O.U.P., 1960)

Feldman, H., *Revolution in Pakistan* (O.U.P., 1967)

Ferguson, J. P., *Kashmir* (Centaur Press, 1961)

Fergusson, Bernard, *Wavell: Portrait of a Soldier* (Collins, 1961)

Gledhill, Alan, *Pakistan* (2nd Edn., Stevens, 1966)

Griffiths, Sir Percival, *The British Impact on India* (Macdonald, 1952)

Griffiths, Sir Percival, *Modern India* (Ernest Benn, 1965 Edn.)

Haq, Mahbub ul, *The Strategy of Economic Planning: A Case Study of Pakistan* (O.U.P., Karachi, 1966)

Henniker, Lt.-Col., M.C.A., R.E., *Journal of the Royal United Service Institution* (Feb. 1948 issue, pp. 117, 118)

Holdich, Sir T. H., *The Gates of India* (Macmillan, 1910)

---

¹ This volume *precedes* that mentioned on pp. 123 and 148, on which Connell is understood to have been working before his death in 1965.

Hunter, Sir William, *The Indian Musalmans* (The Comrade Publishers, 1871, 1945 Edn.)

Huxley, Aldous, *Jesting Pilate* (Chatto & Windus, 1926)

Ikram, S. M., and T. G. P. Spear, *Cultural Heritage of Pakistan* (O.U.P., 1956)

Ikram, S. M., edited by Ainslie T. Embree, *Muslim Civilization in India* (Columbia University Press, New York, 1964)

Ikram, S. M., *Modern Muslim India and the Birth of Pakistan* (Ashraf, Lahore, 1965)

Ikramullah, Begum Shaista, *From Purdah to Parliament* (Cresset Press, 1963)

Iqbal, Md., *Secrets of the Self*, translated by R. A. Nicholson (Macmillan, 1920)

Iqbal, Md., *Reconstruction of Religious Thought in Islam* (O.U.P., 1934)

Ismay, Lord, *The Memoirs of* (Heinemann, 1960)

Jennings, Sir Ivor, *Constitutional Problems in Pakistan* (O.U.P., 1957)

Khaliq-uz-Zaman, Choudhuri, *Pathway to Pakistan* (Luzac, 1961)

Knight, E. F., *Where Three Empires Meet* (Longmans, Green, 1900)

Korbel, Josef, *Danger in Kashmir* (Princeton University Press, 1954)

Lamb, Alastair, *Crisis in Kashmir, 1947–1966* (Routledge & Kegan Paul, 1966)

Lawrence, Sir Walter, *The India We Served* (Cassell, 1928)

L'Etang, H. J. C. J., 'The Health of Statesmen and Affairs of Nations', *The Practitioner*, Jan. 1958

L'Etang, H. J. C. J., 'Ill Health in Senior Officers', *The Practitioner*, April 1961

Lumby, E. W. R., *The Transfer of Power in India* (Allen & Unwin, 1954)

Mackenzie, Sir Compton, *Eastern Epic* (Chatto & Windus, 1951)

Masani, R. P., *Britain in India* (O.U.P., 1960)

Menon, V. P., *The Integration of the Indian States* (Orient Longmans, 1956)

Menon, V. P., *The Transfer of Power in India* (Orient Longmans, 1957)

Mersey, Viscount, *The Viceroys and Governors-General of India, 1857–1947* (John Murray, 1949)

Michel, Aloys A., *The Indus Rivers* (Yale University Press, 1967)

Mohammad Ali, Chaudhuri, *The Emergence of Pakistan* (Columbia University Press, 1967)

Moon, Penderel, *Divide and Quit* (Chatto & Windus, 1961)

Mosley, Leonard, *The Last Days of the British Raj* (Weidenfeld & Nicolson, 1962)

Munir Report; more formally *Report of the Court of Enquiry into the Punjab Disturbances of 1953* (Lahore, West Punjab Government Press, 1954)

Muqeem Khan, Fazal, Major-Gen., *The Story of the Pakistan Army* (O.U.P., Dacca, 1963)

Murphy, Ray, *Last Viceroy* (Jarrolds, 1948)

O'Malley, L. S. S., *Modern India and the West* (O.U.P., 1941)

Panikkar, K. M., *Asia and Western Dominance* (Allen & Unwin, 1954)

Prasad, Rajendra, *India Divided* (Hind Kitabs, Bombay, 1946)

Qureshi, Ishtiaq, *The Pakistani Way of Life* (Heinemann, 'Way of Life Series', 1956)

Qureshi, Ishtiaq, *The Administration of the Sultanate of Dehli* (Karachi, 1958)

Qureshi, Ishtiaq, *The Muslim Community of the Indo-Pakistani Subcontinent, 610–1947* (Mouton & Co., The Hague, 1962)

Qureshi, Ishtiaq, *The Struggle for Pakistan* (University of Karachi, 1965)

Reid, Sir Robert, *Years of Change in Bengal and Assam*, edited by Ian Stephens (Ernest Benn, 1966)

Rosenthal, E. I. J., *Islam in the Modern National State* (C.U.P., 1965)

Russell of Liverpool, Lord, *The Scourge of the Swastika* (Cassell, 1951)

Russell, Wilfrid, *Indian Summer* (Thacker & Co., Bombay, 1951)

Saiyid, M. H., *Mohammad Ali Jinnah* (2nd Edn., Ashraf, Lahore, 1953)

Sarwar Hasan, K., *Pakistan and the Commonwealth* (P.I.I.A., Karachi, 1950)

Sarwar Hasan, K., *The Strategic Interests of Pakistan* (P.I.I.A., Karachi, 1954)

Sarwar Hasan, K., *Pakistan and the United Nations* (Manhattan Publishing Co., New York, 1960)

Sayeed, Khalid Bin, *Pakistan, The Formative Phase* (Pakistan Publishing House, Karachi, 1960)

Sherwani, Latif Ahmed, *India, China and Pakistan* (Council for Pakistan Studies, Karachi, 1967)

Siddiqi, Aslam, *Pakistan Seeks Security* (Longmans, Green & Co., Pakistan Branch, 1960)

Singh, Khushwant, *The Sikhs* (Allen & Unwin, 1953)

Singh, Khushwant, *Ranjit Singh, Maharajah of the Punjab* (Allen & Unwin, 1962)

Singh, Khushwant, *The Fall of the Kingdom of the Punjab* (Orient Longmans, 1962)

Singh, Khushwant, *A History of the Sikhs*, Vol. I, 1469-1839 (Princeton University Press, 1963)

Smith, Vincent, *The Oxford History of India* (3rd Edn., O.U.P., 1958), edited by Percival Spear

Spain, James W., *The Pathan Borderland* (Mouton & Co., The Hague, 1963)

Spate, O. H. K., *India and Pakistan* (Methuen, 1954)

Spear, Percival, *India, Pakistan and the West* (3rd Edn., O.U.P., 1958)

Spear, Percival, *Britain's Transfer of Power in India* (Pacific Affairs, vol. xxxi, No. 2, June, 1958)

Spear, Percival, *India, A Modern History* (University of Michigan Press, 1961)

Spear, Percival, *A History of India*, Vol. II (Penguin Books, 1965)

Spear, Percival, *Nehru* (Article in 'Modern Asian Studies', I, 1, 1967)

Stephens, Ian, *Horned Moon* (3rd Edn., Ernest Benn, 1966)

Stephens, Ian, *Monsoon Morning* (Ernest Benn, 1966)

Stevens, Lt-Col., G. R., *History of the 4th Indian Division* (MacLaren, Toronto, 1948)

Symonds, Richard, *The Making of Pakistan* (Faber, 1950)

Tayyeb, A., *Pakistan: A Political Geography* (O.U.P., 1966)

Tinker, Hugh, *India and Pakistan* (Pall Mall Press, 1962)

Tinker, Hugh, *South Asia, A Short History* (Pall Mall Press, 1966)

Toye, Hugh, *The Springing Tiger* (Cassell, 1959)

Tuker, Lt.-Gen. Sir Francis, *While Memory Serves* (Cassell, 1950)

Tyson, Geoffrey, *Nehru* (Pall Mall Press, 1966)

Verghese, D. G., *Our Neighbour, Pakistan* (Yousuf Meherally Centre, Bombay, 1965)

Von Vorys, Karl, *Political Development in Pakistan* (Princeton University Press, also O.U.P., 1965)

Wheeler-Bennet, John W., *King George VI* (Macmillan, 1958)

Wilber, Donald N. (and others), *Pakistan: Its People, Its Society, Its Culture* (H.R.A.F. Press, New Haven, 1964)

Wilcox, Wayne Ayres, *Pakistan, The Consolidation of a Nation* (Columbia University Press, 1963)

Williams, L. F. Rushbrook, *The State of Pakistan* (Faber, 1962)

Wint, Guy, *The British in Asia* (2nd Edn., Faber, 1955)

Wint, Guy, *The 1958 Revolution in Pakistan*, St. Antony's Papers No. 8 (Chatto & Windus, 1960)

Woodruff, Philip, *The Men who Ruled India*, Vols. I and II (Jonathan Cape, 1953 and 1954)

The following important new works have come out while this book was being printed:

Ayut Khan, Mohammad, *Friends not Masters: A Political Autobiography* (O.U.P., 1967)

Feldman, Herbert, *Revolution in Pakistan* (O.U.P., 1967)

Sayeed, Khalid Bin, *The Political System of Pakistan* (Houghton Mifflin Co., Boston, U.S.A., 1967)

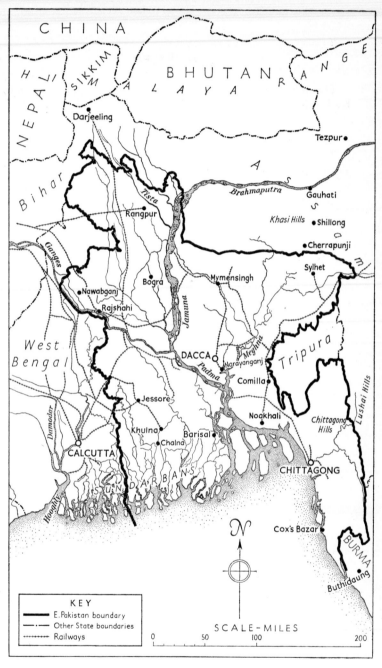

KEY
E. Pakistan boundary
Other State boundaries
Railways

SCALE—MILES
0   50   100   200

East Pakistan
[*Note different scale from West Pakistan*]

Index

Index

T

C

Cabinet Mission (*see* British
    Cabinet Mission)
Calcutta, 36, 38, 39, 42, 69, 70,
    88, 94, 108–11 (*passim*), 135,
    225, 242
    assigned to India, 180
    riots and disorders, 92, 113–15,
    117, 141, 144, 149, 157 169,
    171, 173, 266
    riots and disorders ('great
    Calcutta killing'), 105–7, 181
    university, 56
Caliph, Caliphate (*see also*
    Khilafatist), 14, 23, 25, 58,
    59, 73, 74, 74 n.
Callard, Keith, 27, 236, 236 n.,
    240, 243, 244 n.
Cambridge, 24, 28, 75
Campbell-Johnson, Alan, 123, 126,
    130, 148 n., 155, 160, 161,
    165, 170, 172, 174, 180,
    182 n., 190, 194, 203 n.
Canberra bomber episode,
    Rawalpindi, 254
Cantwell Smith, 23
Caroe, Olaf, 133, 145, 150, 151,
    155
Caste, caste system (*see also*
    Brahmin, Hinduism), 18, 55,
    56, 60, 71, 73, 104, 132, 135,
    224
Cauvery, 15 n.
Cawnpore, 90–1, 105, 110
Celibacy, celibate, 60, 132
CENTO (formerly Baghdad Pact),
    220
Ceylon, Ceylonese (*see also*
    Colombo), 19, 23, 51, 54,
    212, 224
Chagai hills, 45
Chaklala, 145
Chalna, 39
Chaman, 44
Chambh, 41, 271, 272
Chandpur, 36
Chatterjee, Bankim Chandra, 71,
    77
Chauri Chaura, 74
Chenab, 228, 229
Chen-yi, Marshal, 273

Cherrapunji, 37
Chichoki Malian, 228
Chilas, 207
China, Chinese, 13, 19, 31–2, 37,
    38, 40, 45, 84, 84 n., 156,
    196, 222, 223, 254, 265, 272,
    273
    friendship with Pakistan, 223,
    224, 265, 273
    India's border dispute with,
    210 n., 212, 223, 273
    invasion of India by, 223, 264,
    265
Chitral, 39, 40, 53, 207, 227
Chittagong, 34, 37, 39, 52, 56, 82,
    109, 228
Chou En-lai, Mr., 265
Christendom, Christian,
    Christianity, 14, 16, 17, 22–4
    (*passim*), 28, 29. 31, 55, 56,
    58–61 (*passim*), 72, 73, 132,
    134, 202, 212, 239, 246
    affinity with Islam, 18, 19, 56
Chundrigar, Mr., 158, 246
Church (*see also* Christianity), 16,
    21, 23
Churchill, Mr., 123, 126, 232
Civil disobedience (*see also*
    Non-co-operation)
    by Congress, 75, 78, 150
    by League, 129, 142, 152, 155,
    158, 164, 169
'Clause 8' controversy (*see also*
    British Cabinet Mission),
    97–100, 102
Colombo (*see also* Ceylon), 92
Comilla, 109, 110
Common Market, 54
Commonwealth, the (British),
    107, 107 n., 206, 209, 213,
    215–17, 220, 221, 222, 246,
    248, 253, 264, 269, 271
Communal Award, the, 75
Communism, Communist, 14, 16,
    22, 23, 30, 32, 63, 84, 163,
    220, 223, 253, 254, 264,
    265
Congo, Belgian, 85
Congress party, committees,
    Congressmen, 27, 71–3, 76–9,
    81–3, 96–105, 108, 109, 111,
    112, 114–19, 138, 142, 150,

Printed in Great Britain
by Cox & Wyman Limited
London Fakenham & Reading